arts based
research

To Tanya, whose incomparable assistance in preparing this book shines through on every page.

arts based research

Tom Barone
Arizona State University

Elliot W. Eisner
Stanford University

$SAGE

Los Angeles | London | New Delhi
Singapore | Washington DC

Los Angeles | London | New Delhi
Singapore | Washington DC

FOR INFORMATION:

SAGE Publications, Inc.
2455 Teller Road
Thousand Oaks, California 91320
E-mail: order@sagepub.com

SAGE Publications Ltd.
1 Oliver's Yard
55 City Road
London, EC1Y 1SP
United Kingdom

SAGE Publications India Pvt. Ltd.
B 1/I 1 Mohan Cooperative Industrial Area
Mathura Road, New Delhi 110 044
India

SAGE Publications Asia-Pacific Pte. Ltd.
33 Pekin Street #02-01
Far East Square
Singapore 048763

Executive Editor: Diane McDaniel
Editorial Assistant: Theresa Accomazzo
Production Editor: Brittany Bauhaus
Permissions Editor: Adele Hutchinson
Copy Editors: Megan Markanich
Typesetter: Hurix Systems Pvt. Ltd.
Proofreaders: Charlotte J. Waisner
Cover Designer: Gail Buschman
Marketing Manager: Katie Winter

Copyright © 2012 by SAGE Publications, Inc.

Barone, Tom, 1944-

Arts Based Research / Tom Barone, Arizona State University, Elliot W. Eisner, Stanford University.

pages cm

Includes bibliographical references and index.

ISBN 978-1-4129-8247-4 (pbk.)

1. Qualitative research—Methodology. 2. Arts and society. I. Eisner, Elliot W., 1933- II Title.

H62.B3365 2012

001.4'2—dc22   2010048773

Printed in the United States of America.

Library of Congress Cataloging-in-Publication Data

This book is printed on acid-free paper.

11 12 13 14 15 10 9 8 7 6 5 4 3 2 1

Brief Contents

Detailed Contents

Preface

This book is designed to serve as an introductory text for anyone interested in social research within a variety of fields who may not yet feel sufficiently acquainted with the role of artistry in projects of social inquiry. It is meant to acquaint readers with what has, over the years, come to be known as *arts based research*.

The term *arts based research* originated at an educational event at Stanford University in 1993. Elliot Eisner, having written about the connection between the arts and education, thought it would be useful to provide an institute for university scholars and school practitioners that would help them understand what research guided by aesthetic features might look like. Elliot secured the support of the American Educational Research Association for conducting a 2.5 day institute at Stanford that was available to 25 scholars and practitioners.

Elliot asked Tom Barone to be one of three instructors involved in that institute. Noting the enthusiasm that was generated at this institute and the testimony of those who attended, Elliot decided to offer a second institute 2 years later and asked Tom to join him again, this time as codirector. Tom was a former doctoral student of Elliot's, whose dissertation work in the 1970s was dedicated to the development and application of a rationale for an approach to qualitative research and evaluation that employed dimensions of creative nonfiction for inquiring into and disclosing social phenomena. Then, 2 years following the second institute, together, Eisner and Barone, conducted a third and then a fourth. Ultimately there were eight such institutes held from 1993 to 2005.

By the middle of the first decade of the 21st century, many of the leaders in the field of education and other fields currently working in arts based research had been, at one time, students in that institute. We, Eisner and Barone, were surprised to see the level of enthusiasm displayed for the exploration of major themes and other ideas in arts based research. What started with a glimmer became a beacon for many educational researchers looking for another way to think about research and how it can be conducted. We became convinced that the premises, principles, and procedures employed by artists can serve certain purposes for engaging in social research that, in important ways, complement those of the sciences. Throughout a large part of our careers, as authors of books and articles, as university professors, and public speakers, we have strived to advance the field of arts based research.

Over the decades, the place of the artistic and the aesthetic in the process and product of social research has indeed been illuminated and expanded—by us and others. One may argue—as we do throughout this book—that artistry in the social research process is nothing new, that indeed artistry has existed in scientific research from the very beginning. Indeed, before the 18th-century period of the Enlightenment in the Western world, no substantial differences between the arts and sciences were recognized. The ensuing art–science dichotomy that became prevalent in Western thought was described most famously in C. P. Snow's (1993) *Two Cultures and the Scientific Revolution*. This dualism perhaps reached its height in the philosophy of the logical positivists.

For the research traditionalists of the time, the very idea of an approach to research in the social sciences that is based upon a conception of art was an oxymoronic idea. For them, the only means for shedding light on some aspect of the physical world was science, and when it came to issues surrounding human beings, social science was the sole illuminating source. For them, the dominant research paradigm was the experiment and was seen as the gold standard for research. The use of statistics was ubiquitous, and the models to be used in doing research had a mechanistic uniformity: First, you defined the problem; second, you described the theory that was going to be used in the study; third, you identified the sample or population to be studied; fourth, you intervened with some treatment; and fifth, you measured the effects secured and finally determined the level of probability that you had achieved with the treatment that was applied to population or to the sample.

These features were the dominant thematic beliefs that guided research, certainly in education and also, to perhaps not as large a degree, in the social sciences. To do research that was rigorous measurement was necessary, and with measurement came statistics, and with statistics came probabilities, and with probabilities came a reduction of attention to individuals or even to distinctive features of individuals. In the process, the individual characteristics of the human being got abstracted out of reality. There seemed to be much more interest in numbers than in the people being studied.

Within the 20th century, and now the 21st, regard for this dualism—and, indeed, a science-over-art hierarchy—remains but has increasingly been eroded. The idea that the aesthetic was a source of research bias and contamination has, in some quarters, met strong—and creative—resistance. The so-called "literary turn" in the social sciences began as some qualitative research methodologists and practitioners, acknowledged and experimented with approaches to inquiry and representation that had previously been associated with imaginative literature, and other art forms. Consider, for example, a 1976 quote from sociologist Robert Nisbet: The science of sociology is "also one of the arts—nourished . . . by precisely the same kinds of creative imagination which are to be found in such areas as music painting, poetry, the novel and drama." The title of Nisbet's book is *Sociology as an Art Form*.

The dissolution of the art–science dichotomy became increasingly obvious during the historical stage in the development of social research known as the *moment of blurred genres* (Denzin & Lincoln, 2000). In social criticism, journalism, ethnography, and elsewhere experimentations with arts based methods and representational forms yielded literary-style ethnographic essays, New Journalistic reportage, sociological portraits, and so on. For some, social research had indeed, it seems, finally become recognized as being, as Richard Rorty has put it, continuous with literature.

And so it is with us. This book bears witness to our belief in that research continuum. We do acknowledge the utility, at least relatively often, of social science methods for understanding complex social phenomena. But surely complex social messages being made plain through largely propositional language is not the only avenue that one can employ to understand the world or, at least, to describe its countenance. Arts based research was—and is—an effort to utilize the forms of thinking and forms of representation that the arts provide as means through which the world can be better understood and through such understanding comes the enlargement of mind. As proponents and practitioners of arts based research, we find it ironic that what is regarded as empirical focuses upon studies in which numbers are used to convey meaning while studies that deal with individuals as such are often regarded as nonempirical. It seems to us that, in general, we have our conceptions upside down. Indeed, it is interesting to note that the word *empirical* is rooted in the Greek word *empirikos*, which means experience. What is hard to experience is a set of numbers. What is comparatively easy to experience is a set of qualities.

While, finally, other thinkers in the fields of the social sciences have come to accept these premises we have held for so long, we would also note a perhaps important distinction as we locate our own thinking on that research continuum suggested by Rorty. If the relatively recent history of social science research is one of discovery of the literary/artistic side of that continuum by researchers and methodologists who were first trained primarily as social scientists, ours is a journey that for each of us (and especially for Elliot) began at the *artistic* end of the continuum.

At one time in a prior life, I (Elliot Eisner) was a visual artist. My background was secured in schools such as the Art Institute of Chicago and the Institute of Design at the Illinois Institute of Technology. It was visual art that enabled me to succeed in secondary school. I was no prize student since I found most of the material that was being taught of little interest. What did occur to me during my early years as a graduate student at the University of Chicago was that the arts had something to say to people and something to say that was important. If this was true, then why not use the arts methodologically to reveal what the arts make possible in various situations? Why not use expressive form to convey to readers, for example, how it feels to struggle with failure in school, to learn how to delay gratification until such conditions become not only bitter but frustrating as well? In short, why not use the arts as a way of promoting understanding, of diversifying perspective, of securing insight? In other words, why not recognize their epistemological potential, and why not do research in education that features the conditions of the arts in studying schools, communities, and classrooms?

I (Tom Barone) had been interested in writing and telling stories since the second grade. Later, my BA degree in history from Loyola University of the South testified to my view of all human events as emplotted, as storied. But my interests in art theory and literary theory bloomed only after I was privileged to work on my doctorate under Elliot Eisner at Stanford. There and then my newfound interest in literary theory led to a career-long exploration of new forms of qualitative social research.

This book, therefore, is a collaborative effort aimed at exploring the meaning of arts based research, a form of research that is a relative newcomer to the array of conceptions and procedures that are used in doing research in education and in the social sciences. The term *arts based research* is not self-explanatory. At the risk of oversimplifying what is a complex and multifaceted conception, we will try, in this book, to describe the meaning of that phrase in a form that makes it graspable or understandable. We can say now that arts based research is an effort to employ the expressive qualities of form in order to enable a reader of that research to participate in the experience of the author. Put even more simply is this: Arts based research is a process that uses the expressive qualities of form to convey meaning.

Some vivid examples of this process of empathic participation in the life of another can be found at the cinema. Films such as The *Godfather, Pan's Labyrinth, Raging Bull,* and *The Hurt Locker* secure their impact by virtue of the way in which the form of the film has been crafted. By the form of the film we mean the way in which speech, music, and visual imagery interact to express ideas and qualities that would otherwise be inaccessible to language alone. Arts based research is, likewise, a vehicle through which the expressive qualities of an artistically crafted form can come to express meaning and significance. How this occurs and what the issues are with respect to it is what this book addresses.

These movies are mentioned as examples of efforts to transform an artist's (or collectivity of artists') experiences into a script that itself gets transformed into a movie, and the movie itself becomes enhanced with music, movement, scene, and language, including language that is accented. The problem for the playwright and the director is to make the appropriate transformation so that the ideas he or she is trying to render will have a chance at coming to fruition. These films represent works of art, not works of science. They also represent an effort made to raise significant questions regarding the theme of the work. What was America like in the teens? What was the relationship between imagination and resistance during the Spanish Civil War? What is it like to be a famous American athlete in a violent sport in post World War II America? What is it like to be a soldier who is addicted to war? What sorts of visuals are needed to give the viewer a sense of place? What will the music sound like and what should be its pervasive quality? How should the available footage be edited to greatest advantage? These and a host of other questions must be addressed in one way or another in order to create an "authentic" film of an important part of history. And perhaps the most important question one can pose to the work is: Does it raise questions about important social issues, past and/or present?

Of course, these examples of films stand near the very edge of the artistic side of the art–science side of the research continuum. In other examples of arts based research—examples found in this book—there exist design elements that more fully reveal the blending of dimensions of art and science, placing these works on various spots along this continuum. Still, that the emphasis on arts based research is indeed arts-*based* to the *degree* that it evidences, again, expressive qualities of form to convey meaning.

These and other notions are a part of the intellectual agenda in this book. They are identified here to provide a mere foretaste of what is to come. First, however, a more detailed description of the contents of this book.

* * * * *

This book contains two sorts of readings regarding arts based social research. The first sort is found in the main chapters of the book, written by us. In these 10 chapters, the authors attempt to familiarize readers with the approach. We define the term *arts based social research*, consider the purposes for engaging in it, address some of the major controversies surrounding this form of social inquiry, and discuss criteria for judging quality. Here is a more specific breakdown:

Chapter 1 tries to familiarize readers with arts based research by describing just what is and what is not arts based research. What is the relationship between research based in the arts and research that is primarily scientific? Why do we refuse to dichotomize between the two?

Chapter 2 deals with questions regarding the purposes for engaging in arts based research. Why would a social researcher choose to do arts based research and not another form of social research? How does arts based research succeed in prompting readers into the reimagining of dimensions of the social world surrounding them? How can particular examples of arts based research help them "make new worlds"? What sorts of uses may arts based research texts serve?

Chapter 3 addresses the reasons for insisting that arts based research is indeed a legitimate form of social research as opposed to merely a form of inquiry. Phases in the process of doing arts based research are also discussed herein.

Chapter 4 focuses on who the arts based researcher is or can be. Can anyone who so desires do arts based research? Does one need to be formally trained in the arts to do it well? Does one need to be an academic to do arts based research? Within the academy can only arts educators be arts based researchers? Or can arts based researchers reside in other academic fields? How "good" must the work of an arts based researcher be? Can talent for arts based research be developed? What should academic programs look like that aim to enhance capacities for doing "good" arts based research?

Chapter 5 approaches issues related to the audiences for arts based research? For whom are works of arts based research composed? Can arts based researchers hope to expand their audience beyond colleagues within the academy? Can and should arts based research also be composed for lay people, members of the general public? How can arts based research "seduce" members of an intended audience into an engagement with their compositions?

Chapter 6 attempts to trouble the notion of *fiction* as the term may or may not apply to works of arts based research. Questions addressed include the following: What are some possible definitions of fiction? In what senses are (and are not) works of research of all sorts composed, imaginative, fashioned, *fictional*? Is there a strong sense and a weak sense of the term fictional? Is a fact–fiction dichotomy an unhelpful social construct? Which types of "fictional" works should be legitimated as research? Why and why not? What are some specific suggestions for arts based researchers who choose to fictionalize their research texts?

Chapter 7 addresses some of the sticky issues of politics and ethics related to arts based forms of research. A few of the questions addressed here are: Can any social research be *apolitical*? How can works of arts based research successfully confront prevailing metanarratives within a culture by offering alternative "readings" of social phenomena? How can it avoid becoming propaganda in the process? How is the issue of who "owns" a piece of arts based research—the author–artist–researcher, the informants–characters in the inquiry process and arts based text, audience members—be an ethical one? What might a work of good arts based research look like that is both overtly political and highly ethical?

Chapter 8 offers some criteria for assessing the usefulness and quality of works of arts based research.

Chapter 9 investigates the place of theory in arts based research.

Chapter 10 attempts to summarize by providing a cluster of what we consider to be fundamental ideas surrounding the approach to social research that we call arts based.

These chapters are accompanied by the second kind of reading contained in the book—three examples of arts based social research. Indeed, in each of the 10 chapters we attempt to "ground" some of the more abstract notions under discussion by referencing particular examples of arts based research.

Since the number of works of qualitative research identified as arts based have proliferated enormously over the last 2 decades, choosing these three examples was a difficult task. It was done with much care. Still, the works chosen are not meant to represent what we consider to be a "top few" of all existing works. A very large number of good works of arts based social research have necessarily been left out. (Some are cited in the Additional Readings section of this book.) The works chosen, however, were done so because they allowed us to answer the following question in the affirmative: Is the work highly useful to an array of readers insofar as it possesses the capacity to achieve the primary purpose of a work of arts based research—namely, enticing them to rethink an important social issue? This question will guide us as we explore the realm of arts based research.

Acknowledgments

The authors and SAGE gratefully acknowledge the contributions of the following reviewers:

Melissa Cahnman-Tyler, *University of Georgia*

Lynn Fels, *Simon Fraser University*

David Flinders, *Indiana University–Bloomington*

Robert Hard, *Albertus Magnus College*

Rita Irwin, *University of British Columbia*

Carl Leggo, *University of British Columbia*

Margaret Moore-West, *Dartmouth Medical School–Lebanon*

Pamela Stevens, *Northern Arizona University*

Bruce Urmacher, *University of Denver*

Chapter 1

What Is and What Is Not Arts Based Research?

All forms of representation, the means through which the contents of our mind are shared with others, are both constrained and made possible by the form one chooses to use. Sound, which reaches its apotheosis in music, makes possible meanings and other forms of experience that cannot be secured in nonmusical forms. The narrative, as rendered through words, makes possible stories and other forms of prose that are not renderable in music. Arts based research is an effort to extend beyond the limiting constraints of discursive communication in order to express meanings that otherwise would be ineffable. Indeed, an examination of the forms of communication employed in the culture at large reveals a level of diversity of forms that is enough to dazzle the eye, delight the ear, and tempt the tongue. Humans have invented forms within a spectrum of sensory modalities in order to "say" in that form what cannot be said in others. Arts based research represents an effort to explore the potentialities of an approach to representation that is rooted in aesthetic considerations and that, when it is at its best, culminates in the creation of something close to a work of art.

The idea that research can be conducted using nondiscursive means such as pictures, or music, or dance, or all of those in combination, is not an idea that is widely practiced in American research centers or in American schools. We tend to think about research as being formulated exclusively—and of necessity—in words the more literal, the better. The idea that research reports and sections thereof can be crafted in a way not dissimilar from the way in which great novelists write and great painters paint is even rarer. Thus, the idea that we advance is that matters of meaning are shaped—that is, enhanced and constrained—by the tools we use. When those tools limit what is expressible or representational, a certain price is paid for the neglect of what has been omitted. Yet, in American culture, and indeed more broadly in Western culture, the determination of what is true depends upon the verification of claims made in propositional discourse. We have a hankering for the facts—no ifs, ands, or buts! In general, we don't want our prose gussied up with nuances, qualifications, or ambiguous contexts. The cleaner, the better. The clean methodological ideal is what some scholars want to achieve. Reduction of ambiguity is seen as a paramount virtue. It's interesting to note that William James himself suggested in a lecture given at the turn of the century that we should save some space in our mental life for the ambiguous. Creativity was something he valued.

This preoccupation with what we think of as misguided precision has led to the standardization of research methodology, the standardization that uses the assumptions, and procedures of the physical sciences as the model to be emulated. The experiment, for example, is, as they say, the gold standard, and quantification of data is a necessary condition for conducting experiments or so it is believed.

Beliefs about what constitutes legitimate research procedure have enormous ramifications for understanding human behavior and social interaction. The gold standard that we alluded to earlier not only identifies the experiment as the summum bonum of research method. It, by implication, identifies the approach as being scientific. The idea that research could be nonscientific seems to many researchers as oxymoronic. We argue that a great deal of research and some of the most valuable research is not at all scientific, where science means, in general, quantification of data and the application of statistical methods to determine causal relationships. Such research methods have given us a great deal, but they are far from the whole story. The need to provide methodological permission for people to innovate with the methods they use has never been more important. Yet, ironically, so much of what is prescribed leads to a reduction in methodological innovation, rather than an expansion.

The perceptive reader will note that our ambition is to broaden the conceptions not only of the tools that can be used to represent the world but even more to redefine and especially to enlarge the conceptual umbrella that defines the meaning of research itself.

One might well ask how a symbol system without clear connections to a codified array of referents can be useful in doing something as precise as a research study is intended to be. How can clear, concise, and precise conclusions be derived from the use of forms of representation that do little in the way of precise specification? The answer to that question that we formulate is the clear specification of a referent by a symbol is not a necessary condition for meaning. In the arts, symbols adumbrate; they do not denote. When they adumbrate something important happens—people begin to notice. What they notice can become, and often becomes, a source of debate and deliberation. In the particular resides the general—after all, Arthur Miller's (1967) *Death of a Salesman* is not about any particular salesman; it is about middle-aged men who lose their jobs and strain their relationships with their wives and children. The playwright's skill qualities of life are revealed, and the reader learns to notice aspects of the world.

Thus, the contribution of arts based research is not that it leads to claims in propositional form about states of affairs but that it addresses complex and often subtle interactions and that it provides an image of those interactions in ways that make them noticeable. In a sense, arts based research is a heuristic through which we deepen and make more complex our understanding of some aspect of the world.

This last point is of utmost importance in understanding what arts based research is about and what it is likely to provide when it is done well. Arts based research does not yield propositional claims about states of affairs. It tries to create insight into states of affairs whose utility is tested when those insights are applied to understand what has been addressed in the research. For example, in the film *Schindler's List*, a set of moving images makes the experience of Nazi concentration camps palpable. We are afforded an opportunity to participate in those events, and we can debate with others the deep motives of those who managed this center for human extermination. The film, as with other works of art, makes it possible for us to empathize with the experience of others. We believe that such empathy is a necessary condition for deep forms of meaning in human life. The arts make such empathic participation possible because they create forms that are evocative and compelling.

One might ask whether we can trust what we derive from such material. We do not seek for any reader to take such material at face value. Such material always provides a starting point for further inquiry. We are not interested in capturing and then belling the cat. What we are interested in is a provision of a new perspective that makes it possible for those interested in the phenomena the research addressed to have a productive heuristic through which a deepened understanding can be promoted. In that sense, our aspirations are far more modest than those who seek to replicate in prose facts, nothing but the facts. The facts, deconceptualized as they often are, are hardly ever adequate for telling the whole story.

One might ask why an approach to research based upon artistic and aesthetic foundations would be important at an age at which schools in particular seem to be doing such a poor job. Don't we need more rigorous pedagogical methods, more precise quantitative assessments of performance? Don't we need tougher standards and higher expectations? At a time when the ship seems to be sinking, why mess around with the arts, a form of experience and action in which surprise and nondiscursive forms are the order of the day?

We would argue that it is precisely during a period in which precision, quantification, prescription, and formulaic practices are salient that we need approaches to research, and we add, to teaching, which exploit the power of "vagueness" to "get at" what otherwise would seem unrecoverable. It makes no sense to embrace plans that win the battle but lose the war. We need to touch the souls of students as well as to measure their sleeve length or hat size.

THE ARTS ARE OFTEN LARGER THAN LIFE

A second reason the arts are important as a means through which understanding is promoted is because its expansion serves as a marker that diversity in methodology is possible. Methodological pluralism rather than methodological monism seems to us to be the greater virtue.

One of the axiomatic truths in cognitive psychology is that the frame of reference through which one peers at the world shapes what one learns from that world. To the carpenter, the world is made of wood. To the psychometrician, the world is made of quantity. Pluralism and diversity is a virtue not only in race relations but it can be an extremely important virtue in getting multiple perspectives on states of affairs. Without support of the conception of such diversity, it is not likely to be provided.

What sometimes hampers students from getting a handle on arts based approaches to research is a reluctance—or should we say an ignorance—on the part of faculty as to the meaning of the term *arts based research*. Without support from faculty, doctoral students are often left in the lurch. It is demanding enough to do a dissertation well using conventional forms of research method, let alone a research method that is at the edge of inquiry. Yet, it seems to us to be particularly important to encourage students to explore the less well explored than simply to replicate tried and true research methods that break no new methodological grounds. It is better, we believe, to find new seas on which to sail than old ports at which to dock.

The perceptive reader will note that there are two major potential consequences for arts based research. One of these is broadening our conception of the ways in which we come to know. We are trying to open up through this work a new vision of what the arts are about and what educational research can become. We do not see this aspiration as the creation of either an alternative or a supplement to conventional educational research. We do not see it as an alternative because we have no ambition to try to replace conventional methods of empirical research with arts based research; we are not interested in the hegemony of one method over another. We are not interested in a supplement because we do not wish to conceive of arts based research as something one must do in addition to doing conventional research. Arts based research is an approach to research that exploits the capacities of expressive form to capture qualities of life that impact what we know and how we live. We believe we can find such contributions in the poetic use of language, in the expressive use of narrative, and in the sensitive creation in film and video. These options do not exhaust the ways in which arts based research can be conducted or the media that it can employ. We list them here simply as examples of media that have potential relevance for doing research.

Film, video, and various forms of digital and electronic imagery are, relatively speaking, new means through which research can be reported. The term *report* is somewhat too passive. The availability of new media makes possible the generation of new concepts and the creation of new possibilities. For example, Michelangelo himself could not have conceived of what fluorescent tubing as the substance of sculpture might generate in human experience. The movie camera makes possible slow motion to the point where the path of a bullet can be slowed down to the speed of a butterfly. Our point is that the availability of new means has consequences not only for how one addresses the world and reports its features but it has consequences for features to be attended to that might not have been options prior to the availability of these forms. There is an intimate connection between technology and expressivity, and we are certain that in the future the possibilities of the computer and other electronic devices will be exploited in ways that are even more daring than they have been thus far.

How would our thinking, our understanding, and the knowledge that we crystallize and ship around the globe have been affected had writing not been invented? Winston Churchill once said, "At first we build our buildings and then our buildings build us." The tools we design have an impact on how we become designed by the tools of our own hand. The arts, like the sciences, remake the maker and the tools that the maker uses has a profound impact on who we become. It is in this sense that arts based research is a means through which we seek new portraits of people and places. An artist, commented Gombrich (2000), does not paint what he can see but sees what he is able to paint. With the invention of the ax head, humans were able to build forms and perform functions that were simply out of reach before. That general principle applies to the resources used in arts based research.

Given the apparently elusive character of art forms, how will we determine the "validity" of what an arts based research project yields? How will we know if it is accurate or inaccurate? Can arts based research be trusted? We will be addressing these issues more fully throughout this book. But one answer to these questions was alluded to by Wallace Stegner, the American writer, when he was asked what it was that conferred greatness on a work of fiction, he responded by saying that a work of fiction needed to be true in order to be great. The irony is clear. Truth is not owned simply by propositional discourse; it is also owned by those activities that yield meanings that may be ineffable ultimately but that nevertheless ring true in the competent percipient. What we seek is not so much validity as it is credibility. The virtues to be found in arts based research are not located in some isomorphic relationship between a statement and an event; it is to be found in the degree to which, as Geertz says, it makes our conversation more interesting.

What he is driving at is the search for vehicles that allow one into a dimly lit cave that is lightened up—made even bright—by the luminescence of the work. The arts in general teach us to see, to feel, and indeed to know. What we are proposing is that the means through which the arts function as illuminating vehicles may find expression and utility in research activities as well as in the arts themselves.

But what if there are differences in the ways in which different researchers see a so-called common situation or at least a situation common to them? How are differences reconciled? We are reminded of Clifford Geertz's (1974) comments concerning ethnography. He said the aim of ethnography is to increase the precision through which we vex one another. This vexing, this pursuit of intellectual issues, this highly nuanced activity called arts based research, is a way of coming to know that recognizes that differences between investigators is nothing to moan over. Differences lead to challenge, and challenge can lead to debate and insight. After all, one of the characteristics that artists and scientists share is that both groups of individuals are troublemakers. The trouble that they make is trouble for themselves. It is trouble found in the unanswered questions and unresolved problems that serve to animate activity within their field. When there is no problem, there is not likely to be much of an inquiry taking place to resolve it. In short, differences in view may indeed be challenging, but at the same time they may promote precisely the kind of inquiry that expands our awareness of what we had not noticed before.

We realize that the term *arts based research* will appear to more than a few as an oxymoronic notion. Research is the child of science; art is something altogether different. We reject this formulation attesting to the dichotomy between art and science. Science, well done, imaginative in character, sensitive to qualitative variations, and organized according to what aesthetic forms can carry is also the result of artistic judgment. Anything well made, employing skill and sensitivity to form and prized not only for its practical utility but for the quality of experience that it generates can be thought of as an example of an art form. The borders between art and science are malleable and porous. This means that fields like physics and mathematics, the law and history, are fields in which artists work. The artists we refer to are physicists and mathematicians, attorneys and historical scholars. Our aim is to recognize the aesthetic features of fields and their activities, fields and activities previously assigned to realms that supposedly had nothing to do with aesthetic matters whatsoever.

The important point here is that historical portrayals, whether in narrative texts or in film, for example, are occasions for the arts to shine. How a character is represented in a historical study matters significantly in what a reader is likely to take away from the work when it is read. A legal brief, well argued and artistically crafted, may have the result of saving someone's life or making it possible for the state to take it. Artistry as a general process is found in almost any activity, at least potentially, that humans undertake. The so-called facts are seldom "unencumbered" with rhetorical moves. Rhetoric, the art of persuasion, is ubiquitous in virtually every activity designed to persuade or encourage a particular kind of action or to arrive at a particular type of judgment.

One might ask, if artistry in action is ubiquitous, why make a special case for arts based research, or, put another way, why argue a more or less special case for the arts as the basis for doing research when apparently it already exists?

The answer to that question, it seems to us, is that it doesn't already exist in the robustness that it needs to possess to become a respectable and ongoing part of what constitutes research activity. It has taken nearly a hundred years for conventional forms of research to be refined and broadly accepted as ways of understanding individuals and groups. For arts based research to have an opportunity to develop an equal level of acceptance requires articulation of its distinctive and valued role. That is what we are trying to provide in this book.

There is also another factor that must be considered in any justification regarding the value and uses of arts based research. The reason we referred to is related to the evocative nature of artistic form. Arts based research emphasizes the generation of forms of feeling that have something to do with understanding some person, place, or situation. It is not simply a quantitative disclosure of an array of variables. It is the conscious pursuit of expressive form in the service of understanding.

Consider a film such as *The Godfather*. Mario Puzo (1969), author of the book, provided the material out of which a script was written. He needed to learn a great deal about mafia families living on the East Coast of the United States. He needed to understand how their "business" was managed, how profits were made, how killings were ordered, and what the settings and, indeed, some of the history of the mafia families unfolded during the 1930s and 1940s. But learning of these facts is not enough to produce a product that will allow a reader or a viewer to grasp the situations being described and the people being portrayed. For the book, as for the adapted screenplay, plots had to be formed, and portraits of individuals needed be decided upon. For the film, sets needed to be designed, language appropriate to the occasion needed to be determined, pace and tempo of action needed to be judged, actors needed to be cast who were suitable for the role they were to occupy, and the history of the period needed to be revealed in a credible light.

It is the evocative utilization of such data that makes the work expressive and affords individuals who see or read it with the opportunity to participate empathically in events that would otherwise be beyond their reach. A statistical description of the incidence of mafia assassinations or histograms describing the growth of revenues over the period in which these families operated would not, we believe, yield anywhere near as lush a rendering. This is not to say that statistics would be irrelevant; it would depend on the kind of questions that one wants to ask. However, for highly nuanced and expressive renderings of human affairs, the arts are of primary importance.

What the foregoing illustrates is the noncategorical nature of educational research. By this we mean that some research projects will fit comfortably on a continuum that is closer to an evocative orientation to the revelation of a situation than others. Other efforts will be located clearly toward the more conventional and most often mathematical or statistical end of the continuum. We reiterate our point that we are not interested in identifying the necessary and sufficient conditions for arts based research to be identified. We are trying to describe features of inquiry that are examples of research that enable us to pursue that style of work without the encumbrances of a research tradition that often disallows their use. It is in this sense that the orientation we are developing here is thoroughly iconoclastic in character. For that, we make no apologies. As it is said, you can't make an omelet without breaking an egg.

There are a few other issues that need attention if we are to become clear about what arts based research is and is not. One of these pertains to this question: Are we concerned with arts based research or research based art? A second issue pertains to the issue of what "based" means. What does it mean to say that an approach to research or to anything else for that matter is "based" on it?

For us it means that arts based research is an approach to research that we define as a method designed to enlarge human understanding. Arts based research is the utilization of aesthetic judgment and the application of aesthetic criteria in making judgments about what the character of the intended outcome is to be. In arts based research, the aim is to create an expressive form that will enable an individual to secure an empathic participation in the lives of others and in the situations studied. In a certain sense, it is like a travel card, something one can use to get somewhere. Where one is to get when doing arts based research is varied, but despite the variance among examples of arts based research, there is a common feature. That common feature, as we have indicated earlier, has to do with the creation of an expressive form.

The idea of an expressive form has been given attention to by Susanne Langer (1957), who distinguishes between discursive and nondiscursive modes of knowing. Her claim, one to which we are sympathetic, is that the arts are vehicles designed to reveal what someone can feel about some aspects of life. The affective domain, as they say in educational literature, is a salient dimension. Literal language, which is discursive rather than nondiscursive, is not particularly helpful when it comes to matters of feeling and their representation. Thus, arts based research is not a literal description of a state of affairs; it is an evocative and emotionally drenched expression that makes it possible to know how others feel. In the pursuit of such an aim, metaphor will be appealed to, analogies will be drawn, cadence and tempo of the language will be controlled, innuendo will be employed, simile will be used to illustrate meaning, and other such devices will be used to create the expressive form we mentioned earlier.

Earlier we raised the question of whether research based art and arts based research were identical or whether there were important differences between the two. We are here to say that arts based research uses the arts as a foundation for creating expressive forms that enlighten. Research based art is the use of research in any modality that will serve as a basis for creating a work of art. Let us return to the example of *Schindler's List*, the novel. The author of *Schindler's List* had to have done a considerable amount of researching and reading to learn about the Holocaust in a form that would enable him to create a novel about Schindler and his list of workers.

To illustrate, imagine two individuals, one a novelist and the other a behavioral psychologist. These two individuals study the so-called "same situation." Let's assume for a moment that what they study is the concentration camps run by the Nazis in the 1930s and 1940s. No one would disagree that the product of a novel would have literary features, and the product of the behavioral scientist—that is, the study produced by the behavioral psychologist—would differ. It would probably differ in feel, in detail, but mainly it would differ with respect to the kind of phenomena that each was able to bring to the occasion through the methods and assumptions with which each worked.

Our argument is that the literary as well as the scientific have their place, that these two forms of research—and we do want to call the literary a research effort— take different forms and inform in different ways about phenomena that superficially are similar but in reality are quite different. Arts based research is aimed at preparing people who can transform situations into a more or less literary "equivalent." In so doing, the language is likely to be nondiscursive rather than discursive, at least in some significant measure. The criteria for goodness will differ. The prevalence of statistical data would be greater in one form rather than in the other. The kinds of writing skills that one needed to do a literary rendition of the so-called "same" concentration camps would also differ. Our essential argument is that the promotion of human understanding is made possible through the acquisition and utilization of different forms of representation. Some of these forms will be discursive and digital; others will be nondiscursive and of an analog type of language. These forms are nonredundant, and they make possible different forms of understanding. We argue that it is important to have different forms of understanding for understanding complex phenomena that can be viewed in many ways. It is the plurality of view that we seek in the long run, rather than a "monotheistic" approach to the conduct of research.

It should be clear that what we are doing is reconceptualizing the resources that are appropriate for studying human affairs. One can say that we are more interested in paradigm proliferation than paradigm reductionism. We do not believe that there is one road to Rome; there are many, and it is through the exploration of alternative routes—some of which will undoubtedly lead to dead ends—that we exploit our human capacity to experience the world in different ways.

If one looks at the culture as a whole, it becomes clear that in our culture we do use different forms to get on with the business of life and with understanding our colleagues, our families, our friends, in short with understanding others.

Consider the decoding of body language. Here, we observe the visual cues that give us material to interpret. Here, we listen for intonation to decipher meaning that would otherwise be unavailable. Here, we observe comportment, gesture, almost imperceptible visual clues that enable us collectively to understand the implicit as well as the explicit meaning of what is being "said." If these resources or techniques or means are useful in making sense of the situations in which we find ourselves, might they also be helpful in understanding much of the phenomena we address through conventional forms of research? We not only believe that they would; we have evidence that they have already done so. From the observation of 19th century institutions portrayed by Charles Dickens in *Hard Times* (1854/1964) to the depiction of school life made by Jonathan Kozol (1991), in *Savage Inequalities*, we secure portraits of schools in places that reveal what no numbers are likely to contain. We believe that these tools warrant a place in the armamentarium we call research methods.

Those even remotely familiar with controversies within the field of research methodology will recognize that arts based research is, in a sense, a species of qualitative research. Conflicting opinions concerning the features of qualitative research as contrasted with what might be called quantitative research are fast and furious. For some scholars, qualitative research is essentially the use of nonquantitative forms of representation to describe, interpret, and appraise the features of some process, situation, or individual. The essential defining characteristics in this view pertain to narrative-like or artistically critical forms of disclosure. Arts based research as a species of qualitative research fits in to that category.

Research of a quantitative kind is represented by the use of numbers. It is more digital than analog, while qualitative research is more analog than digital. But even these differences pale in the eyes of some who believe that the distinction between qualitative research and quantitative research is an empty one. The argument goes something like this: Anytime someone represents an aspect of the world, in whatever form of representation, it must culminate in experience as a display of qualities. Thus, a description of an automobile accident or a home run with the bases loaded, both nonquantitative descriptors, nevertheless evoke in the reader certain quality of life that can be imaginary but that is rooted in the text or in an array of numbers that was prepared. Thus, what we think of as a literal description, using words to do so, culminates in experience qualitatively. Hence, the distinction between qualitative research, some claim, and more traditional quantitative forms of research is a distinction without a difference.

We speak of digital and analog descriptors for a purpose. In digital descriptions, numbers can culminate in arithmetic or statistical forms in any of several ways. For example, $4 + 4 = 8$ can be represented as $6 + 2 = 8$, $1 + 7 = 8$, $10 - 2 = 8$. In other words, there is, literally speaking, an infinite number of ways in which the number eight can be secured without a change in the meaning of the representation. The representation has a form that can be altered without changing its numeric meaning. However, in qualitative descriptions a change in a part is a change in a whole. Changing a paragraph in a novel, the color in a section of a painting, or the texture of a piece of sculpture changes the meaning of each of those forms. When it comes to the number eight, it can be written 8, or written VIII, or displayed as IIIII III. None of these representations are the same, but the arithmetic meaning remains the same. As a result, paying close attention to the nuances that flow from the perception of qualities becomes a critical feature in qualitative research. Getting each of the words just right, managing the pace of the reading, and attending to the music of the language all matter in qualitative research in a way that makes them not as salient an object of attention in a digital display.

These differences in form and function lead us to conclude that the distinction between qualitative and quantitative research is both viable and useful. In one sense, it seems obvious that to paint a picture and to take a measurement are two different processes that yield information for largely different purposes. If they were the same, one would be redundant.

Chapter 2

Why Do Arts Based Research?

In this chapter, we continue our investigation into the character of arts based research by focusing on issues of purpose. Why, one might rightfully ask, should a researcher in the academic and professional fields of the humanities, arts, sociology, psychology, anthropology, political science, education, social work, women's studies, ethnic studies, communications, journalism, health and medical humanities studies, and justice studies—to name a few—choose to engage in arts based forms of inquiry?

Let us first quickly rule out a few reasons for doing so that are, from our vantage point, insufficient. One is a belief in the inherent inadequacy of other forms of social research. We do not believe that available forms of quantitative and qualitative social research are necessarily inadequate for the purpose for which they are employed. Nor should a social researcher choose arts based inquiry as a default approach, perhaps out of a performance anxiety regarding quantitative or other forms of qualitative research. Alas, arts based research will not necessarily be "easier" than other approaches. An infatuation with or genuine love for the arts, or talent in a particular art form, are also not in themselves adequate reasons for engaging in arts based research, even if they are important attributes of an arts based researcher.

A better reason for doing arts based research may be this: to the extent that an arts based research project effectively employs aesthetic dimensions in both its inquiry and representational phases, to that extent the work may provide an important public service that may be otherwise unavailable. Works of arts based research may, that is, be useful in unique ways. In this chapter (and later in Chapter 7), we elaborate on the character of that potential usefulness and discuss examples of works of arts based research that reside within various fields of study and that employ different forms of art.

TWO WAYS THAT SOCIAL RESEARCH CAN BE USEFUL

The usefulness of any project of arts based research is best understood, in part, in reference to the epistemological underpinnings of this sort of inquiry. Doing some arts based research implies a fundamental shift away from the conventional assumption that all research is meant to bring us closer to a final understanding of various dimensions of the social world. It means abandoning the notion that the research process—whether through the social sciences or otherwise—should *always* result in a more persuasive argument or interpretation of how social and cultural phenomena are best perceived or conceptualized.

A hallmark of conventional social research has been a predisposition toward a kind of closure—even if that is, admittedly, an unachievable goal in any final sense. The aim is to reduce by degree, if never to eliminate or fully dispel, existing uncertainty regarding the truthfulness of knowledge claims. Of course science is always open to the possibility of revision or even replacement of "the highly probably true." But a knowledge claim that is repeatedly replicated and reconfirmed is treated as "certain . . . enough that we act on it as though it were unquestionably true" (Krathwohl, 1993), a condition that is seen as empowering us to explain, predict, and sometimes control the outcomes of similar future events. It allows us to be fairly certain about how to argue about how to act.

Unlike certain postmodernists who dismiss the value of all forms of social science, we believe that there is an important role for (both qualitative and quantitative) scientific research in the human studies that can provide at least temporary answers to nettlesome questions that plague our lives and potentially useful solutions to the seemingly intractable public policy issues that frustrate us. It is, we believe, only human to seek the kinds of reassurance that some social science seems to offer. Prolonged doubt and constant, pervasive uncertainty about important matters in our lives may in fact be psychologically hazardous. Traditional forms of social science may indeed be viewed as a necessary antidote to high anxiety.

Some scholars have noted, however, that a single-minded quest for absolute certainty in human matters has for too long dominated the Western philosophical tradition. Indeed, the first appearance of this quest in the history of Western thought may be located in the writings of the Greek philosopher Parmenides. Parmenides craved a kind of knowledge that evidenced "complete certainty and absolute unity" (Diefenbeck, 1984, p. 10). Much later, Descartes' epistemological project likewise harbored a "preoccupation with the indubitable" (Williams, 1972, p. 136). This preoccupation may be seen as afflicting thinkers from August Compte to the logical positivists and may be viewed as undergirding modern day scientism. Evidence of scientistic views of the world—ones in which only science offers any sort of useful knowledge—may also be found in the socialization process undergone by many doctoral students in a variety of academic fields. Much less evident are inclinations to consider as legitimate those forms of social research based in the humanities and—even more rarely—in the arts. And finally, where and when do future academics encounter identification of an additional, equally important, human need as worthy of pursuit through their scholarship and research? Where in academia are the advertisements for forms of research whose purpose it is to fulfill a need other than the one framed by Caputo (1987) as "the metaphysical desire to make things safe and secure" (p. 7)?

Our mission in this book is indeed the promotion of an additional purpose for doing social research. But before exploring further the question of why "do" arts based research, we are obliged to briefly acknowledge the more than occasional complicity of the arts—and not only the social sciences—in the quest for a safe sort of equilibrium that is maintained through a refusal to ask questions about how things really are. Indeed, one might ask, If a work of art is viewed as a vivid representation of "reality," or as endorsing a singularly "correct" interpretation of social phenomena, then is it really art? And is a piece of social research that aims in that direction really "arts based"? Other characterizations of such sorts of work may include "propaganda" or "kitsch." These are works that tend toward exaggeration and distortion in order to maximize a kind of safety and security. They represent heavy-handed attempts at persuasion, usually in support of dominant, and sometimes sentimental, worldviews.

Some subjectivist aestheticians who deride the possibility of objective "truth" are nevertheless reluctant to abandon the word entirely. They choose instead an inversion of the term to point to what they regard as the kind of personal, inner, subjective "truth" that works of art are meant to embody and disclose. Still, the danger of solipsism hangs over any claim of privilege in knowing and revealing what social phenomena finally mean, whether objective or subjective in character. Arts based researchers, we suggest, are better advised to adjust their vocabularies toward an entirely different purpose for engaging in social research, with notions of persuasion and truth taking on radically different meanings in the process.

What, then, is this alternative purpose for engaging in research that guides arts based researchers? It may be most succinctly stated as the promotion of (at the least, momentary) disequilibrium—uncertainty—in the way that both the author/researcher and the audience(s) of the work regard important social and cultural phenomena. Instead of contributing to the stability of prevailing assumptions about these phenomena by (either explicitly through statement, argument, portraiture, or implicitly through silence or elision) reinforcing the conventional way of viewing them, the arts based researcher may *persuade* readers or percipients of the work (including the artist herself) to revisit the world from a different direction, seeing it through fresh eyes, and thereby calling into question a singular, orthodox point of view (POV).

To promote this revisiting, the arts based researcher may, suggested Caputo (1987), intend "to keep a watchful eye for the ruptures and the breaks and irregularities in existence" (p. 6). This watchfulness implies a willingness to return to the "original difficulty of things" (p. 6) by peering beneath the surface of the familiar, the obvious, the orthodox in a rescrutinizing (re-searching) of the world. It is in adopting this interrogative disposition that arts based research (like much art) promotes a level of dislocation, disturbance, disruptiveness, disequilibrium that renders it sufficiently—even highly—useful, and therefore, in this unusual sense of the word, truthful.

The utility of this sort of research is thereby based on its capacity to fulfill a second important human need. This is indeed a need for surprise, for the kind of re-creation that follows from openness to the possibilities of alternative perspectives on the world. Moreover, the promotion of this disequilibrium through the obviation and undercutting of a prevailing worldview may also mean a useful sort of emancipation of readers and viewers. Nelson Goodman (1968) has written about the way in which art can "call for and then resist a usual kind of picture" and, thereby, "bring out . . . neglected likenesses and differences . . . [and] in some measure, remake our world" (p. 33).

In this chapter, several examples of arts based research, out of the untold numbers available, will serve to illustrate how this approach to social inquiry may assist in this return to difficulty and the remaking of the world. Some of these examples will be projects by researchers who call themselves arts based; some will be by researchers who label their work otherwise but whose achievements closely resemble the emancipatory ones found in good arts based research.

And in later chapters, we will extend and refine the notion of world-making to consider the manner in which arts based research might promote the transformation of public policy and of the institutions which that policy serves and shapes.

EXAMPLES OF ARTS BASED SOCIAL RESEARCH
THAT CAN MAKE NEW WORLDS

The first three examples of arts based research that we reference are projects by academics in various fields who do indeed self-identify as arts based researchers. They also represent three different forms of art: (1) poetry, (2) theater, and (3) photography. First, we discuss the questions that each text seems to raise and later the manner in which each accomplishes that feat.

The first example is an article by Anne Sullivan (2000) entitled "Notes from a Marine Biologist's Daughter: On the Art and Science of Attention" (reprinted in this book). This article incorporates autobiographical poetry into a larger essay on the theme of the nature of attentiveness and its relationship to teaching, learning, and research. Often arts based researchers do not directly identify the questions that their texts are intended to raise. Sullivan (2000), however, did, as she wondered aloud in the introduction to her poetry:

What exactly are teachers asking for when they say, "Pay attention"? What are the relationships between attention and intrinsic motivation? Is it possible to teach habits of attending? How can we enroll peripheral attention to the advantage of education? How can we know the long-term effects of attending? (p. 211)

And then, referring to the realm of social research, she wrote, "What is the nature of the [qualitative] researcher's attention? How do we learn to attend with keen eyes and fine sensibilities? How do we teach others to do it?" (pp. 211–212).

Through her poetry and essay, Sullivan, in our judgment, succeeds in doing that which she suggested, following the novelist James Baldwin (1962, p. 17), is the purpose of art: "to lay bare the questions which have been hidden by the answers" (Sullivan, 2000, p. 218).

A second example of arts based research is performance based—an ethnodrama. An ethnodrama is a written script for a work of ethnotheatre. The latter "employs the traditional craft and artistic techniques of theatre production to mount for an audience a live performance event of research participants' experiences and/or the researcher's interpretations of data" (Saldana, 2005, p. 1).

The ethnodrama entitled "Street Rat" is the result of a collaboration by arts based researchers Johnny Saldana, Susan Finley, and Macklin Finley (2002), the first two of whom are academics. The script was adapted from a research story composed by the Finleys (Finley & Finley, 1999) and from poetry written by Macklin Finley (2000). This story and poetry were in turn the products of participatory and observational social research engaged in primarily by Macklin Finley. Several stagings (under the direction of Saldana) have resulted from this and earlier versions of the script.

"Street Rat" is a work of arts based research that focuses on the lives of some homeless youths in pre-Katrina New Orleans. In attending to the play, one may come to vicariously participate in their daily lives and, consequently, to rethink one's assumptions about various social issues surrounding homeless youth in our culture. These may include the structure of their moral codes and the character of the largely hidden cultural forces that operate to constrain their hopes and aspirations.

For our third example of a project by a self-described arts based researcher, we choose an article by Stephanie Springgay (2003). Entitled "Cloth as Intercorporeality: Touch, Fantasy, and Performance and the Construction of Body Knowledge," the article is available online at http://ijea.asu.edu/v4n5/. In it Springgay blended the following: an analytical essay; photographs of the artist–researcher's studio compositions of (among other things) cloth, human hair, rose petals, and pins; still photos from a video produced by the author; and autobiographical blurbs that express the personal motivations behind her visual creations and that serve as small bridges between the visual imagery and Springgay's elaborate theoretical musings.

The essay into which the visual works are folded is designed to challenge the reader–viewer's preconceptions regarding the nature and place of the body in educational practices. Springgay (2003) extended the work of scholars from other fields who refuse the traditional dichotomy between mind and body through her exploration of the notion of intercorporeality, which, she suggested, refers to "the body in relation to other bodies and the ways in which knowing and being are informed through generative understandings of touch, fantasy, and performance" (p. 1). Springgay contrasted this relational concept of the body and its affiliations with an education of "tactility and felt knowledge," with the oppressive schooling practices that arise out of a notion of the body-in-need-of-discipline-and-control. In our estimation, as Springgay "folds desire and synaesthesia into education" (p. 17), she succeeded in "destabilizing and rupturing [timeworn] boundaries"—an aim worthy of a self-professed arts based researchers.

We agree with the researchers of these three projects that they are indeed examples of arts based research. And we believe that, although these examples are the results of careful scrutinizing of certain aspects of the social world, none makes the sorts of knowledge claims that traditional social researchers offer. None suggests that their view of the highlighted phenomena represents finally correct descriptions, interpretations, or judgments. They are not designed to reinforce stereotypical or taken-for-granted notions of what it means to attend to the physical world around us, to be homeless in America, or to think about the place of the body in educational activities. Indeed, quite the opposite is the case. Each possesses the capacity to disrupt our comfortable assumptions about these thoroughly human phenomena.

Each of these works also contributes to ongoing conversations, both within scholarly subcommunities and in the realms of the public at large, about the themes upon which they focus. But their contributions to these conversations involve more than merely entering them. By questioning taken-for-granted premises, they serve to move them into radically different directions. They do, indeed, contain the capacity, reiterating the words of Geertz (1983), to "vex" fellow conversationalists. They achieve this, however, not by claiming to add to an existing "knowledge base." Instead, they succeed in persuading others to look again at the empirical world—the world of practical experience—out of which human judgments are formed and to experience facets of it in an astonishingly new way.

But how precisely do they accomplish that? This question points us to a discussion of elements of research design—elements found in both the inquiry and representational phases of all research projects.

USEFUL DESIGN ELEMENTS FOR FOSTERING UNCERTAINTY

Some readers may be more familiar with the notion of design elements in regard to traditional forms of social research than in regard to arts based research. Consider, for example, experimental research design. Experiments in the fields of the social sciences tend to be deliberately—and systematically—arranged and conducted to protect against the validation of inferior, "rival" explanations. Random assignment of subjects is just one possible element of design employed to further that desirable sort of control. Such control is important if the ultimate goal of an experiment—the enhancement of certainty—is to be approached. Moreover, in the data representation phase of an experiment, one may find a standardized, systematic format for reporting results. The latter may include a formal statement of the problem, a review of the relevant literature, a methods section, a presentation and analysis of findings, and suggestions for further research.

None of the design elements employed in an experimental social research project is, to repeat, present by chance or whim. Each is included for a clear purpose, meant to ensure a high degree of utility in the knowledge claims that are produced. Other forms of quantitative and qualitative research will, of course, employ alternative design elements for arriving at "valid" and "reliable" knowledge, or at least, in some cases, convincing interpretations of social phenomena.

Arts based researchers also employ design elements in both the inquiry process and in the composition of the research text. Moreover, we see these two dimensions of an arts based project (the manner of inquiry and the aesthetic qualities in the "product") as interrelated, synergistic, mutually reinforcing. They are also often (although not always) engaged in simultaneously, as the process of inquiry may occur within the act of composition and vice versa. But, leaving the inquiry process to be more fully addressed in Chapter 3, we focus here on textual design. Specifically, we aim to link the arrangement of the aesthetic qualities within each of three texts to the alternative, interrogative purpose of arts based research that they serve.

We first pause to note, however, that not only art (and arts based research) offers the kinds of lenses needed to see social phenomena in fundamentally new ways. Scientists, states people, social theorists, inventors, public intellectuals of all sorts, have, throughout history, helped to "make new worlds." But only artists—and among academic scholars, arts based researchers—can achieve that feat through the creation of powerful aesthetic forms. Only the compositions of artists and arts based researchers can redirect conversations about social phenomena by enabling others *to vicariously reexperience the world*. Only they choose to use the expressive qualities of an artistic medium to convey meanings that are otherwise unavailable. But it is only to the degree that its artistic elements of design are employed *effectively* can the work achieve, to that degree, a special sort of aesthetic utility.

This achievement requires the following:

- ■ a careful investigation into dimensions of the social world by the arts based researcher;

- ■ a reconfiguration and re-presentation of selected facets of what that research "uncovers," with those facets now transformed into aesthetic substance upon their embodiment within an aesthetic form; and

- ■ the production of disequilibrium within the percipient of the work as s/he vicariously reexperiences what has been designed.

It is indeed through this reexperiencing—not through a logical form of discourse, nor through the acceptance of a linear argument or explanation—that what we call *deep persuasion* might occur. This is a luring of percipients into the acceptance of alternative values and meanings for facets of social issues and practices that were previously misunderstood as being finally understood.

Let us consider how this persuasion to reconsider the world may operate within our three examples of arts based research.

First, let us look at the Sullivan (2000) text.

In crafting her poetry that serves as the heart of her article, Sullivan (2000) revealed an impressive mastery of detail. Many of the particulars she located were extracted from experiences with her mother, who, she contended, first taught her how to attend seriously to facets of her physical environment. The details she chose to include in her poems were reconfigured into an aesthetic form in a purposeful manner. These minutiae of experience—with their powerful sensory qualities of, for example, the colors of blue on the sides of fish, clamshells, "the oyster blue at my inner thigh," and the "blue-black ink of the squid's soft gland"—are not included for the purpose of replicating a conventionally "real" world once experienced by Sullivan. Rather, the chosen details were recast into an aesthetic form in order to entice readers into a virtual world, one that is a *semblance* of reality (Langer, 1957).

The poems are structured so as to coax readers into the having of an experience that is analogous to (if not precisely the same as) the experience of the researcher/poet. It is through the reexperiencing of powerful mental images that the reader is brought to vicariously inhabit the virtual world of this work of arts based research.

For readers to be willing and able to enter into an arts based text, the virtual world must be sufficiently believable, credible enough for the reader to recognize it as *possible*, if not actual. It must *seem* authentic. (Does this make Sullivan's [2000] article a work of fiction? See Chapter 6 for a discussion of that point.) Moreover, it may be precisely because this world is indeed plausible, as opposed to conventionally "real," that a healthy distance may form between the viewer and her stale images of a taken-for-granted reality. Being transported, at least momentarily, into an "aesthetic remove," the viewer may be coaxed into viewing her own mundane realities from an unfamiliar—and perhaps disturbing—angle.

Again, those facets of the "real world" are associated with the theme of Sullivan's [2000] work that surrounds the nature of attentiveness. When Sullivan's work is successful then the aesthetic distance it has created through its carefully employed elements of design serves to disturb the reader into not merely an imagining of how Sullivan learned to attend to sensory detail through a masterful teacher but, more importantly, a reimagining of how the reader may herself do as much for others.

Other deftly employed elements of design in Sullivan's (2000) poems—rhythm, balance, flow, language choice, thematic control, and so on—also serve to elevate their aesthetic effect above the level of mere technical proficiency. But to the extent that form is associated with function then these design elements are not merely present for "art's sake." Rather, they are brought into a coherence that maximizes their potential for "deep persuasion," achieving that primary interrogative purpose of art as a form of human studies.

Our second example of arts based research—the ethnodrama "Street Rat" (Finley, 2000; Saldana, Finley, & Finley, 2002)—is also structured in a powerful manner. One might, in fact, contend that two forms of art are represented in this example—first, the script of the play, and second, the staged production that brought to life that incorporated script. We will discuss, however, a production of this play attended by Tom Barone in April 2004.

To Barone, a string of carefully arranged, telling details (analogous to those found in Sullivan's [2000] poems) were almost immediately apparent. These included a cascade of concrete images, specific utterances and gestures within particular incidents, both dramatic and mundane, that arose out of the lives of the play's central characters, Tigger and Roach. These incidents suggested, within these castoffs of society, the presence of unexpected forms of intelligence, of strict, if unanticipated, moral codes and of surprisingly poignant hopes and dreams.

These images and utterances were sculptured into a somewhat conventional dramatic form as the action moved from an introduction of the two homeless boys to complications arising from their relationships with each other and their friends to a tense climax and finally a touching denouement in which Tigger and Roach, apparently filling a void in each other's lives left there by others, proclaim their garbage-strewn living quarters as "home."

Visual elements also contributed to the production's effective mise-en-scène. Absent a proscenium arch, audience members were seated in a black draped, rectangular room, its floor shared with the actors. The minimal props, authentic costuming, and background music were all carefully designed and selected to advance the vision of the director and his collaborators and allowed audience members to dwell within a credible world, one that was at once strange and familiar. Within this world were believable characters that, while unique to the play, were paradoxically reminiscent of other distressed, alienated youngsters previously encountered on terrain outside of that auditorium. In that manner did the play achieve metaphorical power for at least one attendee who departed convinced that he would never see homeless youngsters in the same way again.

In "Street Rat" (Finley, 2000; Saldana, Finley, & Finley, 2002), as in the Sullivan (2000) text, that which Iser (1993) called an *imaginary*, an array of "arbitrary apparitions," a set of "diffuse fleeting impressions," were shaped into an "articulate gestalt," thereby providing an opening into a new psychological landscape, into a possible, as *if* world. Entering into such a landscape, the viewer may be rendered at least momentarily disoriented before slowly acquiring a degree of empathic understanding of the inhabitants of that world who are slowly transformed from aliens—"others" with whom it may be difficult to feel a sense of solidarity—into people who live inside of what Rorty (1989) referred to as "the range of us." This sense of dizziness, of disequilibrium, though, is what artists and arts based researchers strive toward as they call into question that which has become the all-too-familiar.

Dizziness and a sense of destabilization may also be appropriate responses to the Springgay (2003) project. A sense of dislocation may indeed arise in one's reading and viewing of this arts based text with its enormously significant implications for thinking about the embodied self and its relationships with other embodied selves. In fostering this dislocation our deeply entrenched ways of thinking about the human (the "social," the "lived") body as existing in opposition to the mind, as dangerous, in need of regulation, are changed.

Springgay (2003) offers a genre-blended text, one in which the written word and the visual image are mutually reinforcing. One might argue that the product, taken in its entirety, is a less unified work than the script of "Street Rat" (Finley, 2000; Saldana, Finley, & Finley, 2002), insofar as the latter offers an aesthetic form *sans* the presence of an explanatory envelope. The part of Springgay's article that attempts to persuade through argument may more closely resemble a work of art criticism with an academic emphasis, one that imports notions from an array of postmodernist, poststructuralist, and feminist thinkers to displace prevailing conceptions of the human body. But unlike most works of art criticism, Springgay's article is studded with artistic constructions of her own making—namely, those powerfully vexing photographs of her studio compositions. More importantly, she avoided relegating those works, with their stunning visual imagery, to a role of servitude as ornamental illustrations for grounding a general "model of intercorporeality."

Instead, the photos themselves—employing various design elements from the visual arts—*embody* that notion. Moreover, these visual components (along with the artfully crafted autobiographical nuggets) are both evocative and provocative, possessing a capacity to engage our imagination in the reformulation of meaning. Enabling us to *experience* her ideas directly for ourselves, Springgay's photos achieve the status of art, thereby legitimating her article, in its entirety, as a work of arts *based* research.

These three examples of social research, all by self-identified arts based researchers, achieve that which we have identified as the oft-ignored, yet absolutely vital, *interrogative* purpose of inquiry into the human condition. Again, they do this by allowing readers and viewers to vicariously reexperience significant dimensions of human affairs through the use of aesthetic design elements. But now here is another often misunderstood notion concerning arts based research: Arts based research is not only practiced by artist–academics who label their research arts based—the Sullivans, Saldanas, and Springgays of the world. Other researchers, from both within and outside of the academy, some of whom see themselves as artists and some of whom do not, may also produce texts that—insofar as they, through their skillful use of aesthetic design elements, convey otherwise unavailable social meaning—may also be identified as arts based.

OTHER EXAMPLES OF QUALITATIVE RESEARCH THAT MAKE NEW WORLDS

The terms *arts based research* and *artistic* research are not, we contend, identical. Rather, the former term implies a continuum that extends from qualitative research projects that, while being officially tagged as science, effectively deploy a few aesthetic design elements to those who exhibit maximum artistry. Aesthetic design elements can indeed be located most obviously in works of art, whether the "high art" of professional artists or "everyday," popular art (including those we mentioned in Chapter 1 by the likes of Arthur Miller, Charles Dickens, and Mario Puzo).

A deep pool of research texts that achieve the important inquiry purpose of raising questions for the sake of generating and redirecting conversations, but which exhibit only a few aesthetic elements, has long existed. But this pool was publicized in the 1970s as the anthropologist–storyteller Clifford Geertz named (and helped to legitimate) the phenomenon of *genre blending*. Later the pool deepened significantly as both qualitative social scientists and arts based research types sensed an enhanced freedom to explore the possibilities within various amalgamations of artistic and scientific research design elements.

Out of the myriad available, we now identify three accomplished published works that are the results of such explorations. We see these works as largely arts based, even if the authors/researchers are unacquainted with the term. Two are by academics; one is not. Some contain more (and more effectively employed) artistic design elements than do others. They are works by Ruth Behar (1996), Laura Simon (1997), and Anna Deavere Smith (1993), and they take the forms, respectively, of a literary autobiographical essay, a documentary video, and an ethnodrama. All, we argue, represent qualitative research texts that are useful in the same way that art can be. Variously labeled, crafted from within or outside of the academy, each is an example of good arts based research that "makes new worlds."

"The Girl in the Cast" is a glorious literary-style autoethnographic essay from the book *The Vulnerable Observer* by Ruth Behar (1996). In it, the ethnographic storyteller reflects upon her time as a child immobilized for 9 months in a body cast following a horrendous automobile accident on Long Island and upon the psychological trauma that lingered into her adulthood. It is only in her fourth decade, upon Behar's return from a visit to her homeland Cuba, back to the country where the accident occurred, that she is finally able to find peace through forgiveness of the reckless teenage driver who had caused her such enormous pain.

The aesthetic elements within Behar's vivid retelling of the ordeal provide a window into the complex psychosocial dynamics that accompanied this particular life incident, but its graceful encompassing of the thoughts of other great artists and essayists adds to the metaphorical power of the essay. The once physically crippled Behar ranges far and wide as she weaves ideas from a wide-ranging group of authors, including the likes of Sandra Cisneros, Oliver Sachs, Carol Gilligan, and Salman Rushdie into a thematically rich tapestry. Her themes include at least two that are familiar to social scientists, especially cultural anthropologists and ethnographers: the insecurities endured by immigrants in a new place, and the coming of age of (here Latina) adolescents. Others include the meaning of confinement and of independence (both physical and psychological) and the usefulness of combining autobiography with ethnography into autoethnography.

That utility for Behar (1996) lies in a capacity to create "forms of embodied knowledge in which the (adult) self and the (child) other can rediscover and reaffirm their connectedness" (p. 135). Through an effective employment of literary elements, this particular autoethnography does indeed foster an empathic understanding of at least a version of the author's "self"—one that serves to interrupt our own sense of safety by calling into question certain dimensions of our own lives. Its capacity to do so suggests its close kinship with arts based inquiry.

The second example is a film directed not by a Hollywood professional but by an elementary school teacher at a predominantly Latino/a school in Los Angeles. First shown as part of the POV Series on the Public Broadcasting Service, *Fear and Learning at Hoover Elementary* (Simon, 1997) traces events that transpired as a result of the passage of California's Proposition 187, a proposal that aimed to deny public education to undocumented immigrants by requiring their teachers to report them to authorities. Indeed, the film dramatically illustrates the dire consequences of the proposition's passage, especially the heightening of mistrust between people of different ethnic groups.

The film achieves this by focusing primarily on the lives of a few individual school people, especially the charming, feisty, intelligent Maira, and her teacher, Simon, herself. Its carefully etched portrait of the rupture in the close relationship between these two victims vividly illustrates how the tentacles of social policy can reach deeply into the realm of everyday human experience. And this picture of deeply personal tragedy serves as the metaphor for the central theme of ethnicity-based mistrust within the society at large.

The film uses careful editing and documentary footage to develop this theme, especially through the elements of characterization and narrative drive. The visual imagery is especially telling, from helicopters hovering over a polluted city's protestor-filled streets, to a close inspection of the tight living quarters of Maira and her family.

By the conclusion of the film, we have been left with disturbing questions about the kinds of social policy that can lead to an enhanced dissolution of community. We are moved because Simon's research and artistry enables us to recognize ourselves as members of that community and because we want to save ourselves. The film's theme is both timely and timeless as it calls into question all social policy that is based on fear and the manner in which that policy can exacerbate estrangement of people who can no longer recognize each other as fellow inhabitants of one world.

The third example is a carefully researched play, somewhat in the style of "Street Rat" (Finley, 2000; Saldana, Finley, & Finley, 2002). "Fires in the Mirror: Crown Heights, Brooklyn, and Other Identities" by Anna Deavere Smith (1993) is a compelling ethnodrama that skillfully explores a variety of complex themes, from racial animosity in America to the nature of truth. (It also, coincidentally, involves an automobile accident in New York.) Having conducted over 100 interviews with people of various backgrounds—from a Lubavitcher woman who was a graphic designer to the Reverend Al Sharpton—all of whom were affected by the 1991 riots following a fatal car accident in Brooklyn, the researcher/playwright shaped excerpts from them into a tapestry of monologues.

In the original production, all 29 roles were performed by Smith herself. This design choice may have diminished any sense of a privileging of some accountings over others, a point essential to the play's thesis about how the cores of worldviews are shaped within the crucible of life experience.

As with "Street Rat" (Finley, 2002; Saldana, Finley, & Finley, 2002), other staging elements added to a heuristic power that is the hallmark of arts based research. Indeed, the lingering questions of playgoers have been so pressing that, within some local venues, opportunities for structured conversation following the play have been prearranged, in order to address directly the disequilibrium felt by audience members.

These examples by Ruth Behar, Laura Simon, and Anna Deavere Smith—alongside those of Sullivan, Saldana, and Springgay—represent only a few of the many available forms of arts based research and adjacent (or overlapping) fields of qualitative research with significant aesthetic features. For word-based, or alphanumeric, texts, the last several decades have witnessed the so-called linguistic, narrative, and literary "turns" in the humanities and social sciences resulting in a burgeoning of literary forms. A short list includes the following: allegory, autobiography, autoethnography, biography, fictional storytelling, layered accounts, life story, life history, literary essay, literary ethnography, memoir, mixed genres, mystory, narrative composition, nonfictional novel, novel, novella, performance science, poetry, polyvocal texts, readers theater, saga, short story, writing-story, mixed genres (see also Richardson, 2000, p. 930). Arts based research may also employ forms of performance and plastic art including, among others, readers theater, collage, painting, documentary films, photography, multimedia and mixed-media installations, and digital hypertext.

Our move in this chapter is, finally, not toward a presumptuous subsuming of all of these aesthetically sensitive styles of social research into an oversized hamper labeled arts based. It is, rather, to advance, discursively and through examples, a conception of *arts based* research as a broad approach to social inquiry. It is also meant to illustrate the manner in which some projects of qualitative research that are not labeled arts based may nevertheless evidence sufficient aesthetic capacity to foster the transformation of worldviews. This can occur when any piece of social research does *not* move to enhance certainty but instead, through the use of expressive design elements, succeeds (in varying measures) in the unearthing of questions that have been buried by the answers, and thereby in remaking the social world. That, in our judgment, is a very good reason indeed for doing arts based research.

Arts Based Research Example

Notes From a Marine Biologist's Daughter: On the Art and Science of Attention*

ANNE McCRARY SULLIVAN
National-Louis University, Tampa, Florida

Through an autobiographical lens, Anne McCrary Sullivan explores the sensory and emotional aspects of attending and their implications for teaching, learning, and research. Her poetry and stanzaic prose attempt to awaken in the reader an artistic engagement with the various meanings of attention. Her use of the genre challenges traditional approaches to representing knowledge.

In an age of attention deficit disorder and of frequent teacher complaints that overentertained children do not want to pay attention, the issue of attention in educational settings is critical. John Dewey's early insistence that curriculum grow out of the interests of the child (Dewey, 1902) included the concept that students would, without coercion, give attention to matters and materials of immediate relevance to their lives. A strong contingency of educators and researchers continues to find this concept critical. More generally, the focus has been on how to get students to pay attention whether or not the curriculum

---

*This article originally appeared in Sullivan, A. M. (2000, Summer). "Notes from a marine biologist's daughter: On the art and science of attention," *Harvard Educational Review*, 70(2), 211–227. Copyright © President and Fellows of Harvard College. All rights reserved. For more information, please visit www.harvardeducationalreview.org.

has interest or relevance—how to trick, entertain, bribe or coerce them to perform (Kohn, 1993). Historically, in the field of education, our concern with engaging and maintaining student attention has been consistent, but our investigations of the nature of attention and its development rather limited.

What exactly are teachers asking for when they say, "Pay attention"? What are the relationships between attention and intrinsic motivation? Is it possible to teach habits of attending? How well can we enroll peripheral attention to the advantage of education? How can we know the long-term effects of attending?

In the realm if educational research, qualitative researchers call for learning about phenomena by giving them sustained attention. What is the nature of the researcher's attention? How do we learn to attend with keen eyes and sensibilities? How do we teach each other to do it? My autobiography is largely an autobiography of attention—learning it, teaching it, discovering its role in research. It's a story that began when I was very young.

I. AN AUTOBIOGRAPHY OF ATTENTION (PART I)

Notes From a Marine Biologist's Daughter

My mother loves the salty mud of estuaries,
has no need of charts to know what time
low tide will come. She lives
by arithmetic of moon,
calculates emergences of mud.

waits for all that crawls there, lays eggs,
buries itself in the shallow edges
of streamlets and pools. She digs
for *chaetopterus*, yellow and orange
worms that look like lace.

She leads me where *renilla* bloom
purple and white colonial lives,
where brittle stars, like moss,
cling to stone. She knows
where the sea horse wraps its tail
and the unseen lives of plankton.

My mother walks and sinks into an ooze,
centuries of organisms ground
to pasty darkness. The sun burns at her shoulders
in its slow passage across the sky.
Light waves like pincers
in her mud-dark hair.

Mother Collecting Marine Specimens

She poles the skiff from sunlight
into the drawbridge shadow, eases
against a piling, its muddy shapes
exposed by lowering tide.

In a cave-like cool, she nudges
grey clusters, crusty forms.
She scrapes, selects,
lays silty bits and clumps
in a bucket of clear water.

Intent, she peers and plucks.
A streak of blood appears on her thumb.
She doesn't notice. She never does.
I slide a finger over creosote blisters,
hear them pop, feel them flatten,
then stare into the realm of the underbridge—
great toothy gears, twisted cables.

Above our boat, the whirr of tires.
No one knows we're under here.
or thinks of these barnacles
their hair like legs kicking
just below the water line.

Bells begin to clang, the hum
ceases, the bridge shudders,
its teeth begin to grind.

When we reenter brightness
and the ordinary pitch of traffic,
I lean to look in Mother's bucket:
green stones, yellow trees,
purple stars an orange flame.

Herding Fiddler Crabs

The sun is high, beginning its downward arc.
Our pits, buckets buried in mud to their rims,

are ready. We encircle the herd, our arms
raised in mud-smeared curves, mimicking
the crabs' outspread pincers. We stamp our feet, close in.
They flee like receding tide

I remember the films shot from airplanes,
The estuary greens blues, blacks
curving around each other's shapes,
and on the mud flats, herds
of indistinguishable bodies
making silent, amebic migrations.

It's different down here. Listen.
Thousands of clicks,
the small collisions,
claws and carapaces,
finely jointed legs landing
in frantic succession
on mud. And there—
so many fallings.

Mother in Water

"Did you see
how she stared and trembled?
If I ever get like that
I want you to row me
beyond the breakers,
push me over.
I mean it. Promise."

Sometimes I see us
in a small white boat.
At the bow she sits,
back erect, facing forward.
Her head jerks lightly.
I row. My arms ache,
eyes sting.
Behind us, land
flattens to a line.

Before she was twelve
she knew these waters,

pooled alone
in a wooden skiff
through the wandering maze
of slough and marsh,
channel and sandbar;
she'd beach the boat,
take off her shirt and swim.

Only water now. Water.
how easily, quietly
it opens. Just
beneath the surface.
I see her gliding,
gills opening,
expanding like sponges,
waving like feathers.
A flash of silver
darts into the green.

How I Learned to Love Picasso

At nineteen, I knew nothing, wanted to know everything,
including why those paintings hung in the Petit Palais,
why people lined up for blocks in the cold,
why I stood with them blowing clouds of breath.

Les Demoiselles D'Avignon. I stared.
At fractured shapes and faces,
pondered all that flesh pink
and then one leg
where a thick blue line
plunged from thigh to calf.

I imagined that line gone.

Learning Blue

My mother taught me blue—
water under the boat,
shadow in the marsh,
blue flashing

at the sides of fish,
blue crabs waving
blue and white claws,
blue speck
at the clam's inner hinge,
just beside
where the soft body lies.
Now I learn blue again—
oyster bruise
at my inner thigh,
blue black ink
of the squid's soft gland
deepening, spreading, tender.

Beware: The Poet Comes for Tea

She sits, rattles the ice in her glass,
laughs at small talk, but
she's looking under your skin.

She sees your bones, that fine crack
in the radius; she hears the blood
rushing out of the heart, leaping

into its hopeful journey,
then limping back to the side door,
knocking lightly, pleading.

She feels that spark at the synapse,
flinches just barely; you don't see.
Later, she goes to her room and writes

your life. She will mail you a poem
which disrupts your breath, makes you weep
for all you thought hidden, interior, safe.

Dolphins

This evening, in diffuse light,
I learn from dolphins what I must know
of poems—how they break the surface

when least expected, make their arcs
in peripheral vision. Startled

at the first glimpse, I jerked to see
their fine motion, the dark lines
tracing their quiet way.
I had been walking, just walking
the curve of the shore, thinking of

who knows what. Who cares? It's gone,
replaced. Oh grace! I turned
to follow their benedictions, my pace
matching the pace of one slow swimmer.
Each time it rose, it rose

beside me, until it turned
to deeper water. I saw
the last blip of its dark Morse code,
then stood and stared,
watching and wanting.

Water and water and water.
Visions cannot be commanded.
The air grows chill now with pink
consolation. One line of light lies
on the nervous surface.

When I Die

Write to my friends.
Tell them what time of day or night
I died and what the weather was.

Tell them, the color of the walls
That last contained me.

Describe the quality of light in the room,
its brightness or grayness. Did light
make a pattern on my face?

Tell them if I closed my eyes myself;
or give the name of the one who closed them for me.

Tell them if there were flowers in the room,
or outside the window, or if there were any scent
that might be called the scent of death.

Tell them the sound of my silence.
Listen carefully for this.

Say who pulled the sheet over my head;
describe the shape of my body under it.

When had I last listened to music?
What was the sound of my last breath?

Was there any small ugliness?
A trail of saliva? A drooping?

Did anyone notice an insect in the room?

Write quickly; avoid nothing.
My friends are poets. They need details.

II. POEMS IN THE ACADEMY (PART 1)

Poems are an anomaly in educational journals. Many readers will be puzzled about the presence of these poems, unsure of their relation to educational inquiry and theory. I would suggest that the relations are multiple, subtle, and complex, and that these very characteristics are part of their potential value.

As a case study of a woman whose life has been grounded in attention, these poems collectively raise significant questions about the nature of attention: how attention to external realities might facilitate awareness of internal realities; how focused attention to an immediate reality may engage memory and/or imagination. "The purpose of art," says novelist James Baldwin, "is to lay bare the questions which have been hidden by the answers" (1962, p. 17).

As a collection of forms that construct their organization from the web-like motions of the mind, rather than in the linear discursive patterns traditionally prescribed by [the] Western academy, these poems invite new ways of engaging with the problem of attention, and complementary ways of mapping such investigations.

As representations of lived states of attention, they resonate with recent brain research related to attentional phenomena, including the roles of peripheral and focused attention (Caine & Caine, 1994; Lozanov, 1978) and the significance of emotion in engaging and sustaining attention (Csikszentmihaliyi, 1991; Damasio, 1994; Sylwester, 1995).

Incorporating highly concrete observations, these poems exemplify a degree of concreteness and detail that has potential of enriching both the accuracy and power of traditional field notes as qualitative researchers strive to evoke the worlds they represent.

As manifestations of a way of processing information and experience that differs from long-established, well-entrenched, but recently challenged academic norms (Barone & Eisner, 1997; Eisner, 1997), these poems, appearing in this particular place, constitute a political statement on behalf of the enfranchisement of artists, whose voices have been marginalized in the academy.

III. AESTHETIC VISION: A COMPLEX ATTENTION

Aesthetic vision suggests a high level of consciousness about what one sees. It suggests an alertness, a "wide-awakeness" that Maxine Greene (1978, 1995) has urged educators and researchers to learn from artists. Aesthetic vision engages a sensitivity to suggestion, to pattern, to that which is beneath the surface itself. It requires . . . a fine attention to detail and form: the perception of relations (tensions and harmonies), the perception of nuance (colors and meaning), and the perception of change (shifts and subtle motions). It dared to address the ineffable (Eisner, 1997). Aesthetic vision adjusts the flow of time. It may seize a moment in order to stare at it and see more fully, more deeply, but aesthetic vision does not assume that what one sees in the moment is what one will always see. It perceives the potential for transformation within any fixity—a block of wood, a piece of clay, a display of words, the configuration of a classroom, or the behavior of an individual or a child. Aesthetic vision is always from a specific point of view, filtered by a specific consciousness. It is personal and situational. It includes emotion, imagination, and paradox. It embraces complexity.

Teachers who function with aesthetic vision perceive the dynamics of a situation and know how to "read" it. They look at details within their contexts, perceive relations among the parts and between the parts of the whole. They look for patterns within disorder, for unity beneath superficial disruption, and for disruption beneath superficial unity. They construct forms and suggest meanings.

IV. AN AUTOBIOGRAPHY OF ATTENTION (PART 2)

My mother, the scientist, taught me to see. She taught me attention to the complexities of surface detail and also attention to what lies beneath those surfaces. She taught me the rhythms of tide and regeneration, and the syllables of the natural world rubbing against each other. In doing [so], she made me a poet.

My mother, the teacher, held classes in mud and water and light. She taught with buckets and shovels and nets. Her students' tennis shoes and hers squished loudly as they worked, discovered, learned. I observed that my mother and her students were happy. I became a 'teacher.'

My mother, the researcher, went into the field twice a day whatever the weather for years, methodically, with her plankton nets. Then she sat patiently at the microscope on the kitchen table, observing, noticing, discovering patterns, making sense. In that kitchen, I learned the patience of research.

My mother made order out of the raggedness of the living world, and I was paying attention. But I didn't know at the time that I was, and I'm quite sure that she didn't think I was. I gave little overt attention to her work. She dragged me along on the mud flats, to the boat docs, under bridges. I went and entertained myself as best I could. While she focused intently on the organisms that grew on pilings, paying such acute attention that she didn't even notice the bleeding cut on her hand ("she never did"), I was distractedly popping creosote blisters.

And yet, there is another layer to this, because years later I remember with a vividness and an intensity that compel me to poetry. On some level, in some hidden and inarticulate way, I must have been attending and recording extremely well. I was learning, internalizing without any direct instruction.

Mother did sometimes offer direct instruction, telling me the [L]atin names of organisms and placing them in their scientific categories. I remember very little of what she taught me in this direct way. What I do remember is so deeply embedded in experience that it has entered my ways of thinking and perceiving, my very way of being, without the intermediary of language—at any rate, without language that addressed this learning directly.

What did physicality and emotion have to do with my learning and with sublingual attention? How important were the tactile impressions of sun on my skin, mud beneath my feet, the water's salt at my lip, the rockings of Mother's wooden boat? How did they matter, those lappings and squishings, the bubblings and "thousands of clicks, / the small collisions, / claws and carapaces?" What did I learn from surprise and the delight at the laciness of the worms she dug up from the mud, the "yellow trees, purple stars, and orange flame" suddenly in her bucket? What are the implications of this for education in a society that demands artificial attention and immediate testable results? What are the implications for researchers who are trying to make visible the invisible processes of cognition?

V. POEMS IN THE ACADEMY (PART 2)

Poems, born of attention, also invite attention. They rarely get it. As a society, we have not been taught how to attend to art, how to "read" it, how to process its content or its potential for generating useful questions. We are relatively illiterate in the arts, even those of us who are otherwise deeply and well educated, unless we have specifically sought those kinds of reading lessons. As a culture, our lessons in art have generally been indirect and have indicated that art is peripheral, an expendable extra. In short, to borrow a term from John Dewey, we have been *miseducated*.

Dewey understood and defended sometimes a bit feistily, the role of art as a way of encoding knowledge about complex relations:

> To think effectively in terms of relations of qualities is a severe demand upon thought as to think in terms of symbols, verbal, and mathematical . . . Production of a work of genuine art probably demands more intelligence than does most of the so called thinking that goes on among those who pride themselves on being "intellectual."

Many in the academic community, not having been taught to read aesthetic forms, reject them as representations of knowledge. If, however, we are to become literate in a wider range of the forms in which knowledge may be encoded, we must give attention to these forms. We must stare at them, ponder them, arrive at an understanding not only of what the forms contain, but also of how form informs.

Walker Evans, the early twentieth-century photographer, an arts-based researcher long before the term became popular, advocated focused attention as a way of coming to know. He advised us, "Stare. It is the only way to educate your eye, and more. Stare, pry, listen, eavesdrop. Die knowing something. You are not here long" (Thompson & Hill, 1982, p. 161).

Contemplating my own autobiography of attention, I become aware of the extent to which I have learned about visual art simply by staring at it, as in "How I learned to Love Picasso." I stood in front of that large painting, *Les Demoiselles D'Avignon*, and stared, allowed my eye to move as it would among the details. I stared with a curious eye, an eye that didn't yet know how to understand, didn't yet know how art could teach me. For rather a long time I stood there, wondering what I was "supposed" to be seeing. Then I allowed imagination to guide my vision. When I imagined that blue line gone and suddenly felt in the painting a shift of energy and balance, a loss that I couldn't articulate but that I undeniably felt as a loss, I realized for the first time that all of the parts of the composition mattered. Any alteration of the part would have an effect on the whole. Nothing was accidental. There was an ecology of the work of art. This was, for me, a revolutionary and long-lasting insight, as was the new understanding that I could learn about art by giving it focused attention.

How do we teach children in school this kind of attention? How often in school were we ourselves encouraged to stare?

VI. TEACHING ATTENTION

How might we teach attention? I've been struggling with that question for over twenty years now. When I taught high school English and creative writing, I was always searching for ways to bring students into attention, the sort of deep attention that would elicit the capacity for poetry that I believed they all had in them. I would do things like take them out on the broad lawn in front of the school, have them spread out, each to sit alone and watch a small patch of grass, to observe and record "what happens there."

The wording, "what happens there," was important. Skepticism about this assignment was generally high among my students. "Just stare," I would say. "Stare at the grass until something happens." No one ever failed to see things happen. Small events became sources of excitement—an ant crawling up a blade of grass, a flutter of motion produced by a breeze, a shifting of light, the crossing of a cloud shadow.

In another homework assignment, I would ask them to "find a place where there's nothing going on. Sit there for ten minutes and recor[d] everything that happens." In response to this assignment, tenth grader Rhonda Rogers sat on her back porch and made the journal entries that led to this:

> Secluded
> and alone
> I sit searching.
>
> The nightly cicadan chant
> converses with itself.
>
> A cricket's flat drone echoes,
> rattlingly hollow.

Zephyrs shudder empty limbs.
Detached leaves scuttle on pavement.

A dog passes,
his nails click, click, clicking on asphalt.
In the distance, one lonely wails.

Forelorn, questing cars
slug into the darkness.

An isolated airplane
dissolves into vacuous night.

In houses nearby,
occasional voices, indistinguishable,
mumble.

Somewhere, a door slams shut,
closing someone in—
or out.
Self trapped moths flutter,
taunts lights
until their muted thuds
interrupt a clangorous quiet.

My mind reaches . . .
Through raucous recess,
damns this solitude. (Rogers, 1984, p. 31)

Clearly, Rhonda had a gift for language that this assignment did not teach her. But with this and other assignments for attention, her capacity for subtle detail and fine distinctions increased, her work as an artist grew richer with particularity and concreteness. She was developing as an artist, and, I would suggest, as a researcher in the world of her experience. As we consider her poem now, we may also find that it raises interesting questions about the researcher's positioning: the role of the subjective perspective in selecting and arranging details, and the inherently interpretative nature of reporting.

ATTENTION, EMPATHY, AND RESEARCH

When I left the world of teaching high school and entered a university context, I continued explorations in poetry and attention as they related to teaching and research. Working with preservice teachers, for example, I gave the assignment: "Choose a student to observe over a period of three weeks. Select a student who is different from you, one you have trouble understanding, maybe one who drives you up the wall. Record the child's actions and reactions, audible language, and body language." It was a traditional sort of case study assignment except for the product it required: "Construct a poem from the point of view of the child you have observed, incorporating at least one fragment of that child's speech."

Students reported that this was a very difficult assignment, not because of the poetic form—I had taught them strategies that related data gathering to [poetry] and we had written poems—but because of the difficulty of getting inside the skin of someone "so different from me." To get under the skin of the other, rather than to simply report observable externals, demanded a deeper sort of attention, an attention that required an imaginative penetration of barriers, and that conjoined with empathy.

Shelley Scholl, one of my students, asked if she might modify that assignment a little. She wanted to write a short poem representing each of the students in the twelfth grade English class in which she was interning, not actually speaking in the first person but representing something of what she knew or imagined of the student's inner life. This is what her short poems looked like:

i.
Silent in the corner,
Luke Pennington
stares at his boot toes,
out the window,
sketches vultures,
wishes he were
anybody else.

ii.
Karen holds her breath each night,
holds Clay in the swaying single-wide,
fingers her engagement ring
and prays for eighteen.

iii.
Stephen's left leg
juts a leaden semi-arabesque
into the aisle between the desks;
Cheek pressed against the unread text,
he dreams of the future. (Scholl, 1995)

When I read Shelly's collection of small poems, it was clear that she had focused a keen attention on these students and that her attention to exteriors had helped her go more deeply into awareness of complex interiors. The class she was teaching was, by many evidences, "difficult." It was a class that could and did try the patience of the supervising teacher as well as her intern. But Shelly reported that her patience grew as she focused attention on individuals and deepened her sensitivity to their contexts. Maxine Greene has proposed that engagement with great works of fine art may open the imagination's way into empathy (Greene, 1995). Making art, "fine" or otherwise, also has great potential.

In the research realm, Elliot Eisner observes, "One job that scholars increasingly want done is engendering a sense of empathy . . . because we have begun to realize that human feeling does not pollute understanding. In fact, understanding others and the situation they face may well require it" (1997, p. 8).

VII. ON ATTENTION, EDUCATION, AND ART

To deny the potential role of artistic attention and artistic representation in investigations of educational issues is to limit our approaches to knowledge. It is the researcher's essential role. Eisner contends, "to highlight . . . to call to our attention . . . to deepen and to broaden our experience . . . to help us understand what we are looking at" (1991, p. 59). There are also essential roles of the artist. Lawrence Stenhouse maintains that "all good art is an inquiry and an experiment. It is by virtue of being an artist that the teacher is a researcher . . . The artist is the researcher *par excellence*" (1988, p. 47).

The artist is a researcher with his or whole organism, inquiring, testing with the body as well as the mind, sensing and seeing, responding and retesting—a multitude of functions performed simultaneously—registering complexity, then sorting, finding a pattern, making meaning. To the extent that the artist is a connoisseur (Eisner, 1991), to the extent that he or she has a rich repertoire of experiences against which or within the context of which to "test" (Schon, 1990), the artist becomes an astute researcher, capable of illuminations and new meanings, new visions of possibility, new questions. We must not overlook the potential role of the artist, alongside that of the scientist and the traditional educational researcher, in our investigations of attention and other critical educational issues.

REFERENCES

Baldwin, J. (1962). *Creative process*. New York: Ridge Press.

Barone T., & Eisner, E. (1997). Arts-based educational research. In R. Jaeger (Ed.), *Complementary methods for research in education* (pp. 73–98). Washington, DC: American Education Research Association.

Caine, R., & Caine, G. (1994). *Making connections: Teaching and the human brain*. New York: Addison-Wesley.

Csikszentmihalyi, M. (1991). *Flow: The psychology of optimal experience*. New York: Harper Perennial.

Damasio, A. R. (1994). *Descartes' error: Emotion, reason, and the human brain*. New York: Putnam.

Dewey, J. (1990). *The child and the curriculum*. Chicago: University of Chicago Press. (Original published 1902)

Eisner, E. (1979). *The educational imagination*. New York, Macmillian.

Eisner, E. (1991). *The enlightened eye: Qualitative inquiry and the enhancement of educational practice*. New York: Macmillian.

Eisner, E. (1997). The promise and perils of alternative forms of data representation. *Educational Reseacher*, 26(6), 4–10.

Greene, M. (1978). Towards wide-awakeness: An argument for the arts and humanities in education. In *Landscapes in learning* (pp. 161–167). New York: Teachers College Press.

Greene, M. (1994). Carpe diem: The arts and school restructuring. *Teachers College Record, 95*, 494–507.

Greene, M. (1995). *Releasing the imagination: Essays in education, the arts, and social change*. San Francisco: Jossey-Bay.

Kohn, A. (1993). *Punished by rewards*. New York: Huffington Mifflin.

Lozanov, G. (1978). *Suggestology and suggestopedia—theory and practice*. Working document for United Nations Educational Scientific and Cultural Organization (UNESCO). (ED-78/WS/119)

Rogers, R. (1984). Secluded. In D. Houchins (Ed.), *Mindflight 4* (p. 31). Baytown, TX: Robert E. Lee High School.

Scholl, S. (1995, November). Untitled poems. In A. Sullivan (Ed.), *Poetry and passion in teacher education: Personalizing and internalizing knowledge*. Papers Presented at the Annual Convention of National Council of Teachers of English, San Diego.

Schon, D. (1990). *Educating the reflective practitioner*. San Francisco: Jossey-Bass.

Stenhouse, L. (1988). Artistry and teaching: The teacher as a focus of research and Development. *Journal of Curriculum and Supervision, 4*(1), 43–51.

Sylwester, R. (1995). *A celebration of neurons: An educators guide to the human brain*. Alexandria, VA: Association of Supervision and Curriculum Development.

Thompson, J., & Hill, J. T. (Eds.). (1982). *Walker Evans at work*. New York: Harper & Row.

The poem "Notes from a Marine Biologist's Daughter" first appeared in *The Gettysburg Review*, volume 7 number 4 and is reprinted here with the acknowledgement of the editors.

Three other poems appeared previously in the following publications: "Mother Collecting Marine Specimens" and "Mother in the Water," 1994, *Tar River Poetry, 33*(2); "Herding Fiddler Crabs," 1998, *Earth's Daughters, 51*(17).

Chapter 3

Yes, But Is It Research?

One of the questions that many people ask when examining arts based research is Yes, but is it research? They often go on to say that such work might be an example of inquiry but not of research. Indeed, we sometimes ask ourselves if it wouldn't be a lot easier if we talked about arts based inquiry rather than arts based research? Obviously we have chosen to walk the latter route rather than the former one. There are a couple of reasons for this. In the first place, the term *research* has a cache that in important ways defines the status of an enterprise. Research, admittedly, has a scientific ring to it. Surely, some still assume, work that is of a research kind will be scientific in character. As we have indicated earlier, we reject such an assumption. Science, we argue, provides one version of research. There are others—arts based research among them.

We want to avoid, however, any form of neat dichotomization between research that is artistic and research that is scientific. That is not to say that there are no significant differences between science and art. If there were not, then we might coin the term *scart* or the term *artence* to cover both scientific and artistic endeavors. But at least since the end of the modernist era the terms *art* and *science* have become more difficult to define; each label lives in a contested zone. Some postmodernists have raised serious questions about just what makes something artistic, and some have struggled to redefine what constitutes science. Within the fields of qualitative research there has been a sustained and growing defiance of rules and conventions regarding the crossing of what were once closely patrolled borders between the realms of the sciences and the arts/humanities. The blurring of boundaries between these fields may have begun in earnest in the 1960s (Denzin & Lincoln, 1998), but the situation has not become less ambiguous since that time.

ART AND SCIENCE: BLURRING BOUNDARIES

In making the case for arts based research as a species of qualitative research—and in our effort to diminish the hegemony that science casts upon the term *research*—we do not want to fail to acknowledge the artistic features of scientific activity. Science, like law or anthropology, can be lifted to an artistic plane when the work is imaginative, sensitive to nuance, expressive in character, and satisfying or moving to experience. The results of what Thomas Kuhn (1970) has called *revolutionary science*, projects of science that result in new gestalts or ways of conceiving of the physical world, seem especially akin to the kinds of world-making that some works of art provide. We believe that an individual (or a member of a group of people) who works at the peak of their powers in shaping a form that has aesthetic characteristics and generates meanings functions as an artist. But then one could say that the aim of preparation for all kinds of research is to do it in a way that makes its features aesthetic. At its very best, a scientific research study also becomes a work of art and the researcher an artist.

To conceive of a scientific researcher as an artist may seem oxymoronic. But it is not. Anything well crafted, anything made with sensibility and imagination, anything that requires skill and the use of technique in order to create something that has an emotional effect is an artistic affair. The arts themselves are not limited to the so-called fine arts but lead their lives among all that we do to make things aesthetic. This is as true in the field of mathematics as it is in printmaking. It is as relevant to those who work in theoretical physics as it is for those who focus on the creation of visual imagery. Art is potentially present whenever humans have intercourse with life.

Likewise, according to some definitions of both art and science, artistic activity can, at least in some measure, be scientific. If, for example, the term *science* connotes an empirical view of the world—one that honors careful attention to the realm of human experience over, say, received wisdom—then there is at least an overlap between science and art. The latter, after all, is also highly focused on dimensions of human experience. Human activities become art when the process of attention is personally moving, when the forms used are imaginatively construed, when there is a sense of coherence and energy in the work. We follow Dewey's (1934/1958) lead in recognizing art as a form of human experience. When human activities achieve that exalted sphere, we can justly claim that we are engaged in or beholding a work of art.

Still, does it matter whether those of us who claim to do arts based social *research* deserve to be recognized as social *researchers*? One reason for not giving up our claim that arts based research is indeed a version of research is that it provides legitimacy to an enterprise that as yet still needs support (even if not nearly as much as in the past). It makes no sense to us to fight hard for legitimacy for a form of work only to find out that the best we can do is to play second string.

The second reason, one less political—and probably, in the long run, more important—than the first, has to do with promoting what might be called epistemological diversity. There are, we believe, a variety of forms of representation available to enrich what one can come to question or to know by virtue of the ways in which the subject matter is addressed. This diversity is, for us, a fundamental consideration in the promotion of arts based research. We find it unfortunate, therefore, that paradigm wars between various forms of qualitative and quantitative researchers have been waged over the decades, with each side disparaging the work of the other. Likewise, there is some contentiousness between qualitative researchers who think of their work as enhancing certainty and others who, as suggested in Chapter 2, aim for the raising of questions within readers and viewers as they reexperience aspects of the world previously unnoticed. Indeed, when it comes to any sort of paradigm war we are pacifists, refusing to fight in a meaningless battle. Again, for us, works of both (qualitative and quantitative) science and art can be useful, if perhaps in different ways—and, of course, *if done well*. Indeed, we believe that each is done well to the degree it is useful in either enhancing certainty in the mind of the reader or in raising significant questions regarding stale, tired, commonplace ways of viewing the world.

ART AND RESEARCH

We now turn to certain characteristics in the processes engaged in by many artists that make it sensible to call their work research. First, however, let us offer a definition of research. Research is, yes, a process of *re*searching—that is, of coming back again and again to perceived phenomena, scrutinizing the world, and thereby reexperiencing it. Within arts based research that scrutinizing may or may not be done in a systematic way as occurs in many forms of scientific research. Or the researching may occur within a more fluid process and even occur serendipitously through unplanned or informal reencounters of phenomena throughout an artist's life—indeed, at least since Fielding novelists have observed the minutiae of human activity, attending to specific characters in particular sociohistorical milieus. Arts based researchers, too, fish for empirical (whether physical or social) evidence in the ongoing stream of everyday life. This is what seems to have been practiced by Sullivan (2000) as she, over an extended period of time, paid "serious attention" to the physical details of the world around her in order to be able to write her vivid poetry. As we also suggested in Chapter 2, this scrutinizing is akin to the kind of watchfulness that

Caputo (1987, p. 6) described as peering beneath the surface of things, keeping an eye out for the "breaks and regularities in existence."

Sometimes the scrutinizing occurs prior to the crafting of the work of arts based research, in a kind of preproduction phase, as with many novelists, playwrights, actors, and nonfictional storytellers, who research their characters and the contexts of their lives. To do so, they may engage in activities such as the following: the reading of archival and historical documents, conversations and discussion with "informants" who represent the actual people whose lives are being represented or who are similar to those people, observations of certain people as they go about living their lives, studies of the physical surroundings and settings of the time and period being portrayed, and so on. Sometimes the studying can occur quite close to home; at other times, they move to strange and distant landscapes to engage in what is traditionally known as "fieldwork." Wherever and whenever it takes place, however, artists and arts based researchers alike call this process of observing and attending to these dimensions of the physical and social world *research*. And the result may indeed be a work of art.

We, in turn, should, however, attend closely to that term *work of art*. For it seems to have two different meanings. In the first, there is an emphasis on the *work* of art. It signals a process of *doing* something that has aesthetic consequences. A second emphasis is on is the work of *art*, wherein the result of the process has features that warrant the assignment of the word *art* to it. It is the latter conception that has dominated our view of art, but it is the former conception—the *work* of art—that provides the theme that holds together human activities of all sorts in various arenas.

There are some delicate issues to be addressed when we talk about art as object, as contrasted with art as an experience. The distinction is one of emphasis, not one of kind. An object becomes a work of art with what it does to experience. An experience is what it becomes because of the features of the object. Thus, the well-designed experiment can have artistic features. The qualitative study that is inelegant, or crude, or ungainly, even though qualitative and artistic in type, may not be a high achievement. What we seek in the end is research that has elegance and subtlety, which promotes meaning not only through its literal or discursive features but because of its metaphorical and qualitative features as well.

THE ARTS BASED RESEARCH PROCESS: AN EXAMPLE

But the *work* of art may, we suggest again, also be seen as a *work* of research. Moreover, it is a process that does not move in a series of linear steps nor as the result of a recipe or formula. Nevertheless, it is a process in which certain phases may be discerned. Indeed, David Ecker (1966) likened the process of art-making to one of qualitative problem solving in which there are five phases. Similar phases may often be found in the process of doing arts based research. Indeed, let us examine them in the context of an example of research included in this book. The example is that of Barone's (2000) literary essay entitled "Ways of Being at Risk: The Case of Billy Charles Barnett." The political and ethical issues and implications surrounding this story-within-a-story-within-an-essay are discussed further in Chapter 7. Here we focus on those phases in the process of researching and writing it. (Readers might first want to read the essay, reprinted in this book.)

Barone's (2000) essay was part of a nationwide study by the professional education organization Phi Delta Kappa (PDK) on the topic of "at-risk" students. Barone was asked by PDK to seek out, identify, and write about a student from a nearby middle school that teachers and administrators deemed highly unlikely to remain in a high school until graduation. The person they chose became the focus of Barone's essay.

As Barone drove down what Kentuckians call a "pike," the highway that would lead to the school research site selected for him—he would later rename it Dusty Hollow Middle School—the researcher Tom Barone had already entered the first of that series of phases in an arts based, qualitative problem-solving process—the phase that, wrote Ecker (1966), is characterized by "an initial haziness and random discrimination of qualities." This is the phase of the empty canvas, one in which the researcher/artist is open, fortunately or unfortunately, to infinite possibilities and therefore one in which the researcher may be beset with great anticipation, anxiety, and confusion about where to focus.

Barone (2000) had been assigned a specific research task: to compose a case study of one particular student who had been identified as being severely at risk of dropping out of school, but that casual characterization was a bloodless one. That is to say, the real-life object of his study, the boy with his own untold life story played out in a cultural context with which the researcher was quite unfamiliar, had yet to be met. Moreover, the researcher brought with him his own existential and cultural baggage, a set of lens through which he would initially attempt to make sense of the life of a teenager who was in possession of his own prisms through which to view the world. But it was in finally meeting Billy Charles in a fast-food restaurant distanced from school that Barone first encountered the "raw phenomena" of his study. It would be the qualities of Billy Charles's personhood that became what Ecker (1966) called "the qualities which achieve candidacy for alternation, reconstruction, or change" within the production of a work of research or art. But at the beginning of that first encounter with Billy Charles, seeing him for the first time, eager to learn from his perspective the manner in which he perceived his supposedly "risky" life in school, Barone felt unmoored, drifting in a sea of possibilities.

There was/is the kind of uneasiness and wonderment that was/is itself difficult, at that stage of the game, to define or articulate. This is an uneasiness that many (even veteran) artists and arts based researchers have come to expect in this sort of research engagement. It is born out of a sense that all phenomena being encountered possess a certain randomness, a lack of coherence or structure. And this lack of focus may lead one to attempt to attend to, recall, and/or record absolutely everything. In other words, there is a mental "block" that disallows the selection of that which Iser (1993) has described as aesthetic content (see Chapter 6, on "fiction"). And this is clearly itself an anxiety inducing, if (almost always) temporary, disability.

In phase two of the qualitative problem-solving process, however, the trouble becomes more defined. That is, a set of potential themes, subthemes, or at least sets of tentative relationships between phenomena, begins to emerge. And often (although not always), these emerge out of a clash in the colors of impressions from various sources about the same set of phenomena. In the case of the case of Billy Charles, some of the colors in which he had been painted were very dark, quite bleak. He was a loser, Barone the researcher had been told by the student's teachers and principal, a young boy hard to talk to, rude and antagonistic, often morose, and not very intelligent. These, then, were Billy Charles's "school colors." And they contrasted dramatically with the sunny, bright, loquacious, even charming youngster who sat across the table from the researcher at McDonald's.

Billy Charles began to appear as if he were one person living two different lives in two different cultures. In the outdoors Appalachian culture, the qualities of his life seemed to be those of mastery, joy, and self-assuredness. He thrived in an environment in which he felt knowledgeable, comfortable, and secure. The reverse was true in an academic setting, where the prevailing qualities were menacing, destructive, and even humiliating. Moreover, at some point it occurred to Barone that Billy Charles was the polar opposite of the researcher himself who felt so safe and secure inside "school," in his tenured university position, but who also felt adrift, unsure, or, one might say, "at risk" in the Appalachian culture of Billy Charles. The delicious irony, however, was this: One of these people was formally researching the life of the other.

For Ecker (1966), in phase three of the qualitative problems process a single pervasive quality emerges out of "the qualitative components being introduced, manipulated, and related to other components." This means that a kind of crystallization occurs as a new gestalt is composed out of the various fragments and sets of tentative relationships between qualities confronted in the research process. The theme was indeed, tied to the notion of "at riskness," but now the notion was given a new twist as it was placed in the larger context of the array of dangers lurking in the life of Billy Charles. These included threats posed by an abusive father as well as from a dysfunctional school system that was itself part of a larger dominant culture encroaching on the safe and secure cultural and physical environs of Appalachia (indeed, the unique way of life of the whole region was at risk of disappearing). This new way of viewing riskiness thereby served as a controlling insight that allowed for inclusion into the research text of qualities (and "data") that were relevant to the theme, and eliminating qualities and data that were not connected to what had become the central metaphor of the research text.

Thereby, the achievement of phase three in an arts based research project represents a moment of great relief and enables the researcher to move on to phase four. For many researchers, this means the onset of the actual writing process, as what Ecker (1966) called a "qualitative control" serves as a patterning principle for composing the research text. For Barone, this meant the ability to decide to omit from his text the descriptions of certain incidents in the life of Billy Charles (example: a fight on a school bus) and to include others (such as the physical abuse by his father) that supported an understanding of the nature of the psychological turmoil that had placed Billy Charles "at risk"—and here, not merely at risk of leaving school but indeed of taking his own life.

Finally, in phase five, writes Ecker (1966), "the work is judged complete, the total achieved—the pervasive quality has adequately been the control" (p. 67). But here we demur. For as we suggest elsewhere in this book, the research process is never really, finally "complete." This is because the text is inevitably turned over to readers (or members of an audience) who will do with it as they will. Some may find it useless. Others, however, will resonate with the central metaphor and be prompted to think of other students—maybe also labeled "at risk"—closer to them whose lives bear familial resemblances to that of Billy Charles Barnett. If they are indeed able to do so, it is because of the carefully observed and arranged details within the text of arts based research. Or we might say that it is because the *work* of arts based research has resulted in a work of arts based research.

To the extent that the literary essay about Billy Charles is indeed a work of arts based research then material will have been used aesthetically but, again, for a very specific purpose. The work will have been an effort to consciously use material aesthetically in order not simply to delight, as important as that might be, but to produce a disequilibrium in the reader or viewer—that is, to enable someone to "get a feel" for a set of phenomena that calls into question previously held perceptions and understandings of that phenomena.

Similarly, in works of art not necessarily labeled arts based research—in works much more powerful than the Barone article—in films such as *Pan's Labyrinth* or in plays such as *Angels in America* or in paintings such as *Guernica*—artists, either individually or in teams, compose stories and construct images that will enable percipients of their work to raise important questions about the conditions under which human beings live. These pieces of art do not offer summary statements about those conditions. Likewise, some of the examples of works included or mentioned in this book, such as those by Saldana (2005), Simon (1997), and Springgay (2003), are—like good films, plays, and paintings—artistic renderings. Indeed, each, as a whole, can be seen as a metaphorical poem dedicated to helping us *remember*—that is, to help us to recall and reconfigure parts of our own past experience, in a sense to interrogate and re-story our own lives.

This does not mean that in the *work* of art through which they were produced each of the five stages in the problem-solving process could be easily identified. Still, in the work that many researchers call arts based, these phases can be located and even felt. And being aware of them may bring a sense of reassurance—perhaps reduce a bit the high levels of anxiety that can be present in engaging in research that is not systematic or formulaic or based on a rigid protocol.

RESEARCH THAT CHANGES THE CONVERSATION

In this chapter, we have offered at least five major points. They may be restated as follows: First, we have suggested that the arts, like the sciences, are concerned with the processes of questioning and knowing. The arts, like the sciences, convey to us images in a variety of sensory modalities through which we come to notice what we haven't previously seen.

Second, the artistic features about which we have been writing are an aspect of science as well as of art. Put simply, science, when taken to its height, can be regarded as an art.

Third, the term *work of art* refers to the features of a product having a configuration or composition that arouses or that is evocative in character. We call such products aesthetic objects. But work of art can also refer to the process of making. "Artings" are processes through which composers and performers, painters and writers, dancers and actors employ their craft.

Fourth, we borrow some ideas from David Ecker (1966) to suggest that oftentimes there are identifiable phases that collectively constitute the features of research activity in various artistic domains.

Finally, we repeat that the end in view is not to arrive at a singular and unchallengeable slice of knowledge; it is to generate questions through which, as Clifford Geertz (1974) noted, will make our conversations more interesting.

We believe that we cannot emphasize this last point enough. There is something very attractive about interesting conversations, even if most researchers working in traditional forms seek considerably more than interesting conversation. They want to know for sure that they have directly affected some facet of the world. Some would even like to understand, in a final way, the aspect of the world that they are able to influence. Yet, as we have said, the quest for certainty that Dewey talked about in 1929 is a hopeless pursuit. We never will know whether what we know is for certain.

This realization transforms research of all kinds—but especially arts based research—into a process that is pervaded by a dialectic activity in which ideas are held tentatively rather than permanently and where conclusions are always partial and temporary. Indeed, the history of science (like the history of art) is a history of changed minds. We once thought that Pluto was a planet. Now we take it to be a star. Who knows whether there will be further transformations as people change their sights and change their minds?

It is comforting to conclude that the changes in our understanding in a changed state of affairs are due to a more adequate conception or theory than one worked with before. This state is, paradoxically, indubitable. We do learn, and we do develop better ideas, more powerful theories, and even small "theorets" to address particular phenomena in the world in which we live. Yet all of these processes are subject to the judgment of a critical community (or community of discourse) that gives ascent to the propositions put forward. This critical community may embrace, for example, an evolutionary orientation to the long-term historical course of human maturation. It might, on the contrary, embrace a theological perspective. Each group verifies its orientation by appealing to evidence that fits the orientation itself. What we are saying is that orientations to the world, the ideas that guide our understanding of the world, are influenced by a critical community that judiciously selects evidence to correspond and to be supportive of the dominant theories that have been advanced historically. Our point here is that the conduct of science, like the conduct of art, is much less a quest for certainty and much more a quest for *plausibility*. The value assigned to any set of processes or ideas is related to a form of social confirmation who some, in some communities, see otherwise. Research is, therefore, itself, a social process that is impacted by an array of beliefs, much of which change over time.

Arts based *research* is not essentially an effort to modify the current conversation; it is, again, closer in spirit to the paradigm shift that Kuhn (1970, 1977) discusses in *The Structure of Scientific Revolutions* and in *The Essential Tension*. That is, it is an effort to establish a new set of perspectives on what the search can be. For many scholars, we believe this will be a difficult road to follow. They are much more comfortable with the tried and true than with the new or with the iconoclastic.

We started this chapter with the following question: Yes, but is it research? We hope by now that it is clear that what counts as an example of research depends upon one's conception of research. If only quantitatively described experiments count as research, then clearly arts based research is not research; it is something else. We reject that conclusion, however. Research in its broadest sense is an effort, as we said, to return again and again in order to shed light on some phenomena of interest. The issues pertaining to how that light is shed is what we have examined in this chapter. Science may or may not continue to be the dominant model for defining research. But that is the result of a social judgment, not a conceptual necessity.

We believe that in many places, as a result of the efforts of arts based researchers working as qualitative researchers in a variety of academic fields, a form of social research is indeed engaged in within the production of a work of art. Many social researchers have come to partake in a more diverse and inclusive view of the purposes for engaging in social research and the various ways in which inquiry processes and research texts may be fashioned in order to achieve those purposes. Later, in Chapter 8 of this book, we address the criteria by which any work of arts based research might be judged to be good and useful. More immediately, in Chapter 4, we turn to the question of who can do arts based research.

Chapter 4

Who Can Do Arts Based Research?

In this chapter, we turn to the question of who can be an arts based researcher. This question identifies a point of contention in the field of arts based research and is related to a number of secondary questions. Among these are the following:

Can anyone who so desires do arts based research? Is arts based research solely a domain of those who are already formally trained in an area of the arts—that is, professional novelists, painters, poets, photographers, etc? Does one need to be an academic, or professional researcher, to do arts based research—that is, someone who has been formally educated in a research program within a field in the humanities, social sciences, or professions? Or can highly sensitive and observant nonacademic artists also engage in arts based research? Within the academy can only arts educators be arts based researchers? Or can arts based researchers reside in other academic fields? Should anyone, whether formally trained or not, be encouraged to do arts based research? How "good" must the work of an arts based researcher be? How artistically talented must an arts based researcher be? Can this talent—to whatever degree—be developed, or is one "born" an arts based researcher? How might academics attain the capacities for doing good arts based research? What would academic programs look like in order to succeed in enhancing capacities for doing good arts based research? In this chapter, we offer our own answers to these questions. In doing so, we want to be both cautionary and encouraging.

CAUTION AND ENCOURAGEMENT

First, here is the caution: We remind readers that we are not relativists. That is to say, we do not hold that doing arts based research is necessarily the same as doing it well. We are not pure "democrats" who believe that all attempts at arts based research merit dissemination. Instead, we believe that a work of arts based research must possess the potential for achieving the ultimate research goal we have already mentioned in earlier chapters: the capacity for inviting members of an audience into the experiencing aspects of a world that may have been otherwise outside their range of sight and to thereby cause them to question usual, commonplace, orthodox perspectives on social phenomena. We believe that someone who can produce such a work—by first carefully observing facets of the world and then recasting them into a meaningful cultural form—is at the time of that creation operating as an artist. The more powerful the work in achieving this goal, the higher the degree of artistry involved in its making.

It seems to us that, generally speaking, the more an arts based researcher possesses the desire, dedication, opportunity, persistence, and support for engaging in activities within a chosen art form and acquiring the technical skills and aesthetic feel for the medium employed, then the more aesthetically accomplished their work is likely to be. Moreover, the more experienced the arts based researcher in carefully, intensely, and persistently studying the social phenomena (the aesthetic content) that are addressed thematically in a particular work, the more likely that the work will be substantively meaningful. Both of those dimensions—stylistic artfulness and thematic significance—are requisites for a good work of arts based research.

We believe that these two dimensions are present in each of the examples reproduced in this book and in examples we have cited but that are not reproduced here.

We noted in Chapter 2 that some of these represent projects by academics in various fields who self-identify as arts based researchers employing different forms of art—poetry, theater, photography, mixed media, autobiography, and the literary essay. Others are the offerings of academics who do not identify themselves as arts based researchers but who also do the kind of research that has resulted in significant works of art. The literary autoethnographic essay by Ruth Behar (1996) and the ethnodrama by Johnny Saldana (2005) are two such examples that emanate from within the walls of the academy. Still other works of arts based inquiry reproduced (or at least cited) in this book are the fruits of research and composition outside of academia. They include, among the multitudes available for recognition, works by Nadine Gordimer, Robert Doisneau, Tony Kushner, Dave Eggers, Truman Capote, Steven Spielberg, Charles Dickens, Arthur Miller, and Guillermo del Toro. All these works, we argue, represent qualitative research texts that are *useful* in the same way that all good art can be. Variously labeled, crafted from within or outside of the academy, each is an example of good arts based research that "makes new worlds."

In previous chapters, we have examined some of the complexities involved in doing arts based research. We have also explored some of the commonalities that such work shares with social science and some distinguishing characteristics of each. Perhaps, in the process of reading these chapters, one may have become more cautious than confident in one's ability to become an arts based researcher. And indeed, we admit that the challenges in doing arts based research well can be quite daunting. Let it never be said that students, or academics, or professional artists engage in arts based research because it is easier than other forms of research! It is not.

But now we move from caution to encouragement. And it may be encouraging to know that while an arts based researcher must be able to meet a certain threshold of quality, not every arts based researcher needs to be a Toni Morrison or a Tony Kushner. We do not believe that good arts based researchers are necessarily endowed genetically with a capacity for doing arts based research. We believe that the skills and talents needed can—to a large degree—be acquired through dedication, practice, and guidance. And we believe that universities and colleges can create and/or modify social research programs that attend to the teaching of those skills and talents, that provide the practical resources required to become a good arts based researcher. And it may be encouraging to understand just what it is that someone must know and be able to do in order to create a work of arts based research that is useful to others. That is the topic to which we turn next.

WHAT AN ARTS BASED RESEARCHER NEEDS TO KNOW

There is a significant sense in which a highly skilled arts based researcher must become an artist in order to create a form that has the expressive qualities that are relevant for understanding the phenomena being addressed. Again, by an "artist" we do not necessarily mean a *professional* painter, poet, dancer, or novelist. But the researcher must exhibit artistry in whatever form he or she chooses. Even an attorney who is preparing a brief to persuade a judge or a jury of the innocence or guilt of his client profits from his ability to render the work that he does artfully. This does not mean that art is an ornament on a form of productive work; rather, it is essential to what it communicates and critically effects its reception. Arts based research is, at its deepest level, about artistic and aesthetic approaches to raising and addressing social issues.

The idea that an arts based researcher must practice artistry, and the idea that arts based research has the potential to illuminate significant questions and issues that might otherwise be neglected in traditional research formats, have practical ramifications for the preparation of researchers. The resources needed for that preparation correspond to the types of knowledge required for doing arts based research. To explore this topic we reference the three kinds of knowledge posited by Aristotle.

One of these types is *practical*. Practical knowledge is knowledge that allows one to negotiate differences in values, courses of action, and commitments in order to resolve a particular situation that needs attention. Politicians, for example, are often said to be highly practical people; their work is riddled with contingencies.

Negotiating the world at a practical level is complicated. One needs to make judgments for which there often is an absence of rule, and one needs to be able to read complex situations so that they are not misconceived. One needs to know *when* to intervene and especially *how*. In short, in a sea of uncertainty, practical knowledge is, at its best, practical; it is, again, useful.

A second type of knowledge that Aristotle identifies is theoretical knowledge. Theoretical knowledge, in his day at least, pertained to those subject matters whose solutions or answers were "of necessity." Theoretical knowledge dealt with the pursuit of certainties. The speed of the earth as it travels around the sun is an invitation to study matter in motion. The motion of the earth can't be other than the way it is. Finding out why some plants provide benefits for those who consume them is another example of a theoretical problem. Again, to understand the reasons why certain plants "work," one needs to employ a framework whose conclusions get tested in application. Unlike the kind of theoretical knowledge associated with arts based research, Aristotle's notion deals with conclusions that had to be what they are. It was not an option. And it certainly wasn't the expression of a mere point of view (POV).

The third form of knowledge that Aristotle posits is productive knowledge. Productive knowledge is the ability to put things together so that they work. To make a table requires productive knowledge if it is going to serve the maker or his or her customer. An example of productive knowledge is knowing how to make a likeness of another person in marble or in clay. Productive knowledge is a making of something, not simply the ability to understand what a person has done. Productive knowledge lives in the universe of action.

Aristotle's triad of knowledges is, one the one hand, informative for considering what an arts based researcher needs to know. On the other hand, Aristotle may have oversimplified the relationship between theoretical, practical, and productive knowledge. Arts based research is a construction; in that sense, it is indeed productive. And arts based research is also practical insofar it deals with contingencies that are temporal and not subject to certain answers. But arts based research may not be theoretical in quite the way that Aristotle thought of theoretical knowledge.

One of the aims of each piece of arts based research is to provide one—but only one of many—accounting(s) of what has occurred. Theories provide guidance in enabling someone to know what to look for. Practical affairs remind one that in the world getting a job done is as important as knowing why something functions the way it does, and no piece of arts based research is likely to find a welcoming reception if it is done without skill or sensitivity to the way in which the form is made. In doing art, or arts based research, we suggest that theoretical knowledge may be better thought of as *thematic*, insofar as themes (and subthemes) within a work of art provide a kind of qualitative control that allows for all parts of the work to cohere into a "whole." Themes also have the advantage of inviting discussion regarding their "fit" and significance and may avoid the suggestion of final interpretations. For indeed, if theoretical—or thematic—knowledge is part of arts based research, it will not necessarily be explicit in the work itself; rather, it may be found in the reflections, interrogations, conversations, deliberations, and debates that effective arts based research generates.

We believe that it is in the arena of discussion and debate that the meanings are made possible by arts based research and that the value of the enterprise is realized. Sometimes those deliberations will be "internal" to the minds of the readers or viewers—for example, one who privately reads the literary essay by Behar (1996) or the poetry by Sullivan (2000) or encounters a theatrical performance of a work by Anna Deavere Smith. At other times, the questions may prompt a search for answers within a community of discussants. In either case, it is at that point that the arts based researcher has been successful in producing a work that is, as Aristotle might also have it, both practical and productive.

RESEARCHERS WHOSE WORKS SHIFT CONVERSATIONS

In order to produce a work that succeeds in luring audience members into having an important conversation about socially significant themes and issues, arts based researchers need to be adept at putting forms and language or music or poetry together to shed light on what is significant but subtle, what is revealing about the aspect of the world being addressed. In that regard, certain strategies and techniques used in the field of drama can, we believe, be productively employed in arts based research.

In some theaters, patrons are afforded an opportunity to read a text that provides a context in which the action of the play is to occur. In a playbill or brochure, they may read about the author and his struggles, the actors and their careers, and the historical period within which the action takes place. Readers get an overview through which they can situate themselves with respect to what is coming. Indeed, such was the case before Barone's encountering, in February 2001, a performance of Anna Deavere Smith's (1993) play *Fires in the Mirror*—programs were indeed distributed to audience members upon entering the theater.

Then came the play itself. The "play itself" is, so to speak, the meat in the sandwich of a theatrical work of arts based research. The play itself carries the momentum, the emotion, the energy for which most patrons have come to the theater in the first place. But complex plays often have themes or ideas that may not be fully appreciated or simply resolved in a single cursory viewing. After some productions, again, as with *Fires in the Mirror* (Smith, 1993), discussion leaders may be present to facilitate discussions among those in attendance regarding the meanings of what they have experienced. What was the message of this play? Was it credible? Did it relate to your life? Did it relate to the lives of people you know? The discussion segment of the evening is a way to engage the patron in the intellectual challenges that good plays make possible. It may be during the third segment of the evening at a theater that there occurs a more thorough exploration of possibility and interpretation that the play makes possible. It may be then that such qualities come to the fore. Indeed, it is happier for an arts based researcher to have generated deeper, more profound questions than to have provided for the superficial comforts of an effort to be correct.

This triadic relationship between context building, the work of art, and the reflections (individually and communally) on the work's meaning can function as a conceptual structure for what is sometimes called "reporting" the results of educational research. Of course, we do not entirely warm to the term *reporting*. Reporting as a term connotes a state of passivity on the part of the recipient as though he or she was to ingest the reports that were offered. It also implies that a single, correct, theoretical perspective offers a final interpretation of meaning.

We prefer to think about communication as an active and interactive process, through which meanings are made and discarded with newer and hopefully more sophisticated understandings of the work that has been created. We believe that this structure of preamble–play–conversation affords a useful programmatic means through which the meanings of the play can be seriously contemplated.

The same might be said of music. In music concerts, program notes at the outset may situate the reader or the listener in the currents and period of the music. The music listener to be is given information for building a context for the music that is going to be heard. The second section of the musical performance is, indeed, the performance itself. And following the performance, it is not unusual for the discussant to provide a minilecture about the music. As with a theatrical production there may be a programmatic structure—one might even refer to it as a pedagogical structure—through which the meaningfulness of the music is enhanced by the conditions that are set up to assist the audience member. Analogously, this structure used for plays and concerts for pedagogical purposes may also be employed in the creation of works of arts based research, which are themselves ultimately pedagogical in character.

RAMIFICATIONS FOR ACADEMIC PROGRAMS

How might academic research programs be designed to create this sort of arts based researcher as pedagogue, one who is sufficiently talented to create a work of art that entices a reader or viewer to reflect and question? We strongly believe that arts based research is not and should not be the exclusive province of arts faculty or faculty and students in arts education programs. There is, however, indeed a sense in which an arts based researcher must become a skilled artist in order to create a form that has the expressive qualities that are relevant for interrogating taken-for-granted interpretations of social phenomena. Again, we do not necessarily mean a formally trained painter or dancer or sculptor, although an arts based researcher could have skills in any of these art forms or others. What we mean is that the researcher must exhibit artistry in whatever form of art or form he or she chooses to engage. As we suggested earlier, an attorney who is preparing a brief to persuade a judge or a jury of the innocence or guilt of his client profits from his ability to render the work that he does artfully. Art is not an ornament on a form of productive work; it is essential to what it communicates and what critically effects its reception. Arts based research is, at its deepest level, about tentative artistic and aesthetic explorations of problems that may not see the light of day in traditional forms of research. Acceptance of the idea that an arts based researcher must become an artist with the potential for illuminating significant questions and issues that might otherwise be neglected in traditional research formats has practical consequences for the preparation of researchers.

One of these consequences is graduate level programs that prepare social researchers will need to provide opportunities to use at least one art form in order to both perceive and represent what one has perceived in the situation being studied. At a practical level, this implies the providing future social researchers opportunities to develop skills in drawing and painting, in videography, in the expressive use of language, and so on. The point here is that what has been seen or experienced requires a symbol system through which experience that is personal is transformed and made public.

We often talk about the desirability of diversity in academia especially as it pertains to racial, gender, or class diversity. But other forms of diversity in academia seem equally important. For example, one can have diverse paradigms employed—that is, theories that provide a distinctive focus on the issue being addressed. For example, a Freudian perspective on a family relationship can reveal qualities that pertain to defensiveness or regression or egoism. The same situation addressed from the vantage point of cognitive therapy conceives of and addresses the phenomena in very different terms. However, these two situations—one cognitive, the other Freudian—all operate within a straightforward linguistic frame. What would someone knowledgeable in clinical matters who uses poetry have to say about the situation? What would a photographer or a painter have to say about the situation? What would their work reveal? In the preparation of social researchers, diversity pertains not only to social categorizations or the use of a variety of theoretical structures; it also pertains to the medium that a social researcher chooses to employ.

The meanings located in a story, the qualities generated by a symphony, and the cadences that are made meaningful in a poem are all sources of enlightenment in arts based research. This suggests that the concept of literacy needs expansion from a process concerned essentially with the making of meaning in language to a process in which meaning is made through the interpretation of forms in whatever media they happen to appear. The ability to deal meaningfully with visual art, for example, is not the same as the ability to deal with music. Each form of representation has its own demands and exacts its own requirements. This suggests that if research methodology is to be expanded and diversified that students will need to be prepared in more than one "language."

What we are calling for are schools and departments in which there is a greater heterogeneity of media used to reveal what one has learned about a situation. We recognize, of course, that this aspiration is daunting. Yet, without at least its partial realization, experience and understanding remains a covert phenomena, knowable only by the person who undergoes the experience in the first place.

The term *medium* is important. What does a medium do? A medium mediates. For a medium to be achieved—that is, for a material to acquire the status of a medium—skills must be available to make that transformation possible: no skills, no technique and therefore no technique, no effect. The development of skills necessary for making the transformation from material to medium is a very important aspect regarding the ability to do arts based research.

We encourage those who are in charge of schools and departments in universities and colleges where social researchers are educated to provide the practical resources needed to become proficient in producing various forms of arts based research. They will then be honoring the second primary purpose of engaging in human inquiry—to raise questions about important social issues by enticing members of an audience into vicariously reexperience dimensions of the social world within an artistic engagement.

Chapter 5

Who Can Be the Audience for Arts Based Research?*

In this chapter, we discuss issues surrounding the audiences for arts based research. In particular, we wonder about the ways in which arts based research might reach an expanded audience, one that includes members of an audience who do not reside only in the academy.

We believe that the potential audiences for works of arts based social research are no doubt more varied than the actual audiences for quantitative and qualitative social science have been in the past. In the academy, hopes for career advancement, along with sheer habit, have ensured that social scientists write primarily toward professional colleagues, fellow members of circumscribed discursive communities who converse in what Toulmin (1953) called the *participant languages* of those who work in specialized fields.

But in recent years, certain cultural observers have expressed discomfort with this narrow audience for scholarly work (Agger, 1990; Jacoby, 1987; Nash, 2004). The concerns of these critics about the tendency of academic writing to alienate readers unprepared to penetrate the opaque prose of disciplinary specialization may suggest a rethinking of research audience. These critics imagine the possibilities of academics directly addressing those who think and talk in the vernacular languages of not participants but *onlookers* (Toulmin, 1953). When that shift in audience is achieved, scholarly writing will have been, as Nash (2004) put it, "liberated." And then scholars may have enhanced their influence through *audience blending* (Barone, 2002), opening up their work to a larger community of percipients and readers.

---

*This chapter is a slightly altered version of the following: Barone, T. (2008). Going public with arts-inspired social research: Issues of audience. In A. Cole & G. Knowles (Eds.), *Handbook of the arts in social science research* (pp. 485–492). Thousand Oaks, CA: Sage.

As we have discussed elsewhere in this book, in the past few decades, some researchers have moved to complement the traditional premises, procedures, protocols, and modes of representation of the social sciences with those of the arts. And since many of these researchers identify themselves as artists rather than social scientists, one might expect a sense of freedom regarding the issue of audience. But while arts based researchers have thus far only rarely abandoned the traditional conception of research readership, some stirrings toward "liberation" can be detected. Toward that hope, in this chapter we are wondering the following: For arts based scholars who no longer wish to disclose their research findings only to their "participant" colleagues, who might their additional audiences be? Might they also directly address onlooker members of the public? And if so, how? What are some of the sticky issues involved in achieving successful audience blending?

MOVING OUTWARD: CATEGORIES OF RESEARCH AUDIENCES

One sort of audience ("additional" because it is not generally considered as legitimate for traditional sorts of social research projects) may be the researcher herself. Drawing upon phenomenologist philosophers, some researchers highlight the self-emancipatory potential of engaging in arts based projects. Catharsis, therapy, self-awakening, self-transformation, self-empowerment, personal growth—these are available subjectivist aims for social inquiry espoused by methodologists who are willing to brave the epithets of self-indulgence, self-absorption, narcissism, and navel-gazing inevitably hurled at them.

Instead of moving directly outward to a wider audience, these researchers first move inward, if often with the assumption that the personal meanings they uncover and disclose will ultimately be appreciated by others. Of course, insofar as writing is inner dialogue, the author of any text may be rightfully seen as its initial audience, the first beneficiary of the personal insights, change, and growth that it fosters. And changing the course of history may indeed occur by first changing oneself.

Most arts based researchers are, however, not unaware of the intersubjective nature of their enterprise, understanding the artistic gesture as primarily a social act, a moving outward into communion with others. And she herself may be one of those "others." Indeed, the arts based researcher-as-her-own-audience may defy dichotomization into self and other. Postmodernist scholars have succeeded in casting doubt on the notion of a totally unified, integrated, consistent self-identity. Instead, they have resurrected Nietzsche's (1887/1968) idea of the multiple self in a form that is fluid, fragmented, and only semistable (if, hopefully, still engaged in some degree of coherent self-dialogue). This view of the self affirms a human capacity to adopt multiple social roles, to compose alternative (even conflicting) versions of one's autobiography. It accommodates the possibility of participating in more than one form of discourse or manner of being. Indeed, the academic reader may often find her own multidimensional self quite capable of engaging with cultural texts that employ languages and imagery both academic and popular, technical and vernacular. When it comes to projects of social inquiry, the arts based researcher may be simultaneously specialist *and* layperson, participant *and* onlooker.

Still, those of us who have not been initiated into the particular idiom employed within a scholarly text may remain frozen out of a participation in its consumption. One set of such onlookers may be the informants whose lives have been represented in the research text. This irony has not been lost on a few social researchers. One is Patti Lather, whose book, *Troubling the Angels* (Lather & Smithies, 1997)—a poststructuralist, if not arts based, work—is aimed at engaging women with AIDS who are not necessarily academics, the kind of people whose lives are revealed in its pages. Similarly, Denzin (1997, p. 101) has identified a lay audience of ethnographic performance texts as those "whose experiences are being performed," those whose life experiences are similar to those of the researcher's informants.

Yet another kind of "foreign" audience might consist of those who commission arts based researchers to produce evaluations of social programs. For example, Eisner's (1979) notion of educational criticism imagined an audience (among others) of consumers of arts based evaluation reports of educational programs. And, as with other forms of qualitative research, some arts based projects have yielded research texts friendly to those involved in professional training programs, as well as those in positions to make policy regarding those programs.

Finally, there is the possibility of sharing the fruits of social research with sets of onlookers who have often been viewed as residing in a realm quite distant from the world of the researcher. This is an audience of the lay public, or better, the various *publics at large*.

REACHING VARIOUS PUBLICS THROUGH ART

Currently, the results of social research studies that do not employ arts based methods are often translated and broadly disseminated to the general public through the mass print and electronic media. But some commentators have noted that a translation of social science research texts into linguistic forms more familiar to lay onlookers is not an easy task (McNergney, 1990). In the rewriting process, meanings can be distorted, and information can be lost. Enormously complex issues may be oversimplified and important ones ignored. Trenchant questioning of subtle but significant assumptions and premises upon which the research project rested may be tacitly discouraged.

For arts based researchers, in particular, a rethinking of audience might result in an elimination of the need for journalistic middlemen. Instead, their research texts might be composed for members of various lay publics as *immediate* audiences, made more formally and substantively accessible, and even alluring, to a wider array of discursive communities.

How might arts based researchers accomplish this feat? How might arts based researchers diminish the discursive distance between themselves and their fellow citizens? Through what venues might target audiences of onlookers be reached? To answer these questions, we might seek out inspirational exemplars. We might consider the works not only of arts based social researchers but of nonacademic professional artists who have reached out to a variety of publics. Activist artists, in particular, have in recent decades achieved some degree of success in communicating with nonacademic audiences.

From Outside the Academy

What has come to be called activist, or public, art is a form of cultural practice begun in the 1970s, and then expanded and institutionalized. Activist artists drew from the earlier birth and growth of conceptual art and performance art. Felshin (1995) described activist art as a "hybrid cultural practice" insofar as it maintained "one foot in the art world and the other in the world of political activism and community organizing" (p. 9). Arts based social researchers interested in addressing a wide audience might learn much from the aspirations and dissemination strategies of this portion of the art world.

Consider venues and locales. Performance based artistic activities in the last quarter of the 20th century took the form of media events, installations, public demonstrations, and exhibitions (Felshin, 1995, p. 10). And prior to the revolution in electronic media, activist artists exhibited their works on billboards, through subway and bus advertising, as newspaper inserts, as photo–narratives, as wall murals and graffiti, and so on.

Currently, public art remains available both as interventionist performance and as exhibitions. Sometimes called *public performance art* or *political pedagogical performance*, these efforts include slam poetry, street fests, and creative mixed media combinations of all sorts. Moreover, the onset of new technologies has meant opportunities for digital and computer based artistry. The Internet is rife with sites devoted to artistic expression related to a myriad of social and political causes. On the web can be found many art galleries of digitalized artworks, online journals, zines, and weblogs. Groups such as Adbusters and Planned Parenthood solicit artwork to be displayed online, and Adbusters often underwrites artists.

Public artists with varying degrees of social commitment have also employed films, videos, and still photography in their attempts to address segments of the general public. Playwrights and theatrical artists have also managed to engage the public in their exploration of important social issues. Those who perform most like qualitative researchers write and stage what, within the academy, have come to be called *ethnodramas*. Prominent nonacademics among this group include Anna Deavere Smith and Moises Kaufman. Smith (1993, 1994) is most famous for her plays *Fires in the Mirror* and *Twilight: Los Angeles, 1992.* The former is a serious exploration of black–Jewish relations in America, and the latter surrounds the civil disturbances following the Rodney King verdict. Kaufman's (2001) stage play *The Laramie Project* about the 1998 murder in Wyoming of gay college student Matthew Shepard became a movie made for cable television.

From Inside the Academy

University scholars, as artists and storytellers, have not explored as wide a range of venues for dissemination as have professional artists. Some, however, are sallying forth into the discursive spaces of the lay onlooker. Just as nonacademic activist artists are performing and displaying (even creating) their works in public sites away from museums, theaters, and other traditional "art-world" venues, some academy based, arts based social researchers are choosing venues for their work that reach a diversified audience over the usual academically oriented presses, and scholarly journals.

We have already referred in this book to the work of arts based ethnodramatist Johnny Saldana. Recall our discussion of "Street Rat" (Saldana, Finley, & Finley, 2002), the play about homeless youth in New Orleans based on ethnographic work by Finley and Finley. In research approach, form, and content, Saldana's work closely resembles that of the aforementioned socially conscientious playwrights who reside outside of the academy and who tend to reach much larger audiences. Indeed, while his work is often presented in campus locales, its themes often attract members of the public into the audience.

University arts based researchers working in other narrative and literary genres are also reaching toward that goal. Banks & Banks (1998) have discussed at length the possibilities of using fiction as social research. In the field of education, novels (especially as dissertations) are becoming much more common (Dunlop, 1999; Poetter, 2006; Saye, 2002). One such educational novel-as-dissertation by Gosse (2005) became the first to be published in Canada. The Edge of Each Others Battles Project (Smith, 2006) employs poetry, narrative, filmmaking, and storytelling as means for bringing together social justice academics and members of local communities scholars to learn from each other and to plan strategies for social action (Smith, 2006). These are goals similar to those adopted by advocates for and practitioners of *applied theater* (Taylor, 2003).

Doing School, the book by Denise Pope (2001), has also achieved demonstrated success in challenging a master narrative by offering the lay public the results of her closely observed research of high school students. According to Pope (personal conversation), it has been, more than any other aspect of the book, the student stories that have accounted for its surprisingly positive reception among the lay public. A significantly better "seller" than most books about educational issues, *Doing School* has received much publicity from interviews of the author on CNN, public television stations, national radio shows, and local news media to the creation of a conference at Stanford investigating the possibilities of school change. During that time, Pope has addressed over 20,000 people who are primarily attracted, she says, to both the substantive topic and the readable style of the book. When it comes to generating conversations, *Doing School* has succeeded enormously.

Equally impressively, the result of Coulter's (1999) work was also increased dialogue within the larger public. Although Coulter was not, at the time, an academic, his research was nevertheless conducted in a scholarly manner. Whatever the source of his credibility, Coulter (1999) reported that when the booklet *Faces of Failure* was presented to the school board, it was picked up by the Winnipeg Free Press, which ran a front page feature on the project, which in turn, generated letters to the editor as well as comments between teachers, parents, and the public. Parents and teachers requested copies of the booklet and research team members were asked to discuss the report in various forums; it became a local best seller. Within 6 months at most elementary schools and some middle schools faculty and administrators had spent time discussing the booklet.

It should be noted that neither of the Pope (2001) and Coulter (1999) studies solved or resolved the issues that had been thematized in them. Many schools across the United States may still be producing stressed out and materialistic students. And Coulter noted that there was no simple change in policy or direction by the Winnipeg School District resulted from the discussions generated by their report. Still, the decisions were the result of more complex dialogue among parents, teachers, and administrators and at least for a while fewer students were repeating grades and courses.

SEDUCING THE ONLOOKER

For arts based researchers, seducing onlookers into encounters with their work may not be easy. Indeed, any arts based researcher (especially those working outside of the popular or vernacular arts) may find that nonartists (both academic and lay) lack a strong desire to engage with their works, the products of their efforts merely replicating the disinterest that members of the public have traditionally held for social science research manuscripts. For, like the traditionalists, they too may be—unlike Pope and Coulter—employing participant languages that relegate some potential audience members to the status of outsiders.

For those arts based researchers who attempt politically overt activist art, occasionally the problem may be a heavy-handed delivery of an intended message, a stridency that hinders efforts at reaching their target audiences. Carol Becker (1994) suggested that a kind of alienation may be the result of some (although certainly not all) activist art:

> Art may be focused directly on the issues of daily life, but, because it seeks to reveal contradictions and not obfuscate them, art works which should spark a shock of recognition and effect catharsis actually appear alien and deliberately difficult. Art easily becomes the object of rage and confrontation. [And artists], frustrated by the illusion of order and well-being posited by society . . . [may] choose rebellion as a method of retaliation . . . [I]n so doing, they separate themselves from those with whom they may actually long to interact. (1994, xiii)

But popular art, including activist varieties, can be inviting and challenging without being off-putting or alienating. Creating a "lay friendly" work might require that arts based researchers enter into the comfort zones of members of an intended audience, enabling them to identify with facets of the work. The artist must manage to pull the lay onlooker into the world of the work, coaxing him or her to participate in a reconstruction of its meaning. The percipient can then place this reconstructed meaning into analogous contexts found in the familiar "real" world outside of the text. If this reading and viewing process results in previously unimagined questions or insights about facets of that "outside" social world, then artistic success is at hand.

BYPASSING OR PENETRATING THE CULTURE INDUSTRY?

But must arts based researchers aspire to interact with everyone within and outside of the academy? Does "going public" with arts based research texts mean reaching as large a portion of the citizenry as have, say, popular films or television shows? Even connecting with a more modest slice of the citizenry might require dissemination though the mass media—a move that raises additional questions about the character of the arts based work to be produced.

The possibility of reaching the masses in this fashion would require more than simply peeling away from the text its coating of what William James once called privileged meaning. Additional compromises might be required. What are they? Commentators on the popular media have noted the stranglehold on the commercially driven media market by the large corporations who comprise the culture industry. To observers such as Agger (1990), this corporate owner-ship and control of the media has meant a displacement of imaginative, vibrant, challenging, transgressive literature and art. This, in turn, he argues, has pro-duced a decline in public discourse.

If Agger (1990) is correct, then it is not merely stridency or mystification through technical jargon that cuts against the possibility of a broad dissemina-tion of the work by the artist–scholar–researcher. Because the culture market squeezes out works that compete poorly in terms of mass appeal, all that fail to attract an audience out of an unwillingness to sensationalize and titillate are in jeopardy. So can broadly based arts based research texts ever be educational in a profound sense? Can they penetrate the center of the public sphere, intel-lectually and emotionally touching large numbers of people and pulling them toward an enhanced understanding of—or least deeper curiosity toward—important educational, social, and political issues?

Might we look to models of great artists throughout history—Dickens? Shakespeare?—whose complex and edifying work has been revered by both the intelligentsia and the working classes? What are more recent examples—in the last half century—of simultaneously thought-provoking and entertaining artworks that have managed to slip past the blockades erected by the gate-keepers of the culture industry to activate the imagination of the masses? The televised adaptation of Alex Haley's (1977) *Roots*? Green Day's punk rock opera and play *American Idiot*? Films such as *Platoon*, *Fahrenheit 9/11*, or *Milk*? Or do some or all of these more recent examples of provocative art fail the stridency test, their appeal and impact thereby diminished?

Ultimately, all arts based researchers, like other artists and writers, must understand that the scope of their audience will always be finite. Referring to literature, the novelist Nadine Gordimer (1989) noted that

> [Any text] will be understood only by readers who share terms of reference formed in us by our education—not merely academic but in the broadest sense of life experience: our political, economic, social, and emotional concepts, and our values derived from these: our cultural background. (p. 59)

Indeed, the general population should never be imagined as a monolithic, homogeneous mass, nonvariegated by cultural background and personal life experiences. And it is obvious that the Zeitgeist can never be transformed by any single arts based research effort. But that is not to suggest that social researchers inspired by the arts should abandon their arduous quest to maintain their scholarly identity and develop their artistic virtuosity while (a la independent filmmakers, playwrights, aspiring novelists, and other storytellers and artists) moving to infiltrate the consciousness of at least some segments of the populace. Nor is it to disparage the strategies pioneered by activist artists to bypass the corporate apparatus of the communications industry, as they target more circumscribed communities within the larger population through the Internet websites and weblogs, or through applied theater, public murals, and other localized, community-based efforts. Indeed, our hope is that all arts based social researchers will continue to experiment with various ways to move their work into the public domain, generating trenchant questions about prevailing societal conditions that might otherwise remain largely unasked outside of the walls of the academy.

Arts Based Research Example

Broken & Buried in Arkansas: A Nonfiction Short Story*

SABRINA CASE, Doctoral Student
University of Oregon, Eugene

THE BEGINNING

> Virtually every corps member you meet will share a similar story of shock, disappointment, and concern from the first days of school.
>
> —Teach For America Diversity, Community, & Achievement 2006 Manual, 35

I sat at my desk, not really sure what to think as I looked around my classroom. *My classroom.* It was not as bad as I'd been told to expect. There were four walls and a ceiling without leaks, neat rows of completely serviceable desks, several windows, and a white board made out of shower board by the previous teacher, another Teach For America corps member now off to law school. They'd told us to expect anything: rooms made out of converted janitorial closets, leaking pipes, backed up sewage, broken windows, graffiti in

---

*This article originally appeared in Case, S. (2010). *Broken and buried in Arkansas: A nonfiction short story*. Unpublished manuscript.

the halls. Maybe some of my acquaintances were now facing those very things. But while this was not a 'nice' school—there was peeling paint, I'd already seen at least one mouse scuttle casually along the back of my room, and the girls' bathroom stall doors had been torn off their hinges long ago—the building was not in itself going to be a daily challenge.

Now if only I could get my computer to work.

"What seems to be the problem?" said Mr. Wilson from the doorway, waving the technical maintenance request slip I'd submitted. He quickly strode into the room, a large man wearing an olive polo T-shirt tucked into belted dress slacks. His eyes moved over my computer, his face already weary—not a good sign considering it was only August and the kids were still two days away from returning from summer vacation. He folded his arms across his chest. "It looks fine to me."

"Yeah, I'm sure it is fine," I said, a little alarmed by his diagnostic methods. "Except that I'm currently locked out because I don't know the last teacher's password."

Mr. Wilson shook his head and emitted a low whistle. "Oh no," he sighed.

"It's not a big deal," I added quickly, sorry to be troubling him over such a small thing. "I just don't have the administrative password to get around it and reset it."

"There *is* no administrative password," he said, standing next to the computer benignly, moving the mouse around for no apparent reason. "You don't have the old teacher's phone number do you?"

"No," I said. "I don't even know his full name. But the office probably has it."

"No, they don't keep records of any of that stuff. He's long gone now," Mr. Wilson said resignedly. "And I'm afraid he might as well have taken this computer with him. It's useless to us now." He shook his head again. "I'll have Fred come by and pick it up later today."

"When will it be back?" I asked, confused. I felt certain this was a fairly minor problem, but I didn't know how to fix the issue. I wondered if Billy, the TFA math teacher down the hall, would know. But before I could mention it, Mr. Wilson was on his way out the door.

"It *won't* be back," he said over his shoulder. "We're sending it off to storage in the Old Gym. I can't even tell you how many otherwise perfectly good computers are over there because of this very problem. If you get another computer, please be sure to write your password down on a post-it or something."

I stared after him, appalled. *If?*

When I returned to my classroom a couple hours later, back from listening to a motivational speaker—the first of five hired by the district to fill up our two days of in-service time—the monitor was gone. The keyboard and hard drive, however, remained on the desk, useless. There was a note beside them in messy scrawl, presumably from Fred, the janitor: "Get you new monter soon."

I had no idea what good a new monitor would do me, since the monitor was never the problem. But that was an issue I never had to confront, since a monitor never arrived that year, and I never saw a point in asking for one.

GROUP THERAPY

It is easy to equate success to race and background, but doing so will be your demise as a teacher. If you show your students that success is attainable through perseverance, and teach them to be self-propelled and self-motivated, then their background will become obsolete. (28)

"I've been *disgusted*, just *disgusted*, with the amount of apathy in my chemistry class," Edward said sharply, the corners of his mouth turned down as if he was being confronted even now with a pile of steaming feces. "I've come up with some really interesting lessons, and they're just *wasted* on them. Short of showing them how to make meth, I can't imagine them ever being interested in learning *anything*."

"Alright, let's talk about apathy," said Sarah in her soothing way, deftly diffusing Edward's customary vitriol. "How have we been addressing that in our classrooms? What's been working for us?"

Sarah was a fourth-year TFA physics teacher at Millcreek High School. That meant she had been living and working in Millcreek for two years of her own volition, which awed the rest of us, who were currently in our first and second years with no intention whatsoever of returning for a third. She struck me as incredibly wise, but what was more impressive was the fact that I never saw her ruffled, even when a stray punch made contact with her jaw during a routine cafeteria brawl one Wednesday afternoon back in September. She was supremely, disarmingly calm. The kids loved her.

"Well, I used one of the techniques described in the Motivation Manual," said Rose brightly. Her ineffable perkiness and thick Georgia-peach drawl had, at first, convinced me she was a bit of a twit, but I was wrong. She was very sharp, just irritating. Her geometry students might have shared my opinion, because they had quickly latched on to her penchant for wildly fluttering her eyes when lecturing, and had made her cry twice by showing off their dead-on impersonations when called upon to answer questions. That issue alone had taken up perhaps two hours of our Tuesday night brainstorming sessions over the last month, culminating in the majority decision that Rose should hold back any student caught making fun of her for a prolonged lunch detention— an idea I was loathe to employ simply because it meant spending lunch with students rather than alone in my locked room as usual. But tonight Rose was cheerful, and I wondered with dread if maybe lunch detention was working. If it was, it would be only a matter of time before I'd be pressured to follow suit in corps solidarity.

"And which technique is that?" asked Sarah.

"I had a problem similar to Edward's—well, probably not *quite* so bad— so after the first week I brought in my diploma and I told them, 'If you work hard and get your homework done and pay attention in class, *you* can get a Princeton diploma someday, too.' I think they were really into that." Rose looked from face to face, smiling, waiting for our approval. "For the next couple weeks I noticed a big difference. A few dropped off again after that, so I keep my diploma on my wall now, and every once in a while, if, let's say, Murray starts nodding off, I'll point to it and say something like, 'Murray, kids who get these didn't sleep in class when they were juniors. I know you want one of these someday, so you'd best sit up and mind.' Because let's face it," she added grimly, "Murray's running out of time to turn things around."

A couple people nodded, commiserating—others who had Murray in their classes, no doubt. I'd never had him, but I had heard so many negative stories about him by then that I felt I might as well have.

"And that works for everyone?" Edward asked, somewhat skeptical but willing to try anything, he was so desperate.

Rose shrugged. "Just about. And, you know, there are some kids you can't do anything for. I never just *let* them sleep, but I think we more or less understand to keep out of each others' way so everyone else can still be successful."

"Excellent," said Edward, jotting something down in his notebook. "I'll give that a shot." He paused, suddenly looking concerned. "My diploma's from Indiana University, though. Do you think that will still work?"

"Sweetheart, I'm sure it'll be fine," said Rose, her voice thick as honey, heavy with self-assurance.

"Aren't you worried they'll steal it?" asked Edward, his own brow knit.

"Nah," she said, tightening her cashmere scarf around her neck. It was late October now, and Sarah's old rented house was drafty. "I lock it up in my desk whenever I'm not in the room."

Edward nodded slowly, like an approving father. "Good idea."

JANUARY

"We're not going to talk about teaching the whole time, are we?" asked Chris, my long-suffering husband, as he was setting the table. He'd not joined TFA, but he'd married me the prior summer and had now found himself marooned in Millcreek, Arkansas, population 1300. He'd taken up a job teaching at the elementary school as a "civilian."

"No," I said, trying to convince myself as much as him. "No way."

But we both already knew that we would. There was nothing else to talk about. The closest city with a movie theatre was two hours away; we did nothing but float between home and school, all of us. And teaching was all we had in common with our dinner guests; they were like the school friends you make because you're forced to share a locker, but with whom any real social activity ends up being awkward. Still, Chris and I were so socially isolated that we were willing to put in an effort with three of the first years at Millcreek High. I was even making a fancy chicken recipe (and a vegetable soup for Stacy, who was vegan). I couldn't stir the soup without chuckling at the idea of a vegan living in rural Arkansas; when I'd arrived the previous year as a bacon-eating "vegetarian," some of my students' parents had told their kids not to trust me because there was "something wrong" with vegetarians. I had taken up hamburgers within months. I wondered if Stacy, clearly more dietarily steadfast, was faring any better.

By six o'clock, supper was on the table and we were seated with Stacy, Edward and Elizabeth.

Elizabeth was a former Peace Corps member and, in her own opinion, a bit of a martyr for deferring her admission to Harvard Law in order to donate another two years of her life to the Millcreek social studies department. Some people resented her for that attitude; we all wanted to be considered martyrs, it seemed, and her résumé out-martyred all of us. But she was a nice enough girl, though very businesslike. Her matter-of-fact tone was not just an affect for her classroom; she was really that no-nonsense, and tonight was no exception.

"I heard Mrs. Winters is going to get fired," she said, almost jovially, referring to the high school principal.

"No way," said Edward, taking on his familiar, professorial tone. "Nothing good ever happens there."

Chris caught my eyes across the table, one corner of his mouth curving upward subtly. I ignored him.

"I think she'll stick around," I said. "I've heard she's the superintendent's niece. And she's already been there, what, six years?"

"Six years too many," Elizabeth declared icily. "That woman has no business being in any school, in any position. Very rarely have I witnessed more profound incompetence."

"Hear hear!" said Edward, raising his glass of iced tea in a mock toast.

"We'll see," I said doubtfully.

Soon the conversation had drifted away from our administration and toward our students.

"You know, I used to feel overwhelmed," said Elizabeth. "I thought for the longest time that it was me, that I just wasn't doing my job well. But now I see it's not me. It's them."

"Who?" asked Chris, casting me another glance. He loved goading them on to little diatribes.

"The kids, to some degree, but especially the parents," said Elizabeth.

"I think you're right," Stacy agreed. She'd spent most of dinner simply listening in silence but Elizabeth's comment had apparently stirred up passionate agreement, for she now leaned in, nodding vigorously. "The parents are awful."

"Not all the parents," Elizabeth added. "But *almost* all of them. Sometimes I think that it's not enough just to try to teach the kids. I feel sometimes like the best thing we could do is adopt them. Just adopt as many as we can and get them out of here, you know?"

Chris raised an eyebrow. I quickly filled my mouth with chicken before anyone could look to me for my opinion. The same notion had crossed my mind with a few favorite students, but nothing so wholesale as what was now being suggested. She must have seen the discomfort in my face.

"You don't agree?" Elizabeth asked. All eyes shifted to me.

"I don't think that's realistic, no," I said hastily, shoving my fork around my plate. "And I don't think it's necessary either. And it sounds . . . well, it sounds really bad."

Elizabeth shrugged. "Yeah, it probably does, but I look at Jerome, who's practically the only decent kid I have in my advanced section, and then I look at his parents. And they are horrible. I mean, complete trash. And I think that the only way Jerome will ever have a chance of getting out of here and *making* something of himself is if I just get him out myself. Like you're doing with Sydney and Emma. I mean, you're planning on taking them with you, right?"

"Uh . . . I don't think that's comparable," said Chris, rather paler than he had been a moment before. "Sydney and Emma are dogs."

"Well, no, it's not *literally* the same," said Elizabeth, clearly getting impatient with us. She seemed to think we were being intentionally difficult. "But you know what I *mean*."

As neither Chris nor I were forthcoming, Edward stepped in. "*I know what you mean*," he said. "But I see what Sabrina's saying, too. This is just one community. There are so many more like it. I just can't see any organized effort ever happening to adopt and move all those kids."

I grimaced. That had *not* been what I was saying.

Elizabeth considered this as she took another bite of her chicken marsala. "No, you're right. I hadn't thought of all the other schools around here. But see, that just brings me right back to feeling overwhelmed. I don't know how we're supposed to fix all this when no one in the community is willing to let us help them. What can you do when it's just a handful of you against so much ignorance? And then I wonder why we're even here. I feel like next year I'll move away and I'll feel like I couldn't save *anyone*."

"Well, maybe once you finish law school you can come back and use that to help create more change," suggested Stacy helpfully.

"No," said Elizabeth at once, irritable. "I'm going into international business law, and you'd need to specialize in education or family law to have any real impact here. So if they want anything from me, it's now or never."

I sat up groggily, still not sure if what I'd heard had been real or in a dream.

"What was that?" Chris asked from his place in bed beside me. "It sounded like an explosion."

"I don't know," I said, pushing my hair out of my face. All I could hear now was the *ting ting* of sleet pelting the windows. Our dinner guests had gone home early to beat the ice. I glanced at the clock. It was 2 in the morning.

Chris moved to the window and peered between the slats of the blinds. "Holy shit," he murmured. "Come take a look at this."

"What?" I asked, drawing up to the window and following his gaze. Our house was on the corner. To our right, across the street, was the school district office. Directly ahead was the immaculate three-story home of our landlords, the Masterson's, a retired white couple who in addition to our single-story brick home owned perhaps 45% of the town's businesses and properties—a small empire built on the success of their extensive farm holdings dating back generations to their plantation roots. Everything was covered in an opaque sheet of ice; the maple branches bent beneath its glittering weight and long icicles hung from the electric and telephone wires. The cars, encapsulated in fogged glass, huddled in driveways.

"No school tomorrow," I said, relieved. Any pardon, even a temporary one, from the endless challenge that was a typical school day was a welcome gift in my book. I was ready to crawl back into bed, a smile on my face.

"No, not that," Chris said, pointing. "*That.*"

Across the corner from us, where the enormous wooden structure of the Old Gym had loomed only yesterday, was a pile of rubble, jagged plywood, and crumpled roofing. The gym, probably seventy-years-old and long suffering in disrepair—a near-forgotten relic from the days when the public schools had still been predominantly white and well-funded, prior to the *Brown v. Brown* decision that had dotted the rural countryside with dozens of all-white private schools—had finally collapsed under the weight of the ice, releasing one final, booming death-groan in the process.

"What a mess," I said. Then, suddenly remembering: "Hey, my computer monitor's in there!"

I felt strangely sad for that perfectly good monitor which, if not already destroyed by the blazing heat of early fall or the leaky chill of winter, was now surely crushed beneath the debris.

"The Masterson's are going to love *this*," Chris observed dryly. "Just one more reason for them to bitch about the declining state of the neighborhood." He sighed, remembering that the next month's rent was coming up due. "I'll bake you a cake if you'll be the one to drop off the check next week."

"Fine," I sighed, too sleepy at that moment to consider the interminable conversations Mrs. Masterson always insisted upon having each month. What had started as pleasant enough visits had become increasingly uncomfortable as she'd come to freely throw out racist comments as if they were casual observations—which, for her, they probably were. We never quite knew how to handle them without coming across as rude tenants. We could tell by her exultant welcomes that we were supposed to be endlessly grateful to have such a nice home. She was the self-fashioned Matriarch of Millcreek, and she was doing us a favor.

"Fine," I said again. "You did it last time anyway. Now let's go back to bed."

School was canceled the next day, but the persistent ice and snow did not discourage people from blocks around from driving or walking down to our intersection to gawk at the wreckage. All throughout the day there were bundled-up onlookers, and the word spread across town quickly so that by the time the sun began to set in the gloomy gray of early evening, it seemed like every resident from both the white and black sides of town had at some point made their winter journey to pay homage to the devastation. No one dared to touch the debris; there seemed an unspoken agreement that it was best to look from a distance.

That is, until one little boy, probably no older than ten, attempted to climb up the one broken wall that was still semi-erect. His mother shooed him off quickly, swatting him all about the head, but it was too late; he'd already done what at least three or four dozen other kids had likely been imagining and, the initial sanctity of the collapsed gym now broken, had pulled down the invisible cordons. By the next morning (with school canceled for the second day) at least ten children would be running from the gym, screaming, their hands or arms or feet pierced and bloodied by the long rusty nails hidden beneath the snow.

"Goddamn idiots," I mumbled over my coffee.

LOCKED IN, BROKEN DOWN & RUN OFF

We all want to respect and appreciate the different cultures and lifestyles that we see in our students, schools, and communities. We must not, however, confuse that important principle with a relativistic view that we have no business "imposing" the value of academic achievement on our students. We are committed to the value of academic achievement, as it will inevitably expand our students' life prospects, giving them more and better choices in life. *(40–41)*

"Mrs. Winters, please report to the office." The intercom crackled, but did not fully obscure the frantic voice of Ms. Myers, the office secretary. "Mrs. Winters, if you are in the building, *please* report to the office immediately."

My students snickered and I also had to suppress a humorless smile. These kinds of announcements were routine and meant only one thing: There was a fight somewhere in the school, and Mrs. Winters had, instead of heading down to confront it, locked herself in her office, turned off the lights, drawn all the blinds, and was watering her plants while humming to herself. In the case of really bad fights, Mrs. Winters could manage to "pretend she wasn't home" for an entire afternoon, foregoing both food and the bathroom, only to emerge at the ring of the final bell, when she would shuffle quickly from her doorway to the exit and into her Buick. This was a reality that the students, teachers, and even Ms. Myers knew—indeed, Ms. Myers knew it better than anyone, as she was always there to hear the turn of the lock—and yet she never gave up on this charade, this farce. She always seemed to reserve hope that, just maybe, Mrs. Winters would not leave her to deal with the bloody aftermath alone.

However, this particular afternoon proved to be the wrong one for Mrs. Winters to play this game, as a boy was beaten within an inch of his life that day with a heavy metal chain before two gym teachers could wrest his attacker off of his unconscious body. Even as an ambulance pulled up, Mrs. Winters was nowhere to be seen. Indeed, no one saw her until Mr. Palmer, the superintendent who had finally had enough, keyed into her office and slammed the door behind him—though that was not enough to keep everyone who entered the office or teachers' lounge from hearing his hollering. That's when I believed she must really be his niece; around those parts, only kin could give you a dressing down like that.

So the rumors turned out to be accurate after all: in February, Mrs. Winters vanished. There was no announcement. It didn't even happen over break or a weekend. She was there on a Tuesday, and on Wednesday she wasn't. Mr. Palmer stood in as interim principal for three weeks—probably the most peaceful, orderly three weeks of the year—and then, without fanfare even in the form of a staff meeting, Mr. Armstrong arrived as the new principal. He was a transplant from a central Arkansas school district, was six-foot-five, had a torso as broad as a tree trunk, and wherever he went he carried with him a large wooden paddle and a powerful disdain for Teach For America.

The Teach For America teachers, nearly the only white teachers in the building, were the first ones he visited.

"Where's your paddle?" he asked the first time he surveyed my classroom.

He hadn't knocked or said hello. He'd just come in and, without acknowledging me, had immediately gone about inspecting the posters and bulletin boards on each wall as my eyes followed him about the room. His voice, rather high and liable to crack whenever he raised his volume, did not seem to match his frame, but I was nonetheless intimidated as he stood over me, arms folded, his own paddle in hand.

"I don't have one."

"You didn't order one from the shop class?"

"No, sir," I said nervously.

"Why not?" he demanded.

"I don't paddle, sir," I answered. "I use alternative disciplinary techniques."

He studied me for a long moment, his brow gradually rising in incredulity. He slowly shook his head and then, without another word, left the room. I blinked at the empty doorway, unsure what to think.

He'd have similar discussions with all the other TFA teachers over the next couple days; none of us paddled, nor owned symbolic paddles. He let us know in the next faculty meeting, in front of all the other teachers, how much this disgusted him; it flaunted his authority and encouraged disorder, he said. At the end of the meeting, he called for a staff prayer in which he asked God to impart wisdom to the staff, especially regarding classroom management.

After school that day, we all gathered at someone's house to complain and to consider in advance the grievance process at Millcreek High School, anticipating trouble.

"I can't believe he made us pray at school," I murmured desolately. "Everything's crazy here."

Mr. Armstrong acted in accordance with his stated views on discipline. Within two weeks, numerous students had been subjected to his paddle in the hallway during passing periods, in front of their peers, for various infractions ranging from grabbing girls' butts to spitting on the floor, yelling obscenities to throwing pencils. There were no disciplinary hearings, no calls home, no follow-up. Students put one hand on the wall, hiked up their shirt with the other if it obscured their bottom, took their "lickings" (the count varied from one to five based on the offense), and got themselves to class. And things did get a lot quieter in the hallway for all but the most perseverant offenders.

Mallory Roberts, a sophomore who was old enough to be a college freshman, was one of that select crowd, and she meant business. Mr. Armstrong, she declared with a haughty sneer in my first period English 10 class, did not faze her. "He's just a fat old man who likes to act tough."

She was in a foul mood that particular Thursday morning, and I felt lucky to dodge the worst of her rage. Sure, she was snappy and rude, sarcastic and cruel—but she stayed in her desk and didn't get in my face like I knew she sometimes did. Still, when she headed out at the end of class, a tense silence followed in her wake; the kids seemed to always know when an eruption was imminent, and they gave her plenty of space as they filed out into the hallway.

Not even five minutes had passed when there was an explosion of shouts. I peered into the hallway but saw nothing. Whatever was happening was occurring around the corner, down by the math wing. I weighed whether or not to venture out, knowing that if it was a fight, I'd be unable to do anything about it. Teachers bigger than me had made trips to the hospital after trying to break up fights, and I'd already been told by other teachers, both male and female, that I was not to try to step into a brawl.

"Ohhhhh snap!" yelled Phineas, one of my Pre-AP English students as he wheeled around the corner and bolted by. "Mallory Roberts just laid out Mr. Clyde! Ohhhh!"

Clearly, Phineas had designated himself a modern-day Paul Revere figure, for he was still shouting these lines over and over as he vanished around the next corner and proceeded to the science wing, his announcement echoing after him.

I pondered his news. Mr. Clyde was a gym teacher, and no small man. I tried to imagine what could have possibly driven Mallory to take him on—and how she'd won, since Mr. Clyde never hesitated to punch students right back, if they started it.

But that was just the beginning of what turned out to be a day preserved in legend. For whatever reason, she ended up in the next class, where she also punched her math teacher, and then she went on to punch her 3rd period home economics teacher out cold. How she was permitted to carry on with her schedule while punching people all the way—especially with Mr. Armstrong in the building—I'd never know. Maybe Mallory had read the new principal correctly, and he had proven too hesitant to take her on. I could hardly blame him; Mallory was truly a force to be reckoned with, and almost universally feared in the school. At any rate, Mallory went free until the end of 3rd period, when—I can only guess how—Mr. Armstrong managed to shove her into a custodial closet and lock the door fast behind her.

I did not know this, of course, until I was passing through the hallway during my planning period on my way to the copy machine and heard a terrible thumping coming from the closet. I looked around; the hallway was empty, but the source of the sound was unmistakable—and, indeed, the door was visibly shaking with the force of her barrage of fists.

"What the—"

I outstretched one hand toward the door, my impulse being to open it, thinking a student had somehow become trapped inside.

"If you so much as touch that door, you're fired," boomed a voice.

I started and wheeled around to find Mr. Armstrong.

"What's going on?" I asked, frightened. This sort of thing was not supposed to happen, and it scared me.

"That's none of your goddamn business. Now if you want to keep your job you had better just move along."

Mr. Armstrong guarded that door for the next three periods, not that it was necessary. No one had any desire to open that door, even if offered money, since everyone was convinced that Mallory would murder the first person she saw upon being released. Only at the end of the day, long after the pounding had ceased and the angry hollers had gone silent, did several men on staff draw slips of paper to determine who would take on the fearful duty of unlatching the janitor's closet. Fred, the janitor, had been wise enough to take the afternoon as a sick day—he had nothing to do without access to his supplies anyway, and Mr. Armstrong was probably not above reasoning that anyone locked in the janitor's closet somehow fell under the janitor's jurisdiction.

But the build-up proved anti-climactic and the precautions unnecessary, for when the door creaked open, Mallory emerged slowly, her hands bloody and shaking, her face swollen and wet from crying. Mallory, it turned out, did have one weakness no one had suspected: she was severely claustrophobic. Only because her mother was in jail did Millcreek High escape a lawsuit. As it was, Mallory did not come back to school for a month.

"The most peaceful month of my life," one veteran math teacher—one of the three who had been punched—would reminisce later at the staff lunch table. "That class was never better behaved than when she was away."

Several other teachers, myself included, cried about it, sobbed about not opening the door despite Mr. Armstrong's threats. At our TFA group meeting that week we talked about it for a while, moralized, and dabbed at our eyes. The following week, we talked about it again, though much more briefly. And then no one really wanted to talk about it anymore.

It had been a month since the Old Gym collapsed. The weather had turned milder and the snow was long gone. Still, the wreckage looked very much the same as it had. Kids were no longer climbing on it—several bandages and tetanus shots at the town clinic had taught them their lesson. Now it was adults who were interested in exploring what remained.

The rummaging had begun shortly after the ice melted, and had at first occurred only late at night. That's when the treasure hunters—usually black, the Masterson's were quick to note, but sometimes white—would arrive on foot or in pick-up trucks. They'd take whatever was of interest that they could either haul or carry: old computers, half-broken school desks, scrap wood, cleansers, miscellaneous electronic parts, whatever they felt they could use. It was free, after all, and the school district had made no show of interest in salvaging any of its property. Most everything over there had been abandoned so long that the district probably scarcely remembered what was there to begin with.

"There it goes," I said to myself one Saturday evening, watching from the back yard where the dogs were out for their bedtime bathroom excursion. A black man in a flannel shirt and baseball cap was carrying a monitor down the street, the cord trailing on the pavement behind him, his shadow long beneath the streetlights. It could have of course been any monitor, but I liked to think it was mine, off on another leg of its dubious adventure, destination unknown.

After a few days the rummaging became bolder. People did it openly, in mid-afternoon, whenever. No one cared. The police certainly didn't; it was clear no one had any idea what to do about this grand old mess, and no one affiliated with the town in any official capacity wanted to show any initiative, since much like the situation with the custodial closet, whoever did first would likely get stuck with, and blamed for, whatever followed. So everyone—the school district, the neighborhood association, the town council, the police— were all laying low, engaged in a bureaucratic game of chicken, hoping some other guy would flinch first.

The Masterson's, disgusted by the ruins and the scenes of "looting" and the "higher potential for neighborhood crime" they felt it engendered, were positively squirming to be rid of it, but also were resistant to the idea of doing the district's work for it, despite what they claimed was its willful and obscene negligence. At our next rent meeting, they seemed genuinely torn about the whole thing. "I just hate that they're going to try to force this on us," said Mrs. Masterson, her tone an odd mix of bitterness and self-congratulation.

"We've done so much to make this town livable as it is, shouldering so much of the burden all by ourselves. We've already given them jobs and homes to rent. Must we be responsible for *everything*?"

She threw up her hands with frustration. "Those people are always so eager to pass the buck. That's what really gets me about 'em. *That's* what really tries my patience and tests my spirit."

The district insisted it simply did not have the funds or equipment to address the Old Gym. Eventually, though, they did hire a couple guys with pick-up trucks to make a half-hearted attempt at loading up and carting off debris. For about a week they came and went, and barely made a dent in the colossal mound of wreckage. Then they stopped coming.

Walking the dogs in the evenings, it seemed like every other front porch we passed now contained at least one old school desk. Houses with larger covered porches often showcased piles of monitors and broken TV sets with "MHS" scrawled across the sides in whiteout. They sat there in the twilight, as still and useless and sad as corpses, the lightning bugs flickering around them in silent vigil.

OBSERVATIONS

Starting a few weeks after the custodial closet episode, Mr. Armstrong began dropping by frequently to observe me. Observations were nothing new, and usually did not fluster me. TFA sent supervisors to observe as often as once a month, and we also regularly videotaped ourselves so that other first- and second-year corps members could offer critiques at "viewing parties." But Mr. Armstrong's visits were not like TFA's. Rather than sitting quietly at my desk, furiously scribbling notes, he would simply come in unannounced and stand beside the door, his arms folded, a contemptuous scowl on his face, his omni-present paddle in hand. He would not move, not speak; his unflinching gaze was always on me, wearing the disapproval of an angry parent, one eyebrow slightly arched as if he had just walked in on his child misbehaving. After five or so minutes, without a word or a gesture, he would leave, letting the door swing slowly shut behind him. We never had follow-ups to these informal "observations." He never offered feedback. Professional improvement wasn't the point of this exercise.

My freshmen and sophomores, sensing this, would collectively exhale with me as soon as he departed, though most seemed more amused by his routine than intimidated. They could tell, after all, that the target of his drop-in investigations was, for once, their teacher and not them.

"Whoa buddy, you must have really pissed him off," Phineas observed one afternoon, positively jubilant. He loved drama, particularly at my expense. "He looked ready to lay that paddle to you."

I shrugged it off as best I could, pretending to dismiss it like any other joke. But the kids weren't joking, and I didn't think it was funny. I thought exactly what they did: Mr. Armstrong had it out for me. But not just me; he observed each of the seven white TFA teachers with the same frequency, in the same manner. We were constantly on our guard. In our evening support meetings we tried to abate our fear by leveling insults at him and his professionalism, his brute menace, his complete lack of civility. We called him a racist, and we believed it. After all, he was jovial and kind to the black teachers at the school, but refused to grant us any measure of dignity. We complained to TFA, who said there was nothing they could or would do, as it was a sensitive issue and they had no desire to strain relationships with the district. Think of the good of the kids, the administrators told us. Yes, they could always place us elsewhere, but if we caused a scene and TFA was no longer invited to work at the high school, the kids would be the only losers.

Begrudgingly, we accepted this as the truth; the kids *did* need us. If we left, who would teach them?

After a couple months, Mr. Armstrong relented and his visits stopped. Sometimes I wondered what his intentions had ever been; I assumed he'd hoped to run us off and, having failed that, was now putting his time to other uses. I wondered if Mr. Palmer had intervened; Millcreek, like so many other districts, had come to be so reliant on TFA to supplement their staffing that burnt bridges might be even less palatable to him than to TFA. I'd heard of TFA teachers who, despite egregious actions that would have gotten any other staff member fired, had not been let go because their districts feared straining their increasingly dependent relationships with Teach For America.

As part of its route to nontraditional licensure, Arkansas had established a two-year mentorship program to complement the battery of PRAXIS tests. While this program was technically accessible to numerous nontraditional educators, it had been established primarily to serve Teach For America's corps members and to smooth the way for hundreds of individuals without any education training whatsoever to teach full-time and unobserved in the state's most challenging, struggling schools. This was the extent of Little Rock's association with the Mississippi Delta, which in numerous professional seminars, conferences and trainings it portrayed as a backwater that unfortunately could not be disowned by the whiter, more affluent central and western regions of the state.

My assigned mentor was Mrs. Ivory, a fifth-grade teacher in the district's elementary school, which was separated from the high school by a narrow staff parking lot. She was supposed to observe me once a month, but she visited my classroom only twice over two years. I visited her classroom much more frequently, as a major part of the program was observing seasoned veteran teachers. However, the practice always left me feeling horrified and angry. Mrs. Ivory was without a doubt incredibly charismatic; her personality was powerful, her face and body animated when she spoke, her tone inspirational. The kids loved her, and the girls admired her sharp sense of style and the elephant-themed accoutrements of her college sorority that she'd hung all over her classroom. She never had significant classroom management issues, not just because of her charm, but because she had no qualms about paddling her kids for backtalk—though, whenever I was in the building, she professed her disdain for the practice and the rarity with which she used it (sometimes *while* paddling a squirming, tearful 10-year-old).

However, while she had an extraordinary talent for disseminating information so that her students retained it, she also had a penchant for teaching patently false, often purely improvised information. During my first observation she had taught her students what seemed to be an entirely self-invented system of proofreading marks—a system of zigzags and swirls and smiley faces that would work in her classroom, but would be unintelligible to anyone else. Another time she chastised a child who had correctly recited the colors in the rainbow, and then launched into a teachable moment about how the rainbow in fact contained pink and brown rather than violet and red. Some of the students seemed confused, but no one challenged her teaching (nor did I, as that was not my role in this arrangement; I contented myself to instead write snide notes to myself about her colossal stupidity).

Mid-April was my final observation, and when I quietly slipped into the room and took my seat she was transitioning into her social studies block. She was just wrapping up a three-week unit on World War II and midway through the lesson, she challenged me to ask her students questions.

"These are some bright bulbs this year," she said proudly. "Go ahead, ask them anything about World War II."

As all the students turned to face me, I squirmed a bit, startled to be called upon when I thought I'd be left to myself. "Well, what kinds of things have you covered?" I asked, unsure what to ask. "Did they learn about the Holocaust?"

Mrs. Ivory blinked twice but did not miss a beat. "Of course!" she exclaimed. "Of course they did!"

"Well, " I said, "how about someone explain to me what the Holocaust was."

The kids looked at one another and then to Mrs. Ivory uncertainly. She did not look anymore confident than the rest of them. "Go ahead, Ricky," she encouraged. "Ricky," she added indulgently over their heads, "is the smartest kid in here. Ricky, tell her the answer."

Ricky, his hands folded neatly in front of him, smiled at this praise. "The Holocaust," he said matter-of-factly, without even the slightest hesitation, "was a giant celebration."

I stared at him, and then glanced to Mrs. Ivory, expecting her to fumble with some excuse or explanation. Instead, she was looking at me as expectantly as Ricky. It struck me that she, too, was unaware of what the Holocaust was. But she must have thought she knew a great deal about World War II, and had done a stellar job—*she* was the one who had, with pride, posed the challenge that had now placed her and poor Ricky in this mortifying position—a position all the more horrifying because they did not even know to *be* mortified.

The anger and disgust rising in me, I could not suppress a streak of cruelty. "A celebration of what?" I prodded with mock encouragement.

Here Ricky shifted uncertainly. "I don't remember," he admitted. He looked to his teacher contritely. "I'm sorry, Mrs. Ivory."

"You've got nothing to be sorry for," she said brightly. "Thank you, Ricky. Now let's move on to partner work."

She never did venture to provide an answer to the question Ricky had been asked, and none of the kids probed for an answer, either from her or from me. Everyone, it seemed, was content not to know.

"This place is so fucked, no one will ever get out," I scrawled angrily in my journal that night. "What are the kids supposed to do when they work hard to learn, but their uneducated teachers teach them incorrect information? No wonder Ricky, a bright kid serious about school, is still scoring 'below basic' on the state standardized test. No wonder the district is on the verge of state-ordered consolidation—their teachers are *making* them fail by passing on a legacy of ignorance. Everyone working here *should* be fired. There's nothing to do here but raze it to the ground and start building all over again."

Mrs. Ivory was, after all, a graduate herself of the Millcreek public school system, as were so many other teachers in the district. "She left knowing nothing and returned knowing nothing," I told my husband furiously over dinner. "But she came back carrying a teaching license from one of the state's fifth-tier universities. And that's immoral. It's a never-ending cycle of failure. If not for TFA, almost *every* teacher here would be like that. Do you know that some of them use class time to preach Bible lessons? Seriously, Bible lessons! I may not be an expert teacher, but at least I know my goddamn material!"

Chris watched me over the rim of his glass. "How does the cycle get broken?" he finally asked.

"How should *I* know?" I spat. "It won't be. It *can't* be! No one with talent would ever want to live here, and anyone from here with real talent leaves. They have no hope. I can't *wait* to get out of this shithole!"

"Some of the teachers are decent," Chris said calmly.

I set my face in my hands. "Not enough. There's no way they'll avoid consolidation."

"Well, maybe consolidation is the best thing. Then they'll get new teachers from whatever school they merge with."

"But *those* teachers," I said sharply, "will still be *Arkansas* teachers."

He was silent for a moment. "That doesn't seem fair."

"I agree," I said stubbornly. "It's not fair to the kids at all."

He shot me a look. "That's not what I meant."

"I know!"

That month, Millcreek was treated to a new bit of drama—and a steady stream of gossip and speculation—when an escaped convict reportedly took up residence in the collapsed gym. Several people claimed spotting him, armed with a handgun and still in his orange jumpsuit, but no one ever could confirm if these reports were reliable. The police drove by with spotlights for five nights in a row and paced around the wreckage ineffectually by day. There was never a formal announcement to area residents; word-of-mouth was enough to get everyone to lock their doors. Absurdly, Chris and I started leaving the dogs in during the day, not to watch the house, but for their own protection—though I don't know what we thought a convict would want with a golden retriever and a beagle mix.

The students seemed much less worried; not only did they not vary their route to and from school to avoid passing by the gym, but many kids started taking that road just to gawk and shout jeers and challenges at the convict, who they imagined was lying low, watching and listening. After a week, interest faded and the police stopped coming by. There was no report of him being caught; everyone just assumed that he had moved on, if he'd ever been there at all.

But though the rumors dropped off, the incident continued to haunt the Masterson's and their middle-class neighbors, who lobbied the school board daily to dispose of the Old Gym. It was a public menace. It had to go. *Now.*

Apparently out of other options and concerned about the possible costly legal action that the Masterson's had threatened, the district sent the men with pickups back once more—this time to douse the wreckage in gasoline and light it on fire. The gym was, of course, still loaded with cleaning solvents, pressurized canisters, various electric components, even the odd tire. And so it was only an hour or so after the fire took that the air was filled with a toxic black smoke and a seemingly relentless series of pops and explosions—some as small at bottle rockets, others powerful enough to rattle the glass in the window-panes. Even with everything shut up tight, the house smelled faintly of burning rubber and other unknown substances. The smoke hung over the neighbor-hood in a haze for days as the fire kept smoldering and the flammables kept popping off.

The kids made up stories of finding a burnt body in the ruins, its charred finger bones still wrapped about a gun.

THE SPIRIT OF GIVING

Even as Millcreek School District had been busily working on the Old Gym problem, Teach For America had been at work organizing and implementing the brainchild of a few corps members for drawing the entire TFA service region's public schools together in a friendly competition. The name of the game was Delta Idol, modeled on *American Idol*, and TFA volunteers across Arkansas and Mississippi had been developing it since the beginning of spring. While the competition was meant to be a fun time, it was also a fundraiser to earn money to launch a Boys & Girls Club in a nearby town. The three corps members heading up the fundraising efforts had already picked a site, had met with a Boys & Girls Club liaison, and had been steadily marketing the project to the current corps as a way to leave behind a legacy in the Delta to serve our kids long after we had all packed up and left. Since Teach For America wasn't going anywhere—in fact, its size was growing every year—successive genera-tions of corps members could pick up where we left off and see the project through and manage and maintain it. This could go on, they reasoned, for decades. It would be yet another way to expand TFA's positive presence and increase our impact.

By April, it was time to advertise and hold school-based auditions for vari-ety acts. Feeling otherwise disconnected from and ambivalent about Teach For America, I signed up to help head the Delta Idol competition at Millcreek. In another couple months, I would be moving away and I wanted to feel like I'd contributed to something bigger than my classroom; I wanted to do something with my students beyond the everyday grind of class work, something just for fun.

After a highly attended audition that brought together both elementary and high school acts, the judges panel—consisting of two TFA teachers and one veteran teacher who we had invited so that the "school's staff would feel included"—designated three groups as finalists to go on to compete at the

Arkansas level. The winners there would compete in the bi-state competition, to be held on a local community college campus and accompanied by a catered, sit-down dinner for the audience. Tickets to attend the event would be priced at $30 apiece. As this price was too steep for the majority of our students' parents and the need to raise money was the whole point, the TFA teachers heading up the project had decided to market the event primarily toward more affluent but charitable white community members and business owners. Despite grumbling by some corps members about the questionable ethicality and mission-compromising nature of such an exclusive fundraising scheme, the plan went off as proposed and the event sold out quickly.

My students were incredibly excited, and the two acts from Millcreek that had made the cut to the final round gained a certain level of celebrity on campus. As the big day approached, the halls were filled with electricity. The groups—both song and dance acts around raps that had been getting a lot of radio air time—rehearsed during lunch and after school with utmost dedication. Since the competition would take place in a neighboring town, arrangements were made to secure rides for them and their families, if they were needed. Sadly, only one of the seven students participating would have their family represented, though, and only his mother was coming while his father and siblings stayed at home; the ticket price was just too much to be affordable for anyone else. But, despite their disappointment that their families would not be able to see them perform in public for the first time in their lives, they were thrilled, hopeful, nervous, and talkative.

I was excited, too, and was happy to allow class discussion to veer into talk of Delta Idol. I felt that, for once, I was involved in something purely positive, something I could just be pleased with without doubt. As my two years were wrapping up, I had mixed feelings about how much use I'd actually been to my kids as a teacher, how much they'd learned, how much they respected me. But this was something that seemed to unite all of us; we were a team.

FINAL PERFORMANCES

Relaxing your expectations for any student—whether out of concern for difficult situations at home or in the community, or out of respect for a culture that is different from our own—in the end only hurts that student by lowering achievement and thereby limiting life-prospects. (41)

The school year ended in mid-May, so I met with my TFA supervisor, Chad, in early May for our final meeting: the year-end report in which I handed over my achievement records. What was most important was that the records demonstrate what TFA called "significant gains." This meant that students could either show an advance of two grade levels in a content area within a single year, or that the majority of classes had achieved 80% of the class's ambitious academic goals. I had selected the latter method of achievement measurements, as I felt it was more attainable. Still, while my two advanced classes had met the 80% mark, my four regular English 9 and 10 classes had not. For some of the skill sets, the numbers were actually quite low, and I was nervous about how Chad would respond. I felt like I was going to be in trouble, and had been dreading the meeting for weeks.

Chad, who was twenty-six and had taught for two years in TFA's South Dakota region, was quiet as he looked over the spreadsheets. I sat in the corner chair of his small office, tapping my fingers on the armrests and watching his face for a reaction. He frowned. "I see you did not meet your goals in your 1st, 3rd, 5th or 6th periods. Why do you think that is?"

I had been expecting this question, and launched immediately into my rehearsed answer. "Well, a lot of the kids in those classes were out a lot. Here's my attendance book. You'll see that these kids, who failed, were also out for nearly a fourth of second semester."

"Why?"

"For reasons having nothing to do with me," I explained. "There were a couple pregnancies," I said, pointing to two names. "He went to jail for three weeks, I don't even know for what." I pointed again to the bottom of the page. "Three of these kids dropped out for months and then popped up at the end of the year so that I had to include them, and that dragged my percentages down. Things like that."

He nodded. "Well, that kind of thing happens. What about this one?"

I shrugged. "She came every day, but had no interest in the material. I did everything I could think of to motivate her, but I just never had any luck. She's not interested in being at school, but someone makes her come."

"What do you think was the major cause for the difference between the performance rates of your advanced classes and your regular classes?"

"Motivation," I said immediately. "The advanced kids just *wanted* to learn more. I didn't really do anything differently with the two groups—aside from using different texts. But they just responded differently. I don't think it had anything to do with me."

"You didn't vary techniques between the advanced and more remedial kids?" he asked.

I shook my head, knowing this was sort of a trick question. "No," I said earnestly. "I used some differentiation, but I didn't want to lower my expectations and water down the curriculum for the more remedial kids."

Chad nodded, pleased with my answer. "Very good. Well," he added, sighing as he placed my reports into my folder and set it into an open file cabinet drawer, "it looks like you've done good work here. Don't beat yourself up about it too much, it sounds like you did everything you could."

And that was that. I considered his words of comfort as I headed out to my car. I hadn't beaten myself up at all, I realized; I had placed all of the blame firmly on my students. They hadn't wanted to learn badly enough, their lives had gotten in the way. They had refused to be helped.

I had expected Chad to give me a harder time. I had wanted him to. But he seemed just as content to let the fault rest on my 15- and 16-year-olds' shoulders as I was. As I drove home, I wondered if I'd really accomplished *anything*. I wondered if my kids might have been better off with someone else, someone who maybe was like me, but better. Someone who actually knew what they were doing. Someone who wasn't such a fraud.

That weekend, we had a small farewell get-together at a second year's home. A lot of people showed up and, despite having withdrawn from my fellow corps members over the previous months for reasons I couldn't really explain, we decided to go. It was the end, after all. Soon we'd be far away from all this.

Everyone was talking about his or her plans. We were moving to Oregon. Why? Because it seemed like the opposite of Arkansas in terms of its liberal-mindedness. No, we didn't have any definite plans. No, we didn't have family up there. We just wanted a fresh start. People nodded.

Elizabeth mentioned that she was still struggling over whether to go to Harvard Law or keep teaching.

"I'm thinking of deferring for another year," she said. "I feel like I'm finally making progress in my room, and I just can't stomach the idea of someone else stepping in and undoing it all, you know?"

"It may be another TFAer," someone offered hopefully, sipping her martini.

"Yeah, probably," Elizabeth agreed. "But what if it's not? It would be as if I was never even here. So I'm thinking of putting in another year, maybe two. Law school will always be there, but these kids need me *now*."

We nodded politely and commiserated with her moral dilemma. Of course, we knew as well as she did that there was not a chance in hell that she would defer Harvard Law for another year. But it was a charade we were all willing to play for the sake of appearances. There was nothing about this strange dance peculiar to Elizabeth; all over the region—probably all over the country—corps members were engaged in this act, this final, hollow display of martyrdom. Serving these kids had been internalized as a moral imperative, so we had to look convincingly torn about leaving.

"I think I may stay as well," said Billy, a math teacher. He had made more of an effort to get to know the community than anyone else we knew, admittedly, and from him it sounded more believable. "I think the school will need us more than ever now that it's definitely going to be consolidated with Chester High School—with everything else that'll be shifted around and shaken up, losing us would be the last straw. I mean, look how many of us they'll be placing in Millcreek next year—we are practically holding the place together. I have plans I've only started to implement, and I don't want to see them go by the wayside. I think they'll make a big difference, not just in my department, but in the school, if I can get them off the ground."

"I understand that," said someone else, a teacher in another town who I didn't know very well. "And I respect that. But we can't just think about what's best for them forever. At some point we have to start thinking about ourselves and what *we* need."

Elizabeth nodded, betraying her own true plans. I knew half of her house was already packed up in boxes. But I didn't have the nerve to point this out; that would have been interpreted as crass and petty of me. It just wasn't done.

A week before the last day of school, the big night finally arrived. It seemed as if most of the corps drove in to attend Delta Idol, more white people among white people. The audience, truly, was a sea of white, most of them middle-aged and dressed in their dinner jackets and pearls, sitting down to their candlelit dinners. Scattered here and there were the black parents and grandparents and younger siblings of the performers, huddled close together like small islands, looking around uncertainly at the white businesspeople studying them.

I was uncomfortable watching the strained interactions and wondered how the whites who made up 95% of the crowd would react to the raps and choreographed dances that my kids were going to present. They were laughing and smiling and waving hello as they recognized one another. They were so damn pleased with themselves for the service they were providing for the black public school kids they fought to keep out of their own kids' and grandkids' private school classrooms.

"This is gross," Chris said.

"I know. Let's go visit the kids."

After picking out a place to sit, we headed backstage. Numerous groups and solo acts were scattered around, studying their order on the program, warming up, tuning their instruments. Some were wearing their nicest clothes while others were wearing their typical uniforms of baggy jeans and jerseys to accompany their acts. My students, huddled in a corner, looked nervous. They smiled when they saw me.

"Are you guys ready?" I asked, trying to be upbeat despite my misgivings about the audience.

They nodded, but with less confidence than they'd had in class the previous day. "They say there's some white girl from a private academy competing," said JaMarcus, one of my sophomores. "Is that true? We haven't seen her."

I frowned, surprised. "I haven't heard anything like that. Besides, this competition is just for the public schools."

"Yeah, we know," said Tyler, unconvinced. "But that's what people are saying."

I shot Chris a worried glance and told them I'd go check it out, and continued to circulate, looking for Jared, one of the two corps members heading up the event. I found him talking to the sound technician, wearing a tux.

"Is there a girl from a private school competing?" I asked point blank. My stomach sank as he grimaced, looking weary of this question.

"Yeah, we had to let her," he said defensively. Apparently I wasn't the first person to confront him about this.

"Jared, what the hell? This is a public school competition only. What do you mean you had to let her?"

"Her dad insisted. He donated a ton of money. We couldn't say no."

"Goddamn it," I groaned. I suddenly felt like crying. "Can't you see what's going to happen?"

"I'm sure it'll be fine. And remember," he said magnanimously, "they'll get a Boys & Girls Club."

We stared at him, stunned.

"Well where is she?" I demanded, scanning the performers. There was not a single white child among them.

Jared exhaled before speaking. He clearly didn't appreciate my tone. "She's going to wait at her parents' table."

"Why?"

"Her dad wanted her out there with them," he said brusquely. Like he was just reporting the facts.

"He didn't think she'd be safe back here with the black kids?" I asked, my voice an angry hiss.

Jared paled. He said nothing.

I took a moment to breathe and force back the heat in my cheeks before I marched back to my kids and, hugging them each in turn, wished them luck. They saw in my eyes that the rumors were true. Their faces fell, and the disappointment seemed to roll across the kids like a shockwave. *Then what's the point*, their faces seemed to say. *One white girl and a white audience of voters. What's the point?*

We sat in the back with the rest of the non-paying TFA members in the audience. Our kids performed admirably, with energy and enthusiasm. Act after act went by, some funny, some absolutely stellar. There were ballads, raps, juggling acts, magic tricks, puppet shows. But I couldn't get into it; with each act—followed by restrained applause by the white audience and hoots and hollers from the students' sparsely represented families—the vote neared and my dread deepened.

Finally, a petite white teenager, her blonde hair falling in delicate ringlets over a satin ball gown, emerged from the audience and mounted the stage. With lace-gloved hands she lowered the microphone and the classic, melancholy song from *Les Miserables* filtered through the air. Her voice was high and clear, but not any more remarkable than most of those others that had come before. Objectively, she was better than some, and not as talented as others. But when her last trembling note faded, the auditorium filled with thunderous applause. She smiled meekly and took a bow, and then wound her way back to her parents' table, where they raised their glasses in a toast to her.

I watched, my insides roiling. The black families, who had been visibly startled to see a white performer emerge from the audience, watched with mixed expressions as she returned to her seat among the diners. I detected surprise, anger, betrayal, resignation, despair. But I didn't know what they were feeling at that moment. Not really. And even if I did, I couldn't really understand. I couldn't fully comprehend how this was just one more in a long series of slights, of unfulfilled promises. I squeezed Chris's hand under the table.

There were two other acts after that, but the wind seemed to be gone from their sails. They got through and walked off stage with little ado. And then it was time for the audience to vote.

In a movie—in one of those inspirational, feel-good films about education—fairness would have prevailed and the best act would have won. But this was not a movie, and the results came out how my students knew from the start—how they had been taught through long experience—that they would. The white girl from the private academy—one of many academies founded in order to maintain segregation and to let whites benefit at the expense of my students—won. Later, the corps members in charge of counting would awkwardly admit that it was a landslide. The second- and third-place acts accepted their trophies with smiles, determined not to let the audience see their heartbreak and furious indignation, but everyone felt it nonetheless.

Even the white audience seemed uncomfortable at the resulting spectacle caused by their collective choices. Some couples gathered their jackets and made an early exit. What was occurring on stage was no different than what could be seen in the private and public classrooms all across the Delta every day, but it was rarely so immediately *visible* as it was right now. The openness of it seemed somehow indelicate, crass. It simply didn't seem polite to force them to sit in its presence. It simply wasn't *done.*

By the start of school on Monday morning, the story of Saturday night's events had spread through the student body. Everyone on staff—but especially the TFA teachers—were confronted with a mix of anger, sorrow, defeat, and resentment. Some of my kids started to cry in class.

I didn't know what to say. There was nothing *to* say. We—Teach For America in general and all its members specifically—had betrayed them and confirmed their very worst suspicions of us and our motives. We had grumbled, but had not stopped the production. We had not relentlessly challenged the fundraising methods or the voting system. We had not stormed the stage to prevent the violation of the competition's stated rules. We had sat there at our tables in mortified silence, benign, ineffectual, useless.

It didn't matter what we said about equity; Delta Idol drowned out our words with our actions. And there was nothing that could ever make it right. Not an apology, and certainly not a Boys & Girls Club.

I had never felt more ashamed in my life.

As if Delta Idol had broken the will to resist of more than just the students, Millcreek School District resigned itself to selling the Old Gym property to the Masterson's that very same week. The old farmer and his wife had finally worn them down, it seemed.

Deed in hand, the Masterson's brought a small army of bulldozers to the site within a day of the ink drying. Rumbling and spitting exhaust, they handily razed the Old Gym to the ground within hours and, by the end of the evening, had shoved all the wreckage into a compact mountain on the far corner of the lot. The next day, the bulldozers were parked to one side and digging equipment rolled in. Within two days an enormous pit had been dug. The bulldozers shoved everything into this dark hole—desks, computers and all—and once more set it afire. Once reduced to ashes, the bulldozers shoved all the dirt over the top of it. Yet more equipment came in to moisten and level the ground. Within a week, there was no sign that the Old Gym had ever existed. All that remained was a large rectangle of freshly tilled soil.

The Masterson's were proud of themselves indeed. Neighbors brought them gifts in gratitude. They had saved the day yet again.

On our last full day in Arkansas, Chris and I walked over to the Masterson's house together to deliver the keys and to thank them for allowing us to rent their home. We sat awkwardly in their cool foyer as Mrs. Masterson brought us tea and freshly baked sugar cookies on a porcelain platter decorated with rosebuds.

Chris looked out the window, which faced the final resting place of the Old Gym.

"So what will happen to the lot now?" he asked, trying to strike up small talk that would not get them going about what saints we were for teaching "those little animals at the public school." That was always Mrs. Masterson's default topic for small talk, since she had once been a teacher at the same school, and had tried to "weather it" after the academy had been founded, but eventually had joined all her white colleagues at the new school after finding that "there was just no working with them."

Mrs. Masterson's face brightened. "I am *so* glad you asked!" she exclaimed. "We've got something real special in the works. A few of the ladies and I have decided to turn it into a community garden. Mostly flowers, but maybe a vegetable garden in one corner. And we're going to have a playground installed."

"Wow," said Chris. "People around here could really use that. The school's playground is broken."

Mrs. Masterson's eyebrows leaped up in surprise, and then she chuckled as if she'd decided he must have been making a joke. "It's not going to be for *those* kids," she said matter-of-factly. "They'd only wreck it. That's why *their* playground is broken. No, no, we're going to put up a nice white picket fence around it and give out keys to families in the neighborhood. It's a *community* garden, after all, not one for the whole town. Besides, those kids have the run of the all of Millcreek—and Lord knows it shows on the buildings and in the trash all over the place. And that's fine, let them have the whole town. But what about *our* kids? They need a space of their own, too. They need someplace safe and clean to play. I want the grandkids to have someplace nice when they visit us."

I swallowed hard and busied myself with my cookie. Of course, I thought. Nevermind that they already have a private school and highly trained teachers and a library and an all-white 'community' pool and nice homes to live in and college funds. What about *their* needs?

"Don't get me wrong, I hate that it has to be this way," she continued with what seemed to be genuine, heartfelt regret. "But I don't see any other way we can keep it nice. It's one thing to clean up a lot, and quite another to clean up a town."

I envisioned the Masterson's hiring a brigade of bulldozers to raze all the houses on the other side of the highway. Because that is surely what she meant. There wasn't a hole big enough to bury all that brokenness, she seemed to imply over the rim of her teacup. Alas, it just wasn't realistic.

"As it is, it'll be enough of a handful to keep painting over the graffiti that's sure to pop up on the fence," she said, clicking her tongue. "We might as well stock up on the white paint now. But I'm determined not to let them ruin it."

I sipped my tea, grateful to have something to do with my hands. I felt sick with despair. And then I realized it didn't matter what I felt. *I* didn't matter at all; all my feelings were self-indulgent. My whole life here had been self-indulgent. It dawned on me that maybe Mr. Armstrong had a point in trying to drive us off like a bunch of carpetbaggers; he didn't want what we were selling. He didn't want it for his kids.

Mrs. Masterson finally noticed our silence, but misinterpreted it. "Look at me, going on and on about all this depressing stuff. What about you! Here you are, getting ready to leave and go on new adventures. You must be thrilled!"

"We're excited to see what Oregon's like," Chris agreed. "It'll be nice to be close to the ocean."

Mrs. Masterson smiled wistfully. "We talk about moving out West sometimes, Jim and I. But we're just so tied to this place. I mean, we've come to hold the town together in a lot of ways—this whole gym debacle is a prime example of that. Sometimes I think that if we left, the whole place would finally come crashing down." She sighed, her face filled with a strange mix of regret and pride. "So I just don't think we'll ever end up doing it."

Chapter 6

Can Arts Based Research Be Fictive?

Among the trickiest issues confronted in considering the possibilities of arts based forms of social research is the one involving whether they might include works of fiction. In this chapter, we consider that issue.

For many traditionalists, merely thinking about a project of social inquiry as, in any sense, "fictional" disqualifies it from consideration as legitimate research. Indeed Banks and Banks (1998) have noted that in conventional academic discourse, "fiction remains a no-no, a mode of expression . . . that is simply off-limits" (p. 17). Asking methodological gatekeepers who have only recently begun to warm to creative forms of *nonfictional* research to also value *fictional* works may represent "a bridge too far." Some arts based researchers might understandably feel too intimidated to cross a line in the sand onto the territory of what is commonsensically regarded as fiction. It may be indeed safer and easier to avoid a moniker that appears to some critics of arts based research as a "red flag."

We urge resistance against that intimidation. This is because a good case can be made for fictional works of social research that exhibit a potential for achieving what we have described as one of two primary purposes for engaging in inquiry into human affairs. This is the potential of the text for enhancing meanings of social phenomena that run counter to final, orthodox, seemingly settled interpretations and conclusions. Works of fiction may indeed, through their recasting of the empirical particulars of the world, achieve extraordinary power to disturb and disrupt the familiar and commonplace, to question and interrogate that which seems to have already been answered conclusively, and to redirect the conversation regarding important social issues.

DEFINITIONS OF FICTION

We begin our attempt at justification, however, by asking the following questions: What is fiction? And what is not? The answers, it seems, depend on the definitions one honors. There is, for example, a sense in which all cultural artifacts are fictional insofar as they are fashioned by human beings. This thinking follows the etymological origins of the word *fiction—fictio*, "to fashion or make." Clifford Geertz (1974) noted that, within works of literature, a description in which actors and events are represented as (presently or previously) real and actual is as much a fiction—a "making"—as one in which "actors are represented as not having existed or events as not having happened" (pp. 15–16). In this sense, a work of social science is as fictional as a folktale.

A second definition of fiction is more prevalent within Western cultures, both academic and popular. This one demands a harsh dichotomy between two categories of cultural artifacts. Here, fictional works are seen as the opposite of factual (or nonfictional) ones, much as fantasy is regarded as the opposite of truthfulness. The factual exhibits a literal rendering of worldly phenomena; in the fictional, qualities of experience are, for artistic purposes, purposefully recast—fashioned—by the "maker" of the work.

Within this neat compartmentalization, a line is indeed drawn between, for example, documentary and fictional films; between literary works classified in best seller lists as fiction and those labeled nonfiction, or elsewhere as imaginative versus factual; and between representational and nonrepresentational works of visual art.

This dichotomy seems to flow out of the antipathy toward ambiguity within our culture that was discussed in Chapter 2: There is indeed a deep desire for categorization that offers a precision and clarity to relieve us of an anxiety born of ambiguity, however misleading or dysfunctional such a facile distinction may be.

Within this dichotomy, fiction is equated with the world of the unbridled imagination, a world of pure aesthetic form. Artists are viewed as bracketing off the real world while residing within a fantastic realm, an "aesthetic remove." The work produced there is seen as psychically distanced from the mundane realm of everyday commerce, as sealed off, self-contained, and infatuated with illusion. And the formalist critic Northrup Frye (1967) has noted that illusion is "fixed and definable, and reality is best understood as its negation" (p. 169). The purpose of art is thereby construed as something to be admired for its aesthetic beauty, sought out for the pleasure it offers but not used for deciding about how to act regarding "real-world" social issues.

This notion of fiction may indeed seem frightening to researchers and methodologists who regard the first purpose of research discussed in earlier chapters—approaching (if never quite reaching) an objective "reality"—as the only useful one. Mistaking a fictional (or nonrepresentational) work of art or research for one that attempts to accurately mirror an external world can be problematical. In addressing the realm of storied accounts, Phillips (1994) described that problem as follows: "If an action is taken on the basis of an incorrect narrative, even if disaster does not always ensue, [we will likely] end up with consequences that we neither anticipated nor desired" (p. 174). For Phillips, actions that rely upon nonfictional ("correct") accounts of events—events that "actually happened"—are more likely to be "successful" at making decisions about what to do next than those based on stories that are "incorrect," not literally "true."

We do not deny that this distinction can be a useful one in certain circumstances. We also suggest, however, a third way of thinking about fictionality—in general, but especially in regards to arts based research—one that moves beyond both of the previously given definitions. In this view, fiction is neither a term that encompasses all works of arts based research nor one that represents the useless, effete, "fantastic" half of an often inadequate dichotomy.

In articulating this definition, we consider various sorts of design elements present within all "cultural artifacts" (including research texts). We consider the alternative purposes for which (a) a research text is composed by its "maker," (b) the contexts surrounding its publication or display, as well as the ways in which (c) it is used by percipients or readers.

In so doing, we attempt to ground our otherwise lofty discussion with examples. These examples will include texts we have already referred to in this book, as well as two short stories (one by Nadine Gordimer [1985], another by Sabrina Case [2010]), a work by the professional French photographer Robert Doisneau (1973), and a book by Tom Barone (2001) that is fictional, factual, or both.

PROBLEMATIZING THE DEFINITIONS: THE FICTIVE

We begin our reconceptualization by problematizing the dichotomous relationship between fantasy and fact, thinking instead in terms of a synthesis of these apparent dyads that occurs within any act of fictionalization, indeed in any creation of a work of art. In this act of fashioning, substantive and formal qualities are merged, elements of aesthetic content embodied within, an aesthetic form. And the result is the production of what Iser (1993) labeled the *fictive*.

Selection

Iser (1993) highlighted three acts in the production of the fictive. In the first, *selection*, elements are chosen from the "given world," or "referential fields outside of the text," including "social, historical, cultural, and literary systems." These are elements of what Iser calls the *real*, although we prefer the term *empirical*, insofar as they are experienced by the researcher. These are details within the physical and social environment that are transported into the text from the outside. Other empirical (or "real") elements, meanwhile, are *not* selected; they are excluded from the text.

Empirical details may, in fact, be acquired precisely in the manner that information is "collected" within science based forms of social research, that is, through interviewing, participant observation, document analysis, and so on. Empirical elements may also arise out of careful reflections on the previous experiences of the researcher with social phenomena. The research may occur within a preproduction phase, prior to the fashioning of a text; more often it will occur within the process of composition.

Within qualitative social research, the inclusion of a surfeit of available empirical elements may result in a "data dump," an indiscriminate depository of too many of the phenomena experienced in a research project. For works of art or arts based research this may mean the inclusion of extraneous elements that do not contribute to the advancement of a controlling insight, or central thesis, or that which Dewey (1934/1958) called a "pervasive form." Each of these terms is meant to describe the "glue" that holds together (and allows for the advancement of) meaning within the text—a meaning that the reader or percipient may reexperience in their encounter with the work as a whole.

We have previously discussed this selection and importation of particulars in arts based works by Sullivan (2000), Saldana (2005), Springgay (2003), and other qualitative research texts by Behar (1996), Simon (1997), and Deavere Smith (1993). (Reread, if you will, the poems by Sullivan, with this act of selection in mind. More pointedly, revisit her poem "When I Die" with its final line of "My friends are poets. They need details.") But as participants within various social research traditions—academic or otherwise—these authors and artists may not be viewed as engaged in producing works that are clearly identifiable as fiction. Rather, assumptions to the contrary may be made, their texts seen as accurately portraying individual persons and documenting actual events in a real world external to the text. But let us visit, temporarily, a work by someone clearly identifiable as an author of imaginative literature. While the short story by the South African writer Nadine Gordimer (1985) entitled "A City of the Dead, A City of the Living" is labeled as fiction, we nevertheless recognize an apparently "real" physical and social environment in this story. Consider this highly detailed portrait of a house in which the protagonists live their lives:

> The house provides the sub-economic township planner's usual two rooms and kitchen with a little yard at the back, into which his maquette figures of the ideal family unit of four fitted neatly. Like most houses on the street, it has been arranged inside and out to hold the number of people that the ingenuity of necessity provides for. The garage is the home of sub-tenants . . . The front door of the house itself opens into a room that has been sub-divided by greenish brocade curtains whose color has faded and embossed pattern worn off before they were discarded in another kind of house. On one side of the curtains is a living room with just space enough to crate a plastic-covered sofa and two chairs, a coffee table with crocheted cover, vase of dyed feather flowers and oil lamp, and a radio-and-cassette-player combination with home-built speakers. There is a large varnished print of a horse with wild orange mane and flaring nostrils on the wall. The floor is cement, shined with black polish. On the other side of the curtains is a bed, a burglar-proofed window, a small table with candle, bottle of anti-acid tablets and alarm clock. During the day a frilly nylon nightgown is laid out on the blankets. A woman's clothes are in a box under the bed. In the dry cleaner's plastic sheath, a man's suit hangs from a nail. (Gordimer, 1985, pp. 10–11)

Within the traditional dichotomy, empirical details that are assumed to be selected from outside of the text while directly and accurately re-presented within the text are generally considered to be the exclusive hallmarks of non-fiction. In traditional forms of qualitative social research, these details may be thought of as research "data." But the Gordimer (1985) excerpt suggests that the fictional storyteller also observes the minutiae of human activity in the manner of a qualitative social researcher. Indeed, as Roiphe (1988, p. 840) has noted, "the basic talent of the novelist is to observe social behavior—the way a person furnishes his house or makes love or reacts to death or folds an envelope or constructs his sentences or plans his career."

Again, we have already noted examples of selected empirical details in works by arts based researchers that while not appearing as traditional as most qualitative "social science" also are not readily recognizable as fiction. Two other such examples to be discussed later in this chapter are a short story by Sabrina Case (2010), entitled "Broken and Buried in Arkansas" (reprinted in this book), and a book by Tom Barone (2001). As with a photograph by Robert Doisneau

(1973), each of these texts will seem suspended somewhere in between the two categories of fiction and nonfiction—a conundrum to be further explored.

Combination

Iser's (1993) second act in the production of the fictive is *combination*, and it occurs simultaneously with that of selection. Here the chosen particulars of the text are understood not in isolation from but, in relation to, each other, in a process that may indeed be described as a fashioning or a making. Indeed, in order to recognize the fact that these points in a portrait act primarily as correlatives rather than isolates, Pepper (1945) labeled them not data but *danda*.

In Gordimer's (1985) text, each word, as a *dandum*, does seem to be weighed carefully in terms of its potential contribution to the whole (much like each note, line, or gesture in accomplished works of nonliterary art). For example, her descriptions of the interior and exterior of a house, simultaneously lean and elaborate, taut and skillfully drawn, containing no more danda than necessary, are crucial to understanding events that transpire later in the story. The protagonist Nanike, barely surviving in apartheid South Africa, ultimately betrays the identity of a fugitive whom her more idealistic husband is harboring inside their home. Later we come to understand that she sees her house and possessions, however modest, as necessary for the survival of the infant who is her fifth child. Without intimate knowledge of this setting and the characters that inhabit it, the reader cannot fathom the complex motivations behind a later act that may be considered, depending on one's point of view (POV), as either cowardly or brave.

For Iser (1993), as for some other aestheticians and literary theorists, the presence of artfully arranged particulars in a work that achieves fictive status may no longer serve the *primary* purpose of mirroring facets of a "real" world. Indeed, the house in Gordimer's (1985) story may or may not have existed quite that way outside of the imagination of the author. That story's clear designation as a work of fiction serves to cancel any claims of direct correspondence between elements of the "given world" and the words in a text.

Nevertheless, familiar elements of experience do help to lure the reader into the text and enable her to vicariously inhabit the world recreated therein. Indeed, so vivid is the Gordimer's (1985) description of the small, cluttered house that we feel cramped in reading of it. For this to be possible, however, the imported "realities," while recast as danda, must nevertheless remain identifiable and familiar, seen as believable, credible, lest readers no longer be able to relate the recreated world to their life experiences outside of the text.

Again, having read Chapter 2, the act of combination is familiar to us. We have described, through examples, how the selected elements of various social research texts, assumed to be nonfictional, are recast, rearranged, and reorganized. Indeed, privileged particulars may be, in varying degrees, carefully combined in any cultural artifact, whether a product of art, craft, or science. But for Iser (1993) (if, again, not exactly for us), it is the *third* act of fictionalization that clearly separates a work of fiction (or art) from all other artifacts. This is the act of *self-disclosure*.

Self-Disclosure As Fiction

The self-disclosure of which Iser (1993) writes happens when a text identifies itself as fictional. This occurs through the presence of certain signs—some obvious, some subtle—that are available to a percipient of the cultural text. Some of these signals may reside "within" the text, while others will make themselves known through the context in which the work is situated. Iser (1993, p. 11) suggested that these signals invoke conventions that are shared by author (or artist) and public. They form, he wrote, "the basis of a kind of contract between author and reader" (p. 11).

These signals suggest to the reader that the work is not merely "discourse" but "enacted discourse," that selected and recast elements are no longer to be taken for reality but as particulars operating as correlatives within a structure that performs a figurative function. In other words, they come to reference something other than (or in addition to) themselves. As a result of an act of self-disclosure by the text as a work of fiction, therefore, "reproduced reality is made to point to a 'reality' beyond itself" (Iser, 1993, p. 15). Insofar as it does, the text becomes, simultaneously, an empirical enterprise *and* a work of the imagination.

How does the Gordimer (1985) text point to a "reality outside of itself"? While open to other interpretations, the theme of Gordimer's story seems to focus on issues of privacy and surveillance in a police state, on the ways in which oppression can produce in subjugated individuals a fear and defeatism. This is a fear that causes them to act myopically as they move to guard their meager possessions rather than risk them for the seemingly distant hopes of a greater freedom, hopes that may be fueled by information from afar (such as that found in newspapers). They may, moreover, abandon these hopes without realizing why they do so.

This theme serves a kind of controlling insight that surely operated within acts of selection and combination in the production of this text. But the presence of the theme may also signal the emergence of a metaphorical power within the text. For upon reading this short story, one may come to understand that it does not point merely to local settings and conditions—here, apartheid South Africa. It may call to mind analogous circumstances in other settings; indeed, it may cause readers to wonder how they themselves might or should act in similar circumstances of curtailed political and personal freedoms.

How, for Iser, can the story by Gordimer (1985) legitimately be called a work of fiction? Interestingly, Iser (1993) recalled Geertz in his suggestion that all activities of human cognition and behavior contain a fictive element. But Iser went further, suggesting that some works mask their fictional nature while others refuse to do so. Both the maskings and the refusals are accomplished through the invocation of conventions that suggest that the work is either literally true—a mirror of nature—or the opposite, a text fashioned in accordance with aesthetic principles.

What are some of these conventions by which a text reveals its fictional or nonfictional status? They are, suggested Iser (1993), legion, and they vary according to culture and history. Some may be disclosed subtly within the text itself, as discussed above in relation to the Gordimer (1985) story—that is, through any of an array of linguistic signs that promote an understanding that the world being entered into should or should not be acted upon as if it were a reproduction of reality. Other conventions are as obvious as the labeling of a work, such as in the prominent imprint of the word *fiction* on the back cover of the Gordimer anthology of short stories—or "nonfiction" on an autobiographical work. Still others operate within the context in which the work is observed. For example, the nature of the venues of manuscripts by traditional social researchers—academic journals and book presses—signal which epistemological attitudes are appropriate for approaching the textual content of articles therein; or a staged play is removed from the world outside by the presence of a proscenium arch; or sculptures, paintings, and sometimes photographs are likewise framed and separated from "reality" by their location in a museum.

The message conveyed to readers and viewers by these signals is, for many phenomenological aestheticians such as Iser (1993), one of responsible attitudes. Strangely aligned here with the postpositivist Phillips (1994), Iser noted that the attitude adopted by a reader in approaching a fictional work is indeed important if an appropriate reaction is to ensue. This attitude toward the text involves bracketing off the "real" world of the text, seeing it not as a literal representation of reality but as presenting a credible and believable, quite possible, but hypothetical world.

Most significantly, Iser (1993) noted this bracketing allows for a particular pragmatic purpose to make itself felt. We heartily agree with Iser that fictional works do indeed serve a pragmatic function. That purpose is the one that we have described as is the second primary reason for engaging in human inquiry: the enhancement of alternative meanings. Or as Iser (1993) put it, the fictive text could direct the reader toward the

> empirical world from which the textual world has been drawn, allowing this very world to be perceived from a vantage point that has never been part of it . . . [thereby] making conceivable what would otherwise remain hidden. (pp. 16–17)

DOUBLE READINGS

The bracketing that Iser (1993) and other phenomenologists evoke is meant to stringently demarcate works of fiction and imaginative art from others that are decidedly not. Of special interest here, however, is social research that may not be clearly designated as either fiction or nonfiction or that emits confusing or mixed signals about a fictional/factual status. Consider, for example, the ambiguous appellations invented (from within and outside of academia) to describe works that straddle the fact–fiction border—creative nonfiction, the novel as history, the nonfiction novel, faction, ethnopoetics, ethnodrama, ethnographic fiction, evocative autoethnography, artful science, docudramas, infotainment, and, yes, even arts *based* research. A Hollywood film may be introduced as being "based on a true story," or "inspired by actual events." Or we might reference the various "creative" design elements that have been employed by researchers—even those who persistently self-identify as "social scientists" or "arts based researchers"—as they engage in what is called "genre blurring" (Geertz, 1974).

These design elements may indeed serve as devices for enhancing the artistry of a manuscript published in venues traditionally associated with "social science research" (whatever, nowadays, *that* term might mean). These devices include (among others) the use of composite characters, invented dialogue, "revealed" inner dialogue, connotative language, plot, narrative drive, tone shifts, the purposeful alteration of details about settings, events, or characters (sometimes for ethical more than aesthetic reasons, such as hiding the "true" identity of vulnerable informants). Most convincing might be the presence of what are called *gaps* in the text: "the unwritten part [of the text], elements of indeterminacy [without which] we should not be able to use our imagination" (Iser, 1980, p. 58). These are the purposeful elisions in the construction of the text that create spaces for ambiguity of meaning.

But other devices may point in a different direction, suggesting mimetic replication of the real world, a tight, literal correspondence between word and world. The presence of some of each of these elements alongside those afore-mentioned may complicate the possibility of a definitive "self-disclosure" by a text as fictional or nonfictional.

A dialectical tension within a work may indeed be the result, one that offers conflicting clues about its preferred reading. The prestructured devices and dimensions within a work that seem to suggest a literal reading may stand in conflict with opposing features that point toward a kind of usefulness that is associated with the exploration of an artistically crafted, possible, hypothetical world.

A work of creative nonfiction may therefore be read simultaneously both literally and metaphorically. Back to Sullivan's (2000) text: Are we not at once learning about an actual person's (the author as a youngster's) growth in attentiveness to the world, while also being propelled into wonderment about the same process in the children in our own lives? A return to Saldana: Do we not believe that the ethnodramatist remained inwardly faithful to specifically located individuals, informants who were then transformed into characters in a play that escaped the "tyranny of the local" (Goodson, 1995), pointing outward toward analogous people and places and events? What attitude is the finally correct one in which to read such texts as Sullivan's and Saldana's?

Now we ask this same question about an example of artistry that is not directly identified with the academic world of social (including arts based) research but from the world of professional photography. This example may reinforce the idea that the fictional/nonfictional status of a work ultimately depends at least partly on the interplay between text and percipient. But in presenting this example we will further problematize the idea of self-disclosure as suggested by Iser (1993), as we refine the notion of context in which the cultural artifact resides.

The Case of Doisneau

Here we refer to Barrett's (1985) triad of contexts that may inform the inter-pretation of a photograph (or other cultural artifact). The first is the internal context of the work—for photos, Barrett says, this includes the title, date, and maker, as well as interpretations of the apparent "internal meanings" meanings of subject matter and form. The second context is the "original context"—that which was "psychologically present to the maker at the time the picture was taken" (p. 59). The third context is the external or presentational environment, the context in which the photo is displayed—or what Barthes has called its "channel of transmission." (Note the similarities between Barrett's first and third contexts and Iser's (1993) two kinds of signals of self-disclosure as fiction.)

The basic details of the internal context of our photographic example are as follows: The title is *At the Café, Chez Fraysse. Rue de Seine, Paris*. The date it was taken was 1948. The photographer was the renowned Robert Doisneau (1973). And here is a brief description of—and interpretation of meaning within—its subject matter, formal qualities, and the internal interplay of empirical elements, or danda.

The black-and-white photo captures some sort of encounter between a young woman and an older man at a bar. The body language and facial expressions may suggest the precise moment of a sexual proposition. The art critic Sarkowski (1973) elaborated nicely, shifting, however, from pure description of the photo's contents to an interpretation of their meaning:

> The girl's secret opinion of the proceedings . . . is hidden in her splendid self-containment; for the moment she enjoys the security of absolute power. One arm shields her body, her hand touches her glass as tentatively as if it were her first apple. The man for the moment is defenseless and vulnerable; impaled on the hook of his own desire, he has committed all his resources, and no satisfactory line of retreat remains. Worse yet, he is older than he should be, and knows that one way or another the adventure is certain to end badly. To keep this presentiment at bay, he is drinking his wine more rapidly than he should. (p. 172)

And what are the "facts" surrounding the original context—what the author "knew" about the making of the photo (Barrett's [1985], second context)? That which is to be discovered in investigating this context may or may not correspond to what is interpreted from within a reading of the "internal" details of the photo.

According to Barrett (1985), Doisneau (1973), fond of cafés, discovered the pair drinking in a Parisian bar and asked if he could photograph them. His original intention was indeed to use the picture for a photo essay on Paris cafés in a popular magazine. Still unclear, however, is what the photographer knew about the precise nature of the relationship between the pair, of the events leading up to and following this encounter. For example, might the gentleman *not* be propositioning the young woman but simply telling an employee that he no longer needs her at the shop, due to slow business (Sarkowksi, 1973, p. 172)?

Moreover, the degree to which the photo was staged or composed is still in dispute. Indeed, a scandal ensued when it was learned in later decades that

Doisneau's (1973) most celebrated photo, *The Kiss at City Hall*—widely regarded as an iconographic expression of the *joie de vivre* that pervaded postwar Paris—actually involved a contrived recreation of a spontaneous gesture between the same two lovers that Doisneau had previously observed kissing. How can the romantic spontaneity of an era be conveyed in a work that has been revealed as duplicitous? The fuel for the scandal over *The Kiss* was, of course, the willful violation of the tacit contract between photographer/artist and public/viewers, a misrepresentation of a staged photograph as a work of "nonfiction." (This is, of course, the same contract that we have discussed as important within the field of social research.) Does the willingness by this photographer to violate this contract once not call into question the trustworthiness of his other works, including *Chez Fraysse* as naked, "undisturbed," "naturalistic" glimpses of realty? Could some sort of fiction again be being passed off as some sort of nonfiction?

If the facts here offer no final clues as to how to "correctly" regard this work, the confusion is compounded as we look at the third context suggested by Barrett, the context in which it was displayed.

Interpretations of the meaning of a work may indeed shift in accordance with the place where it is made public. Although originally published in a mass circulation magazine, Barrett (1985) reported that this photo was later reprinted in a brochure on the evils of alcohol. Then the same photo appeared in a scandal sheet under the caption "Prostitution on the Champs-Elysees." Still later the photo was hung on the walls of prominent art museums.

It is easy to see how within each of these venues alternative signals about meaning, purpose, and appropriate use were conveyed. Moreover, the alternative reading suggested by one particular placement was the source of another controversy, one that may illustrate the dangers involved in a misconstrual of a work of fiction as fact. For upon the photo's appearance within that scandal sheet, the *real* gentleman in the photo—no doubt convinced that, to paraphrase Phillips (1994), an incorrect interpretation had been made and undesirable consequences had resulted—successfully sought *real* recompense by way of a lawsuit. This particular channel of transmission, with no alteration of the photo's internal content whatsoever, had (falsely? irresponsibly?) signaled to readers that specific people had been engaged in illicit activity.

TEXT, CONTEXT, READER: THE DANCE

We are left, therefore, with this question: How can a viewer ever know with certainty what this or any photo is "finally" about? Indeed, we suggest that no work of art (or work of arts based research—to the extent that it is a work of art) ever *finally* states anything. Of course, any useful interpretation of meaning within a photo—as for arts based research—must surely be responsible to, and to some degree influenced by, the choice of, arrangement of, and interplay between, the empirical elements within the composition of the text as well as the context in which it is displayed.

But there is one final layer of complexity to the issue of whether a work of arts based research is to be read as a work of fact or fiction or both. The additional element is that of readers or percipients—their backgrounds, inclinations, values, worldviews, and purposes for attending to the work.

Some artists and social researchers may indeed take great care in sending clear (internal and external) signals about how appropriately to use their work, while others may purposely choose to blur the line between fact and fiction (sometimes to make the point that such a line is itself a fiction, a social construct). Still others may violate the contract between author and reader by, for example, failing to imbue a document marked as fact with a high degree of validity or by willfully labeling as fiction a work based on demonstrably real characters and events that they refuse to disguise.

The possibilities always exist for discontinuities between an author's preferred reading and the experiences of the reader in a textual reconstruction. The reader may be misled about, or misconstrue, or ignore, or purposely override that preferred reading. For genre-straddling works, the challenges regarding classificatory signals may be magnified. Still, no matter how careful in signaling their intentions for the reading of the text, most artists or authors will ultimately release control over their work to a public. Nor may they have control over the context in which it is displayed. Works of art (and social research) may be misappropriated through a change of context and thus send alternative signals about how it is to be used.

Indeed, this authorial release of control is, to some degree, inevitable as a reader or viewer confronts a work—of nonfiction, of art, of arts based research—from their own unique worldview. Dewey (1934/1958) emphasized the inevitability that the viewer or percipient of any text, but especially works of art, will fashion their own experience in the process of reconstructing that which is formally embodied in a work.

That reconstruction may, for some viewers and readers (such as formalist and structuralist art critics), focus primarily on getting aim at discovering the "internal" meaning of a cultural text and perhaps the manner in which the formal qualities of the work synergistically convey and reinforce that meaning. For other viewers and readers, however, the reconstruction of the text might differ drastically from the original experiences of the artist. They may not be content to remain within what Iser (1974) called the "frame of possible decisions" (p. 55), as ordered through "means of communication by which the author is brought into contact with the reality represented by the author" (p. 57). These readers have been called "revolutionary readers" (Belsey, 1980). These are readers who employ their critical faculties to reinterpret the meaning of a text from within a worldview that is significantly different from that of the artist.

Indeed, throughout the ages, works of art have been interpreted and reinterpreted in accordance with shifting historical and cultural conditions. But revolutionary readers come in different stripes. Some observers have noted a process of co-option as the transgressive nature of a work of art is "tamed," made to fit within and support prevailing (often orthodox) ideological frameworks. Others may attempt to "uncover" meanings that are not easily supported by textual content, offering interpretations not readily acceptable or convincing to other members of a critical community of discourse. Still others may employ their analytical powers to simultaneously "understand" the intended meaning of the text and unpack it in order to reveal the nature of the power relationships between characters as portrayed within the work. (To that end, certain variants of feminist theory could surely be brought to bear on the contents of the Doisneau [1973] photo.) All of this may suggest that the greater the existential/historical/cultural/ideological distance between artist and viewers, the greater the potential divergence between the original experience in the production of the work and the reconstruction of meaning upon viewing.

This returns us to the possibility that a cultural text's identity as a work of fiction or nonfiction ultimately depends on the interplay within an act of reading or viewing between (a) features of the text, (b) its context of display, and (c) the reader. If this is the case, then the line between fact and fiction is not merely a line at all but a boundary that shifts within every encounter of the text by a viewer. The identity of a work of arts based research as fact or fiction may depend on a complex dance between textual signals—located both within the design elements within the text and in the context in which these elements are confronted—and the purposes for which the viewer/reader is enabled to—and chooses to—use the text.

The Case of Case

For two last illustrations of this possibility, we turn to works of arts based research. First we consider the short story by Case (2010). The story is an account of one year in the life of an Ivy League-trained Teach For America teacher in a rural Arkansas school. The characters within the story are sharply drawn, as in this excerpt describing a less than attentive school principal:

"Mrs. Winters, please report to the office." The intercom crackled, but did not fully obscure the frantic voice of Ms. Myers, the office secretary. "Mrs. Winters, if you are in the building, *please* report to the office immediately."

My students snickered and I also had to suppress a humorless smile. These kinds of announcements were routine and meant only one thing: There was a fight somewhere in the school, and Mrs. Winters had, instead of heading down to confront it, locked herself in her office, turned off the lights, drawn all the blinds, and was watering her plants while humming to herself. In the case of really bad fights, Mrs. Winters could manage to "pretend she wasn't home" for an entire afternoon, foregoing both food and the bathroom, only to emerge at the ring of the final bell, when she would shuffle quickly from her doorway to the exit and into her Buick. This was a reality that the students, teachers, and even Ms. Myers knew—indeed, Ms. Myers knew it better than anyone, as she was always there to hear the turn of the lock—and yet she never gave up on this charade, this farce. She always seemed to reserve hope that, just maybe, Mrs. Winters would not leave her to deal with the bloody aftermath alone.

However, this particular afternoon proved to be the wrong one for Mrs. Winters to play this game, as a boy was beaten within an inch of his life that day with a heavy metal chain before two gym teachers could wrest his attacker off of his unconscious body. Even as an ambulance pulled up, Mrs. Winters was nowhere to be seen. Indeed, no one saw her until Mr. Palmer, the superintendent who had finally had enough, keyed into her office and slammed the door behind him—though that was not enough to keep everyone who entered the office or teachers' lounge from hearing his hollering. That's when I believed she must really be his niece; around there, only kin could give you a dressing down like that.

So the rumors turned out to be accurate after all: in February, Mrs. Winters vanished. There was no announcement. It didn't even happen over break or a weekend. She was there on a Tuesday, and on Wednesday she wasn't.

Careful selection and combination of details as those found in this passage of the Case text leaves us somewhat ambivalent about its classification as fictional or not. But we can see the dialectical tension, the conflicting clues about its preferred reading within the text. Regarding "internal meanings," the story has the ring of "truth' as a harrowing autobiographical tale of a first year teacher. (So was, of course, the story by Gordimer [1985] credible or believable, albeit, unlike Case's [2010] story, labeled as fictional.) Indeed, the simultaneously lifelike but literary-style story by Case seems to easily lend itself to a double reading, perhaps designed both to reproduce the realities of characters in actual settings while also making us wonder about a larger theme regarding the im/possibilities of school reform being promulgated from outside a local culture. But what were the author's stated intentions for the story—its "original context"? Did she intend this story to be fiction or, as labeled, creative nonfiction. Again, the answer is complex, indeed. Here Case, at some length, reminds us of the literary ploys of the genre blurrers. (And again, a fresh reading of the Case story, reproduced in this book, may further understandings of the author's points.)

As the title states, this work of educational autoethnography is conceptualized as a nonfiction short story. While this may strike some as a contradiction in terms, I made this decision to reflect the nature of the work as one that is simultaneously autobiographical, built of real events, and yet occasionally afforded creative license in order to bridge time between chronological events, reconstruct remembered conversations, and allow for thematic ties between what may otherwise seem to be disparate elements. Every attempt has been made to create a story as "true" to the events the author witnessed and experienced as the author's flawed memory, retrospective interpretations, and potential projections can allow. Nevertheless, once filtered through the numerous lenses of observer, participant, and finally, writer (over the passage of six years), this account cannot pretend to be entirely "true," as the label "nonfiction" implies. More importantly, as I have not corroborated the piece with other participants or "characters," I felt it was better to term it a "short story," reflecting my exclusive and imperfect authorship.

Prior to my arrival in rural Arkansas, I had been trained in creative writing and literary criticism, and carried with me the intention of returning to writing after my two-year teaching commitment as a Teach For America corps member. Thus, I often viewed events with the perspective of a writer vigilant for material, and immediately committed observational accounts and dialogue to paper in the form of a journal I diligently maintained over my two years in the Mississippi Delta. I had, at the time, imagined that this journal might provide material for later works of fiction, but have since—as a doctoral student in the field of Critical and Sociocultural Studies in Education—recognized the value of more nonfiction-oriented accounts cast in a literary style.

While, as the writer of the piece, I have brought an altered, years-removed understanding of many of the events I participated in or witnessed, I did draw heavily upon accounts written at the time, when my memory was fresh (though still, admittedly, subjective). In some cases, such as descriptions of the activities surrounding the Old Gym, I recorded my entries in a very detached, even journalistic manner. In the story, I attempt not only to preserve this tone of detached neutrality in some places, but also to juxtapose it with the more emotionally charged experiences of the first-person narrator.

Most of the characters are real people, though their names (with the exception of mine and my husband's) have been changed along with the name of the town. Others are composites—particularly in the case of fellow Teach For America corps members portrayed, who often assume the words of multiple, merged actual corps members. I also portray two principals at XXX High School, one resigning and being replaced mid-year. In reality, these principals worked in the two schools of the district over the two years I worked in XXX, but having taught at both schools, I selected moments with each that seemed relevant to my story. I have chosen to manipulate time and consolidate characters in order to create a more cohesive central narrative. These authorial manipulations contribute to the "storied" product, which cannot be labeled nonfiction, though neither can it be termed fiction. All of the events portrayed did occur, and have been rendered as near to "accurate" as possible. I had no interest, however, in providing an explicit interpretation of the events or their meaning. I felt that by selecting the short story format—in which, by definition, the author must leave the work open to multiple interpretations—I was taking the clearest path by which to avoid analysis or didacticism. This piece, though "real," is meant to stand alone as an experimental autoethnography, a literary work that rests on the uncertain reliability of its narrator. My hope is that the story's events and characters will largely speak for themselves, and the reader can conclude what he or she will.

Of course, a reader's "conclusions" will also depend on the context in which the story is read—its "channel of transmission." But for those who are encountering the story here in a chapter that is suggesting that the membrane between fiction and creative nonfiction is semipermeable, the reader is left with ambiguity about its aims. Some readers may, for example, be prompted into a discussion of the merits of Teach For America as an organization that may seem to fit nicely into the dominant educational metanarrative discussed earlier and whose aura is therefore rarely interrogated. Others may simply read the piece as a "true" isolated incident with little metaphorical resonance. Still others may "double read."

The Case of Barone

Finally, there is the methodological dance of Barone (2001) as he problematized the notion of a clear demarcation between truth and fiction in the joint construction of the life stories of several former students of a high school arts teacher. The actual name of the teacher (Don Forrister) has not been changed in the book. The names of his former students have. The details of incidents inside and outside of school were selected and arranged carefully by the author into life stories but remain (the author insists) faithful to the themes identified by his interviewees. But from one storied account of teaching–learning events to another, empirical details regarding the same actual incident sometimes differ from, even conflict with, each other, in accordance with the varying perspectives of the informants. Nevertheless, the author refused to "triangulate," relishing instead the possibility of a plurality of meanings within the same set of social phenomena.

Moreover, in addition to the life stories of former students and their teacher, the author included a chapter devoted to analysis of the life stories—and the degree to which they evidence the effects of good teaching—from two conflicting, but perhaps equally convincing, theoretical perspectives. This refusal to privilege one theoretical vantage point over another creates an uncertainty that demands an imaginative participation by the reader in the textual reconstruction, demands a refashioning of the work in which the reader participates.

This uncertainty lives within the "gaps" in this experimental, postmodern narrative/arts based text. The presence of these "gaps" signal a refusal of literality (or "closed meaning") that in turn nurtures a kind of productive ambiguity. And this ambiguity suggests a particular pragmatic purpose for which the text may be used. That purpose, insists the author, is a heuristic one: to stimulate reflection and conversation regarding the central educational issue of quality in teaching.

Nevertheless, despite his methodological cautions, but because of the genre-blurring qualities of his work, Barone (2001) understood that the text that he intended to be read as primarily fictional may be reimagined by a revolutionary reader as nonfictional. Such a reader would (irresponsibly) read the text as primarily about the actual characters within it. As in the case of the Doisneau (1973) photo (and the works by Case [2010], Sullivan [2000], Saldana, and others), literalists who would insist that each text is primarily about the "real" characters portrayed in it may go about making summative decisions about their deserved fates. Some literalists in France at the time of the Doisneau

(1973) photo's publication might conceivably have demanded further investigation of that apparently illegal incident as evidence of a crime: Those perpetrators at that particular bar should have been arrested! Literalists reading the Barone text might similarly decide, on the basis of this manuscript, that Forrister either deserved a raise in pay or—as literalists reading the Case story may feel about the cowardly school principal—deserved to be fired.

Still, Barone (2001) took pains to explicitly recommend for his work of creative nonfiction a *fictional* reading. Indeed, to avoid misunderstandings about his preferred reading, Barone elaborately explicated the reasoning behind his methodological and compositional choices. Those misunderstandings themselves may be otherwise understandable in a professional realm of social science where all traces of the fictional reside outside of the prevailing norm. For ethical reasons, therefore, we suggest that arts based researchers send explicit, indeed, crystal clear signals about the purposes that they would like their text to serve. This is especially the case when harm may come to actual persons or specific institutions portrayed in the text.

There is indeed a danger present when a text intended to serve a fictional purpose is considered literally truthful than vice versa. The fictional should be identified as such to protect actual innocents. But what about the possibilities of using a text labeled nonfictional for the interrogatory purposes of good fiction?

In the case of Barone (2001), those readers who bring themselves to think metaphorically about the qualities in this work would use them to engage primarily in discussions about, not merely the formal qualities and the particular characters portrayed therein, but the broader themes that transcend a world crafted out of carefully selected and recombined empirical details. Readers may choose to reflect on—and enter into conversations about—the teaching of the "Don Forristers" who they have experienced in their own lives, and, further, on the ideological positionings that inevitably inhabit the evaluation of teaching. Those who do so will achieve an elevated order of utility that only fiction can provide. Or as Iser (1993) would put it, the "imaginary" will have been "pragmatized." And as Rorty (1979) might suggest, the second fundamental purpose of human inquiry will have been achieved—not the delivery of truth, but the enhancement of alternative meanings of social phenomena.

CHOOSING FICTION? SOME SUGGESTIONS

We conclude by offering a few recommendations surrounding the creation of arts based research that relate to the topic of this chapter. We suggest that arts based researchers do the following:

1. Decide on the purpose or purposes for which the research is being undertaken. Do you intend for the text to be read as a factual version of the truth or as imaginative literature? Or—since some arts based research can document the activities of real people and still promote the interrogatory purposes of fiction—both?

2. Employ methods and compositional design elements that are likely to achieve the intended purpose or purposes. These design elements, we suggest, may be drawn from genres thought of as primarily fictional or primarily nonfictional, or (again) somewhere in between. But textual fashioning in studies that rigorously aim solely at factual truth will, to one degree or another, differ from projects aimed toward the kind of ambiguity and uncertainty that produces metaphorical power.

3. Disclose a clear and honest indication of your intended purpose or purposes. Be aware of the various signals, both internal and contextual, being sent in that regard.

4. Be brave: Release control of the work, understanding that others with alternative backgrounds, ideologies, and worldviews will do with it what they will. Understand that ultimately the manner in which the work is used will depend on a complex interplay between text, context, and reader that occurs within each specific "reading" event.

In closing, we revisit our primary question posed in this chapter by asserting yes, arts based research can indeed be fictional and not merely in the diffuse sense that all human artifacts are "fashioned." Some works can (even if "double read") end up disrupting the commonplace and suggesting new worlds, as only good art—as fiction—can. But for those arts based researchers who decide to label their work fictional because it does indeed aim toward an interrogative (as opposed to, or in addition to, a factual) end, we have one final suggestion:

Be prepared to articulate a defense of your choice against incredulous traditionalists who are unprepared to hear the words *fiction* and *social research* in the same sentence.

In the end, we do indeed urge resistance against the impulse to retreat from the possibilities of producing arts based (and other forms of qualitative) research with the capacity for the kind of enhancement of alternative meanings within social phenomena that has long been identified with works of fiction. And we hope that this chapter will assist you in that articulation.

Chapter 7

How Might Arts Based Research Be Both Political and Ethical?

In this chapter, we address the places of politics and ethics in arts based research, social research that exhibits important aesthetic features. We have chosen to address these two dimensions of arts based research in the same chapter because we see them as intimately intertwined. Even further, each has implications for judging the aesthetic quality of a project of arts based research. We will, of course, elaborate on those perceived connections. First, however, we comment on the political in arts based research, and its relationships to the aesthetic.

To suggest that the political can or should play a role in any form of social research remains, for some research traditionalists, a call to argument. Since its inception and throughout most of its history, social research has been identified exclusively as a kind of apolitical science, one meant to serve not as a form of advocacy, but as a neutral, objective adjudicator of the competing values undergirding various positions taken on social issues.

A detachment from the political has, likewise, been a hallmark of several schools of aesthetics. The search for the "beautiful" within art has been undertaken in a supposedly transcendent realm, one therefore unsullied by the power relationships that reside within the affairs of daily commerce. It is not surprising, then, that some commentators would assume that any form of social *research* that honors the premises, principles, and protocols of the *arts* must be *twice* removed from the realm of the political.

We do not make the same assumption, however. To the contrary, we hold with many other theorists that power relations are evident in all human activities and artifacts, including artistic ones, although some more obviously than others. Arts based social research is, therefore, inherently political, and we will describe the ways in which it may indeed be seen as simultaneously artful *and* political.

We will do this both in theoretical terms and, more importantly, through the use of extant examples of arts based research and other works of art.

But even as we do so, we will also reject an equally fallacious assumption, the one that would legitimate all obviously political works of arts based research as useful research.

This fallacy states that there is—or should be—no distinction made between art and agitprop, that arts based research may be didactic, polemical, dogmatic, or even propagandistic. Instead, through examples and argument, we will insist that if art based social research—like art itself—may interrogate an entrenched ideological stance regarding social phenomena it must do so without imposing a "correct" alternative ideology. Instead, good examples of arts based research accomplish the previously identified purpose for this sort of inquiry—the artful posing of questions regarding important social and cultural issues—by allowing them to be seen in a previously unavailable light.

In this chapter, as we seek out the places of the political within arts based research, we stop at two locations. We find the political, first, within the content of arts based research texts—that is, in *themes* that suggest the manner in which power and privilege is distributed (or maldistributed) within specific cultural settings. Second, we address the *politics of perspective* within works of arts based research. We discuss the usefulness of truly democratic arts based research in which no single point of view (POV) regarding textual content is privileged over others—whether that of the author/artist/researcher or of any of the various research participants (e.g., informants who become the characters within the text). Each of these two facets of the political in arts based research, therefore, pertains to issues of power. And it is there that we will find connections with ethics, insofar as we see unequal power relations to be undemocratic and ethically troublesome.

CONFRONTING METANARRATIVES: SOME EXAMPLES

How might arts based research, in an artful manner, directly or indirectly address unequal power relationships prevailing within a culture? And how might the disclosures made lead to the enhancement of previously undisclosed meaning within social phenomena that we have identified as a primary purpose of arts based research? To answer these questions we redirect our attention to five literary works of arts based research—three that are quite obvious in their social commitments, one that is moderately so, and one that is not obviously committed to an issue that is political in nature. The first three works are by Nadine Gordimer (1985), Johnny Saldana (2005), and Denise Clark Pope

(2001). The fourth is by Tom Barone (2000) and the fifth is by Anne Sullivan (2000). Four of the five have already been described in previous chapters—all except the Pope piece.

The short story by Nadine Gordimer (1985) and the ethnodrama by Saldana (2005) are examples of works that operate within a tradition of literature identified by Jean Paul Sartre (1988) as *socially engaged* (*literature engagee*). Socially engaged literature is a genre that flows out of concerns for inequities found within sociopolitical relationships in a culture. For Gordimer, that was the apartheid culture of 20th-century South Africa: The relationships between a dominant white master class and the subjugated indigenous African population served as the backdrop for her assertively political novels and short stories. The social scene explored by Saldana, Finley, and Finley in "Street Rat" is one in which alienated young people eek out an existence in the alleyways of a Southern U.S. city.

As politically engaged artists, both Gordimer and Saldana focus on the effects of social conditions and practices on particular sorts of human beings. Gordimer represents one novelist in a long stream of such writers, from Victor Hugo to Charles Dickens to Richard Wright, while Saldana (a self-described arts based researcher) might be seen as working within a tradition of socially conscientious works of theater in which Bertold Brecht, Augusto Boal, and even Sophocles, participated. Indeed, artists of all sorts—from painters such as Francisco Goya and Judy Chicago, to filmmakers such as Spike Lee and Ang Lee—have, throughout history, artfully critiqued social practices and cultural conditions that operate within the interests of the powerful over those of the much less powerful—the marginalized, excluded, neglected, and dispossessed. Consider the photographers Lewis W. Hine and Dorothea Lange who offered startling contrasts between haves and have-nots within an America of the not-so-distant past. Consider also the work of more recent activist art, approaches which, in turn, provide sustenance for some arts based social research.

What all of these artists and researchers apparently have in common, then, is a yearning for social justice that is pursued though various forms of art. In doing so, they transgress against deeply entrenched discourses, habits, and practices that have become commonsensical, taken for granted as "natural" within the belief systems of the dominant culture. These belief systems are supported through images and language that are lodged within the public consciousness and accepted therein as fundamentally true and rarely questioned or challenged. It does not matter that the images are skewed, distorted. It does not matter that the symbolic language consists of a set of abstract words, devoid of concrete referents, to which meanings are nevertheless assigned. These words and images live in a mutually supportive relationship within an overarching storyline that is legitimated as part of what we refer to as a master narrative. In discussing this notion of the master narrative, we draw inspiration from and loosely follow some of the ideas of the theorist Jean-Francois Lyotard (1979).

Master narratives presume to provide explanations that bring final meaning to cultural phenomena and therefore the comforts of certainty, stability, and order to a frightening world that seems riddled with ambiguity, instability, and disorder. They are, moreover, understood not as authored by individual subjects but by a transcendent, infallible metasubject that is seen as giving "voice to a common grounding" (Lyotard, 1979, p. 34). The master narrative therefore operates as a set of preunderstandings—about, for example, science as the single source of knowledge—that come to be taken for granted as truthful. Master narratives are, therefore, totalizing, insofar as they attempt to bring final meaning to cultural phenomena, refusing the possibilities of alternative explanations of, or additional perspectives on, those phenomena.

But these master narratives may nevertheless be revealed by critics as political insofar as they, disguised as "objective," nevertheless serve to legitimate, normalize, and therefore empower certain social values, vantage points, and discourses (ways of being) over others. These norms may, moreover, serve the interests of certain segments of society—including those that control the sources and dissemination of legitimated knowledge—at the expense of others.

One important attribute of works of art, and arts based research, can be their capacity for enhancing alternative meanings that adhere to social phenomena, thereby undercutting the authority of the master narrative. This may make art appear inconvenient or even dangerous to those who have become familiar and comfortable with the prevailing, dominant, exclusive worldview legitimated within the metanarrative that a work of art or arts based research may serve to question. Those with interests in the maintenance of that narrative may, in various ways, attempt to dismiss or even banish transgressive works of art.

Within Western culture, master narratives about a variety of social themes can be identified. We have mentioned earlier that race, gender, social class, sexual orientation, childhood, aging, colonialism, and intellectualism may represent a few of these themes. Certain of these themes can be identified as playing a role within both the Gordimer (1985) and Saldana (2005) pieces. In Gordimer's short story, the themes of race, gender, and social class are all intertwined, as an oppressive master narrative within an apartheid society produces a kind of fear among of one's colleagues that are themselves the victims of that master narrative. But this narrative is challenged by the author of this story's revelation of its presence, marking the artist–storyteller Nadine Gordimer (although a white South African woman) as subversive to the regime of truth supported by it (and, indeed, analogously tyrannical regimes in other times and places). Similarly,

Saldana's carefully researched and crafted ethnodrama enables its audiences to vicariously experience a kind of life lived on the edge of an abyss, revealing (among other things) the structure of moral codes in alienated young people who, the master narrative insists, lack all moral bearings.

Nurtured within the broader master narratives just identified are offshoots, derivatives, and secondary metanarratives that can be identified within particular sorts of endeavors within the culture. Still another example of arts based social research, this one (Barone, 2000) arising from within the field of education, illustrates the undercutting of this sort of secondary metanarrative.

Part of a prevailing metanarrative within the field of education may be formulated as follows:

> An educational crisis exists in the land. One of the primary causes of this crisis is the lack of character in students themselves. These students are, to an undesirable degree, dull, lazy, undisciplined, drug addicted, even violent. They are largely to blame for the educational crisis, the perpetrators, not the victims, of social crimes.

Against this cultural backdrop, Barone (2000; reprinted in this book) researched and wrote that story-within-a-story-within-a-literary-essay described in Chapter 3. Recall that it focused on one poor, white, troubled Appalachian adolescent named Billy Charles Barnett (pseudonym) who had been singled out by his school as most likely to drop out before graduation. However, Barone soon discovered a student who was quite unlike the one that his teachers and school administrators had described as "slow" and "hard to talk to." Indeed, prior to meeting Billy Charles, Barone had been led to imagine the stereotypical vision of an "at-risk" student deeply embedded in the cultural/educational metanarrative—an angry youngster disinterested in schoolwork, lacking discipline, and not very smart. But upon meeting Billy Charles in person, Barone was startled to encounter a loquacious 15-year-old in possession of great personal charm and a keen intelligence. Indeed, the sudden realization of the high degree of cultural knowledge (albeit literacy of an Appalachian subculture) possessed by this student jolts the researcher into

> a sudden realization of my vast ignorance about the ways of people who live within a two-hour drive of my home and about the fundamentals of a world no longer honored in the dominant culture. (Barone, 2000, p. 180)

As the story/essay continues, the reader learns more about the difficult life and remarkable character of Billy Charles and about the journey of discovery taken by the arts based researcher. Billy Charles, Barone (2000) discovered, was not merely at risk of dropping out of school but at risk of taking his own life. Moreover, the author posed the question—without supplying an answer—about whether Billy Charles would be personally better off if he left school. Indeed, the researcher/essayist began to wonder about whether and how the menacing and destructive qualities within the institution of the school as well as the larger dominant culture might be implicated in the production of the quandary within which Billy Charles finds himself. Could it be, Barone asked himself and his readers, that—the metanarrative notwithstanding—the school and the middle class cultural norms it promotes and enforces are the guilty parties in this case? What, after all, are the various ways of adolescents being "at risk" that are masked by the official language adopted by the educational establishment?

Like Saldana and Gordimer, Barone (2000) promoted a reexamination of official forms of discourse by luring readers into reexperiencing life through the eyes of the dispossessed—New Orleans street kids, South African blacks, a poverty-plagued Appalachian adolescent. And like the Saldana (2005) and Gordimer (1985) pieces, the story of Billy Charles Barnett is deeply political, even if it may seem somehow less so than the others. Indeed, Barone has called "Ways of Being at Risk" a kind of critical story, much like a piece of moral fiction (Stone, 1988) that "establishes the connection between political forces and individual lives."

Arts based research that does so may be seen as transgressing against the prevailing metanarrative, which can lead readers to become more "wide-awake" (Greene, 1977) to unfortunate conditions within institutions and cultures and ultimately into informed conversations about bringing about more responsive, just, and democratic social arrangements.

And again, whenever we see conditions of society that suggest it is just and democratic, we would argue that an ethical set of conditions prevail. By engaging in a project that operates in favor of such conditions may be said, at least on that level, to have conducted herself in an ethical manner. But do all forms of arts based research indeed operate in such an overtly political and ethical manner?

The neopragmatist philosopher Richard Rorty (1989) has distinguished between two kinds of literature. One, he suggested, is the sort that helps us become less cruel. This is the sort that either helps us see deleterious effects of our social practices and institutions on other people or that helps us see the effects of our private idiosyncrasies on others. A second kind is that which helps us become autonomous, to redescribe ourselves and thereby "make ourselves new" (p. 101) to become more "wide-awake" to ourselves and to whom we can become. The first sort seems to be classified as "political," while the second may be seen as oriented toward the "personal" or "private." One might extend that distinction to all works of art, literary and otherwise.

Remaining within Rorty's (1989) dualism for a moment, we might classify works by Saldana (2005), Gordimer (1985), and perhaps Barone (2000), as examples of the kind of literature and art that deals obviously and overtly with political issues. The less overtly political essay/poetry by Sullivan (2000) might not and could therefore represent the second of Rorty's two kinds of literature/art.

It seems to us, however, that Rorty's (1989) distinction is too neat, that indeed the political inevitably resides within the personal and vice versa. Compared with the pieces by Saldana (2005), Gordimer (1985), and Barone (2000), the article by Anne Sullivan (2000)—reprinted in this book—may indeed seem less focused on overtly political matters and more concerned with personal, experiential growth. The Sullivan piece of arts based research seems rather introspective, contemplative in presenting how she learned from her biologist mother to be attentive to the nuances of the physical world around her.

It may indeed be true that the Sullivan (2000) article does indeed portray the growth of an individual (here, the author Sullivan herself as a child) through autobiographical renderings. Stone (2005), however, has argued that the Sullivan piece does indeed potentially hold political consequences. Using the feminist framework of Kristeva (1982, 1996, 2000), Stone insisted that poetic language itself can indeed be revolutionary. More specifically, Sullivan's poetry moves to "reclaim the maternal," values the acceptance of "a radical kind of otherness" identified with women and motherhood. One who embraces this "otherness" can become in Kristeva's words "a deviser of territories, languages, works . . . that impel him to start afresh (Kristeva, 1982, p. 8; cited in Stone, 2005, p. 313). A poet, with her new languages, especially one who moves to resituate the place of the maternal in a culture that marginalizes it is, therefore, potentially a political revolutionary.

Indeed, taken together, then, these four works—by Saldana (2005), Gordimer (1985), Barone (2000), and Sullivan (2000)—suggest that Rorty's (1989) neat distinction between the private (or personal) and the political may be, in fact, a less than useful approach to classifying works of art or arts based research. This is because all of these works may be seen as honoring the emancipatory aim of art as expressed by Nelson Goodman (1968): They can indeed serve to free us from entrenched, commonsensical ways of viewing the world. Art, writes Goodman, can present and then resist "a usual kind of picture." Art" may bring out neglected likenesses and differences . . . and in some ways, remake our world" (p. 33). They may remake the world, again, in a manner that is more sensitive to existing power relations and therefore serve as ethical projects as well as political ones.

ARTS BASED RESEARCH OR PROPAGANDA?

Indeed, we believe that arts based researchers may never escape the fact that, in addressing social issues, they will inevitably, in one way or another, explicitly or less so, be dealing with power relationships and therefore ethical issues that exist within the sociocultural landscape they choose to portray. Some will suggest, perhaps rightly so, that a kind of intellectual honesty requires arts based researchers to attend overtly to—and even explicitly reveal—those power relationships.

But there is a clear danger for arts based inquirers in approaching issues of the political in social research, using an approach that may not be seen as ethical. This is the danger of becoming ideologues, advocates, partisans, and propagandists in their striving to avoid becoming political eunuchs. This is the danger that high-minded arts based researchers will, in their passion for challenging familiar, comfortable, dominant metanarratives, proffer an arrogant, totalizing metanarrative of their own. This is the danger that arts based researchers, in their dedication to eradicate cruelties, may become strident, exclusionary, monologic, and authoritative—and therefore off-putting to readers and self-defeating. This is the danger that arts based researchers may (to paraphrase Sartre [1988]), in their zeal to make history, forget to make art. And they may simultaneously, in a certain sense, be acting unethically in the process.

Let us now return to the works of Gordimer (1985), Saldana (2005), Barone (2000), and Sullivan (2000) to ascertain how each author managed to walk the ethical line between, on the one side, abnegation of the political self, and, on the other, the pitfalls of activist artists who stridently assert what they hold to be true in a manner that (unethically) serves to overpower other points of view.

Some people do indeed move to make art—and therefore arts based research—in this manner. Fearing that they will fail to emphatically deliver a message about social affairs and conditions, they refuse to see a second trap, antithetical to the notion that art must never be political. They refuse to recognize the difference between art and agitprop, holding instead that arts based research may, if necessary, be didactic, polemical, dogmatic, or even propagandistic.

We reject any such apologia for propaganda as equally unfortunate as the idea of apolitical art and as unethical as well. Through examples and argument, we will insist that arts based research—like art itself—may interrogate an entrenched ideological stance regarding social phenomena without obvious attempts at imposing a "correct" alternative ideology. Instead, good examples of arts based research accomplish the previously identified purpose for this sort of inquiry—the artful posing of questions regarding important social, political, and cultural issues by allowing them to be seen in a previously unavailable light. To do this, the researcher must adopt a stance of epistemological humility, one in which she challenges orthodox views without insisting upon a new orthodoxy.

We will elaborate on what we mean by epistemological humility by first focusing on literary forms of social research and the issues of textual politics that operate within them. These are issues involved in which versions of events are privileged over others in the conduct of the research and in the arrangement of the research text.

To consider these, we return to the notion of the master narrative, more specifically to the educational master narrative that we just described. We have suggested how master narratives often stand against the imagination, against the composition of partial, local narratives of human growth and possibility.

We have noted that the educational master narrative may consist of a series of distortions designed to manipulate social reality toward a desired end. In other words, at the very outset of a work of research there may *already* be a privileged view of who the characters in the study will be, what the events will mean. Again, from an ethical standpoint, that seems to us to be very unfortunate. We have seen how works by Barone (2000), Saldana (2005), and Gordimer (1985) transgress against the totality of the master narrative. But how can this be achieved without the researcher/artist/author herself assuming, albeit with sterling intentions, the role of unethical totalitarian, positing a correct(ed) single view of social phenomena?

They do so by, yes, first offering more closely observed images and stories that defy the easy distortions and stereotypes of various sorts of people in our society, especially the challenged, underprivileged, and dispossessed, that have come to be taken for granted by members of the public as accurate. But they also achieve this by refusing to present an alternative master narrative in their own work. Indeed, they may, like the authors of this book, think it highly arrogant and unethical for an arts based researcher to purport to have discovered a final truth, an unmediated reality about the essence of any inhabitants categorized within a society. The epistemologically humble arts based researcher desires instead to offer small, closely observed, local stories and portraits that invite readers (and viewers) to look again at what they think they have already seen. But they achieve this by offering a degree of ambiguity—as opposed to an attitude of certainty—in their research texts. This ambiguity arises within a recognition of the value of a variety of alternative perspectives within a research text. These are the perspectives of the author/artist, the various views of the characters, and the perspectives of the members of the audience of the work.

WHOSE RESEARCH IS IT?

To elaborate upon what we mean here, we turn to yet two other examples of arts based research. The first comes in the form of a book about the lives of students in an affluent high school in northern California. The book is *Doing*

School by Denise Clark Pope (2001). Its subtitle reveals its transgressive intentions: *How We Are Creating a Generation of Stressed Out, Materialistic, and Miseducated Students.* The book explores the culture of competition in a comprehensive California high school as it traces the tensions between the felt needs of students and the materialistic brand of success expected of them. The author maintains an eye for telling detail as she transforms her informants into quasi-literary characters, transmuting her own concerns into the form of biographical portraits of five ethnically diverse students—Roberto, Eve, Kevin, Michelle, and Teresa—fashioning for inspection the idiosyncratic life worlds of these students and the common social forces that operate to diminish them.

The master narrative describes success in school largely as the achievement of high GPAs that should lead to academic success in either the world of work directly after high school or, as is the case in *Doing School*, in the world of college and then in the world of work. This success should, in turn, result in the fulfillment of the American dream of either high-paying jobs and an affluent lifestyle or at least in attaining work that offers a livable wage. But Pope (2001) cut against this metanarrative by offering Lyotardian style stories that question its authority.

Graphically, with telling details, Pope (2001) demonstrated the price that each of these students pays in their all-consuming quests to succeed in an intense, stressful, materialistic school culture. While each of the stories advance Pope's theme as the writer of the book, the story of none is identical with that of any other. For at least some of the students the costs involve, in different ways, the relinquishing their own sense of identity and their desires to change the world around them for the better. As we read this book, we do not feel that we are entering into the lives of strangers who populate a vague and distant campus but encountering specific human beings who harbor recognizable dreams in the face of debilitating circumstances.

Pope (2001), to her credit, we believe, insisted upon no final solutions to this dilemma presented to students by the master-narrative. No alternative master narratives are advanced. No simple policy solutions are recommended. Instead, as a good narrative researcher she subtly invites readers in to feel their own doubts and allows for questions about the status quo to emerge.

Interestingly, Pope (2001) did not claim to be engaged in arts based research. And while it is clearly a work of qualitative research, the book does defy easy labeling and categorization. Still, at its quasi-literary center, the composed biographies of the five students serve as a core out of which Pope's analytical content is extrapolated. The diachronic, or storied, data is important, and so we think, then, that the project can indeed be identified as arts based.

Storied data is at the heart of another example of research, one that is labeled, not as arts-based, but as *dialogic* research. This is a study of former students who happened to be retained in grade at least once in their tenure in the public schools of Winnipeg, Manitoba, Canada. The study, by David Coulter (1999), also asks to be ethically justified by its intentions to move beyond the caricatures of students within the master narrative through careful observations and the telling of their stories of school based experiences. Moreover, it is another study designed to question facets of a worldview about children and schooling that was—and still is—firmly planted in the realm of common sense. But unlike *Doing School*, this study is one that was not originated by an academic. It was begun instead by a school administrator in conjunction with some teachers in his district. And here is where another set of ethical/political issues rears its ugly head. These are the issues of who owns the research project.

David Coulter was working in the school district of the Winnipeg Public Schools in the late 1990s, at a time when groups of teachers and parents were being passed on to the next grade level without actually mastering the skills necessary for that level. The controversy about local promotion, or a no-fail policy, was picked up by the local media and Coulter was asked by the school board to study and report on the issue. Coulter asked for others to join him in his research, and six teachers and administrators volunteered to do so (Coulter, 1999).

The research plan agreed upon went approximately like this: The research team began by reviewing the existing literature on retention in grade. The team was struck first by the massive amount of studies already available. Most of the studies were traditionally scientific. In fact, it turned out that this was and is one of the most thoroughly researched topics in education. Moreover, the team found near unanimity among the research conclusions, which can be summed up as follows: On average, retained students are worse off than their promoted counterparts in terms of both personal adjustment and academic outcomes. Few topics researched in education, the research team discovered, had such clear-cut, one-sided findings (Coulter, 1999).

But as Coulter (1999) pointed out, retention in grade has, despite the overwhelmingly disapproving body of traditional research, been a common practice in schools throughout North America for about a century, even as its popularity has webbed and waned. Within the master narrative, nevertheless, the term *social promotion* is a pejorative. The master narrative insists that students who are the equivalent of lemons in the automobile industry should be moved down the assembly line and allowed to go out into the market when they are clearly defective products.

But the Coulter research team asked themselves the following question: Who needs one more traditional study that is likely to support the findings of

62 previous ones that cut against the prevailing master narrative, when the 62 previous ones have been so roundly ignored by both the public and policymakers in favor of that entrenched master narrative? And so they took a different research track, one in which the stories of individual former students would serve as a base.

It is true that, as in the Pope (2001) study, the issues researched in the Coulter (1999) study were not identified by the students who were the victims of the master narrative. But Coulter's work did result in a research booklet entitled *Faces of Failure*. In that document, included alongside the passive, third person, technical prose of standard research reports were placed the stories of some informants in their own vernacular voices. These were the tales of several recruited former students, now adults, who had repeated at least one grade in school and who were willing to discuss the experience. They were the specific stories of Mary, Alex, David, Suzanne, Lorie, and Linda who helped ground the official language and images of the master narrative in the experiences of children.

Both Coulter and Pope (2001) apparently entered into their studies with good intent, for what might be called counterhegemonic purposes—that is, to get closer to the lived stories of real people in order to question the dominant understandings embodied within the master narrative. But how ethical was it for each of them to initiate the study from, as it were, outside of the research locales and the interest zone of their informants and collaborators? Would it not be more ethical if the study had percolated from the bottom up, from the felt needs of and live concerns of the actual victims of the master narrative?

So this set of ethical issues encountered by arts based researchers may involve the manner in which the researcher justifies the initiation of and engagement in a research study that reveals the deeply personal stories of other peoples' lives. Pope (2001), for example, had much to gain professionally in her research for *Doing School*. This book was, in fact, a redrafting of her dissertation work. It helped her to become credentialed as an academic and educational researcher. But was it not the intimate details of the lives of the five students she portrays that served as a means to those ends? What are the ethical responsibilities of the researcher to her informants when it is the researcher whose career may benefit from the intimate information offered up by her collaborators in the work? This issue was surely heightened in the Pope project as a kind of trust and rapport developed between the researcher and the students whose lives into which she was probing.

Some would argue that, in order to be ethical, the origins of all arts based research storytelling must be indigenous—that is, originated by those being stereotyped by the metanarrative. The life stories of the oppressed, this argument goes, must not be told by the privileged researcher—even a liberal with noble intentions—on behalf of the victimized.

One counterargument may be that students, in particular, often do not have the cultural capital—the means, the access, the political finesse, the maturity—to have their stories told, heard, and disseminated. But is that true or is it overstated? Perhaps students could be taught how to tell their own stories, make their own works of art, disclose their own perspectives rather than having them disclosed for them? Some studies, such as that of Chappell (2009), demonstrate that many students can and do make public their own emancipatory-oriented artworks. The same is certainly the case for adults who have been shoved to the margins of our culture: There are untold numbers of examples of individual and community based activist artists who have achieved this, without the encouragement and assistance from well-intentioned academics. At any rate, it is our sense that, when it comes to vitiating the power of a master narrative, it is less important who originates an arts based research project than who *ultimately* owns the project.

THE PROCESS OF BEING POLITICAL AND ETHICAL

Ethical and political questions about the ownership of a study do not, after all, arise only at the origins of the project but during the entire research engagement. They are not finally resolved once a project has, for example, been approved by a Human Subjects Review Board. They pop up throughout, arising, often unexpectedly, from outset to end, in all forms of qualitative research. But what these questions may have in common is that they involve issues of privilege and power.

Consider a few questions that may arise during the compositional process: Who gets to decide what themes are developed within the research texts? What details should be included and excluded from the emerging portraits? Whose voices are "heard" in the composition? These are all important questions, but the overriding ones, we believe, are these:

How can one create arts based texts with the greatest catalytic potential for engendering a conversation, texts, that is, in which there is not inscribed a single, monolithic, static, privileged, authoritative, dominant POV? How can we offer a multiplicity of perspectives, each of which is fragile, fluid, tentative, and epistemologically humble? How can we create a text that is simultaneously owned by all collaborators, one that discloses the multiple perspectives of the researcher and the various perspectives of the characters inhabiting the text? And how can the text serve to raise questions about the dominance of the master narrative in the minds of readers as they imagine characters and events outside of the text as analogous to those portrayed within it?

That last paragraph is a mouthful and deserves to be broken down:

First, regarding the researcher/artist, we believe that in a truly ethical process of arts based research and composition, the researcher must be a writer rather than an author. This distinction suggests that the writer (or artist), unlike an author (or propagandist), does not have an ideological agenda (Wicomb, 1991). A researcher/artist must, of course, accept ultimate responsibility for the arts based text. But to avoid an agenda an artist/researcher must understand making art as a process of discovery. She or he must be willing to be educated—indeed to be transformed—in that process. The arts based researcher is therefore incomplete and developing, a reader of her own writing. (In some literary style arts based research—in fact, some of our own—the researcher himself may become a character in the text, although one who is seen as changing within the process of researching and writing.)

And the ethical arts based researcher must be open to engaging—sharing power with—informants and readers in a textual conversation. This means forgoing a tone of certainty and finality that (sometimes strident and sometimes subtle) freezes out the possibilities of alternative meanings to social phenomena.

The voice of the writer, we suggest, should not overpower those of her informants-turned-characters in the text—the people with whom she is collaborating—by signaling through the presence of various textual design elements a revelation of final meaning. This may require, for example, a refusal to overwrite the vernacular idioms of informants with the specialized languages of academia, a domination that is evidenced in, among other places, texts of well-intentioned critical ethnographers who may ironically denigrate the perspectives of their informants in their zeal to correct what they may see as a false or constrained consciousness.

This is not to say that lives of participants-turned-characters are portrayed within a moral and political vacuum; linkages must indeed be established between those lives and the debilitating structures that exist both inside and outside of the research setting. The conditions of oppression experienced by these characters are not declared or directly stated; they are instead embodied within portraits of lived events, allowing for readers to vicariously experience those oppressive conditions.

Indeed, the perspectives of participants/informants are critical in an arts based text. But always beware the reminiscence. In our view, no one is the sole proprietor of his or her own story or POV. Indeed, we have discovered in our own work that presenting various drafts of a biographical account to informants—for what is called in qualitative research a *member check*—will often result in conflicting details in the reading of successive drafts. Recollections of details of our own lives can indeed shift dramatically, sometimes from moment to moment.

This is one important reason why the ethical arts based text avoids mining the perspectives of its storied characters for a kind of subjective truth about who they really, really are and what they really, really know. These characters themselves only understand events from their partial, tentative, shifting perspectives. For this reason, we understand the initiation of a member check not as an epistemological gesture but as an ethical one. While arts based researchers will never be recipients of final truths from their research collaborators, it seems only fair that the latter are granted final approval over the contents of their life stories.

Of course, this in no way diminishes the value or significance of the perspectives of informants-turned-characters. Coulter (1999) addressed this point directly in quoting Mikhail Bakhtin's (1984) insistence of the autonomy of the characters in what he called a polyphonic, storied text. These characters must be, Bakhtin wrote, "free people, capable of standing alongside their creator, capable of disagreeing with him and even rebelling against him" (p. 6).

In encountering a responsible arts based text, one may sense that the characters have, as they say, taken on a life of their own. This may seem paradoxical, insofar as the researcher remains the writer of the text. But consider how Pope (2001) and Coulter approached this issue, each in slightly different ways.

Pope (2001) carefully gathered data from the lives of five students in the research process and then crafted them into vividly drawn biographical portraits through which they are transformed into characters who may then indeed live freely in the minds of readers. Coulter (1999) included the actual words of former students who speak directly in their own voices. In each case, the stories of the students were variegated, each slightly different from the other, even occasionally standing in contradiction to each other. Coulter, especially, was quite careful to include the stories of a few former students who believed that being held back in school was the best thing that ever happened to them educationally.

Moreover, the ultimate importance of such a textual arrangement allows for the presentations of life stories of those (such as the students and the former students in the Pope and Coulter studies) whose perspectives have been marginalized or absent in more traditional forms of research. This produces what Bakhtin (1981) called a *carnival* of characterizations, a research text in which the commonplace becomes strange and the accepted state of affairs is defamiliarized.

GOOD ARTS BASED RESEARCH: ETHICAL POLITICS FOR A BETTER WORLD

The presence of this mix of often conflicting perspectives of the researcher and the various characters in the text works to diminish the possibilities of an overbearing, totalized, ethically challenged monologue in favor of a democratic conversation. With no one final "truthful" master narrative dominating the text, the result may be a tension or friction in the text that may serve as an invitation to the reader to enter into the conversation.

The writer offers a text that is partly unwritten, replete with gaps, or as Iser (1980), put it, "elements of indeterminacy without which the reader would not be able to use his imagination" (p. 87). These gaps are designed to entice the reader into wondering about that which she may have once, under the sway of the master narrative, taken for granted as true and real.

In the process of reconstructing the text within the act of reading, the reader is both conditioned by the text and in turn conditions it. The reader may choose to refuse the so-called "internal validity" of the text, refuse to see it as a mirror of reality, even as she resonates somewhat with the various perspectives of the writer and of the characters. She may thereby take the text home into the realm of her daily experiences to see what it might suggest about familiar social conditions, conventional cultural practices, and the limitations placed on the perspectives of writer/researcher, informants/characters, and reader. She may self-identify with those characters or recognize in them people she knows in her world outside of the arts based text. She may relate the oppressive conditions lived by the characters to nearby social settings. She may in that sense put this ethically sensitive and democratic text to use as an imaginary, an opening into a possible, more just, truly democratic, world. She may even been lured into an epiphany, a major transactional moment that disrupts the ordinary flow of experience, and as Denzin (1997) put it, alters and shapes the meaning within her life project. Or at the very least she may feel the need to continue the conversation generated in her own mind with others in a community of discourse for whom the text has been similarly challenging and disturbing.

The end result will then be a politically powerful work of arts based research that stands on firm ethical grounds, an aesthetically powerful work of arts based research with the potential to change the world for the better.

Arts Based Research Example

Ways of Being at Risk:
The Case of Billy Charles Barnett*

TOM BARONE
Arizona State University

We are the representatives of two subcultures, meeting at a McDonald's along an interstate highway in northeastern Tennessee. Sitting across from me is Billy Charles Barnett, a tall lanky boy with dark hair, green eyes, a pug nose, and an infectious grin. He is a member of the rural "disadvantaged," a fifteen-year-old nominated by the vice-principal as the student least likely to remain in Dusty Hollow Middle School. I am a middle-aged urban academic who, secure in a tenured university position, will never leave school.

I am inclined to believe the warnings of others like me—teachers and administrators at Billy Charles' school—that this teenager from the hills will be "slow" and "hard to talk to." I am, therefore, surprised to discover almost immediately a keen intelligence and an eagerness to share his knowledge about his world. Even more jolting is a sudden realization of my vast ignorance about the ways of people who live within a two-hour drive of my home and about the fundamentals of a world no longer honored in the dominant culture.

*This article originally appeared in Barone, T. (1989). Ways of being at risk: The case of Billy Charles Barnett. *Phi Delta Kappan*, 71(2), 147–151. Bloomington, IN: Phi Delta Kappa International, Inc. Reprinted with permission of Phi Delta Kappa International, www.pdkintl.org. All rights reserved.

Between slurps on a straw, Billy Charles speaks:

You don't know what jugging is? When you go jugging, first you take a jug that bleach comes in. You rinse it out and tighten the lid and get some soft but strong nylon string. Then you need to get a two-inch turtle hook, real strong . . . and a three-or-four-foot line. The best bait is a bluegill, cut in half. You know, you really should use the head part. It's better than the tail, because turtles always go for the head of the fish first. But you can [also] catch catfish, bass, like this. I caught me a seven-and-a-half pound bass once, jugging. The jug just hangs in the water and nothing can get off the line unless they break it. I can catch a mess of turtles [this way], and then I make turtle soup. Do you know how to make turtle soup?

I find myself squirming in my seat. But why should I be the one feeling inadequate and defensive? No, I didn't know—until Billy Charles told me—that the market was bearish on coonskins this year, and that I could expect no more than $40 for a flawless one of average size. The topic had simply never come up in any graduate course on curriculum theory. Moreover, E. D. Hirsch and his co-authors had included no such items in their *Dictionary of Cultural Literacy: What Every American Needs to Know.* So I take comfort: not only am I the better educated, but also apparently the better *American* of the two strangers chomping on their cheeseburgers on this unseasonably balmy January afternoon.

Although I know nothing about the price of coonskins, I am better informed about Billy Charles than he is about me. For example, I know that Billy Charles is spending a second year in the seventh grade. I know that he has expressed on numerous occasions his intentions to drop out of school as soon as he can. And I know that, on occasion, he has entertained fantasies of dropping out of life, as well.

The last item is, of course, the most troublesome. *Specific suicidal ideations* is the phrase used by the school psychologist to characterize Billy Charles's morbid fantasies. Having ventured forth from my cozy, book-lined office to conduct a case study of what I thought would be a typical at-risk student, I would soon be forced to rethink my tired notions about such fundamentals as, oh, the meaning of life, the purposes of schooling, and the various ways in which an adolescent can be at risk of not being educated. To explain what I mean, let me tell you my own short version of Billy Charles's life story.

Billy Charles Barnett was born in the hills of northern Tennessee on 28 March 1974. When Billy Charles was two, his parents were divorced, and his mother received custody of him. His father moved to another part of the state, where he remarried and divorced several times, never receiving custody of any of the children from those marriages. When Billy Charles was eight, his father returned to live near Dusty Hollow. Billy Charles began to visit his father a few times a year. At age thirteen, in the seventh grade, he began to spend more and more time with a dad who passionately loved to hunt and fish and trap. Billy Charles decided to move into his father's house, located in (he still insists, even today) "paradise": a densely wooded area, thoroughly distanced from the world of convenience stores, gas stations, and book-lined classrooms.

What had begun to stir in Billy Charles is easily remembered by most former thirteen-year-olds. Billy Charles was beginning to think about who he was: the son, the grandson, the great-grandson, and maybe the great-great-grandson of frontiersmen in the upper South who remained in that region as the frontier moved on. Perhaps the sons of each succeeding generation felt what Billy Charles has hinted to me: violated and abandoned, as "civilization" barged in to distort the shape of their lives. But even today the allure of the woods remains intoxicating to many of the menfolk, who have traditionally been charged with providing their families with the necessities of life.

Some of these men (Billy Charles's stepfather among them) have managed to relegate outdoor activities to the margins of their lives, taking to their shotguns and fishing gear only on weekends. But not Billy Charles. At least not since he started to become a man. Billy Charles has always loved the outdoors, but what his mother calls his "obsession" with hunting, fishing, and trapping began a couple of years ago and accounts (she insists) for his initial desire to live with his father.

That was a glorious time, according to Billy Charles. He was ecstatic to finally have for his very own a father to connect him to the past that lived within him, a male parent versed in the ways of the wilderness to guide him into his own Appalachian manhood. Almost daily Billy Charles and his father went out in the wilds, the two of them together, teacher and apprentice. Billy Charles was joyously receiving an education in the *real* basics, eagerly learning the time-honored skills of survival (as opposed to such pale school-honored imitations such as how to write a check or fill out a job application). He was absorbed in the fundamentals of the world around him. Almost daily for more than a year, rain or shine, this wilderness school was in session. Even after the master turned on his eager pupil. Even, at least for a while, after the beatings began.

The friction started early in the summer when Billy Charles's father introduced some female strangers into the household: a new wife and a nine-year-old stepdaughter. Billy Charles's version is that he was now burdened with cooking for four instead of for two. ("It was a lot more work and all she [the stepmother] ever did was eat ice cream and watch TV.") The resentment probably runs even deeper, rooted in the slight Billy Charles must have felt as his father's attention was divided and shared with others. Whatever the cause, tensions rose, and the beatings increased in frequency and in severity, reaching a peak when his father attacked him with a horsewhip.

So a father turns viciously on a son who, in a time of delicate adolescent need, is reluctant to leave—until the final incident of abuse when the new family decides to vacation in Florida.

While in Florida Billy Charles wrote a letter to his mother, describing his increasingly unhappy life. His father somehow managed to read the letter, and Billy Charles awoke, he says, to the pain of being pulled from the couch by his hair and slammed across the room. Not even the memory of the exciting encounter with a hammerhead shark on a previous day's deep-sea expedition could prevent a second change of custody. Not even the image of his father's face that, as Billy Charles poignantly admitted to me, now makes him depressed when it appears before him unbeckoned. So, on the verge of manhood, Billy Charles went back to Mama, back to a place strewn with so many obstacles to his escape.

Billy Charles has always resisted any encroachment of the school world on his freedom outside. Rarely, for example, has he deigned to do his homework. But he is frequently reminded of his sins of omission, as his mother and three sisters collaborate on school assignments in the crowded kitchen. So he retreats further inward, into a bedroom shared with two young men in their early twenties—his cousin, Carl, and Teddy, a friend of Carl's. (Only temporary boarders, says Billy Charles's stepdad, only until Carl's parents "work things out.") What does he do there all night? Billy Charles corroborated what one of his teachers told me: "I asked him and he said, 'I crawl into bed and I die.' That's what he said, 'I just die.'"

If Billy Charles feels cramped, is he ever tempted to create some artificial space for himself through the use of drugs? His mother once caught him using an amphetamine. He was promptly hauled off to the police station, and this experience, his mother believes, was sufficiently traumatic for him to swear off any further drug use. Maybe so. But an earlier, much more stunning incident seems to have produced a deeper fear, at least of harder drugs. Several years ago, as Billy Charles tells it, a good friend, while sitting right beside him, had injected himself with an overdose. Just a couple of nine-year olds in northern Tennessee, one watching the other die, 1980s style. Recently the memory was revived when Teddy's girlfriend died in an identical manner. This, too, has depressed Billy Charles. I have wondered (but have lacked the courage to ask) about the possible relationship between these morbid memories and his own "specific suicidal ideations."

Billy Charles's imagination is his only source of escape during his self-described "imprisonment" by day. The school bus deposits him at Dusty Hollow Middle School at 8:15 every morning, and by second period—math, the period when the cage seems the smallest—Billy Charles is gone. He leaves through his mind—but always on foot. "I am walking in the hills," he says, recalling the leaves and the ground and the foxes and the possums. "I love to walk." Before meeting Billy Charles I had never known a fifteen-year-old without the slightest desire to drive a car. But driving is simply not of interest to him. Says Billy Charles, "I can walk to wherever I want to go."

Although Billy Charles is rarely present in spirit at school, he drifts less often out of his social studies and reading classes. The social studies class is taught by Billy Charles's favorite teacher, a bright, inventive young man who attempts to inject some liveliness into classroom activities with various simulation games, films, and student-centered projects.

Billy Charles's interest in reading class may be surprising, for Billy Charles has never been an avid reader. There is an encyclopedia in his house, and there are dictionaries. But there are few books and no daily newspaper. Billy Charles has not been raised in a home in which reading is seen as a delicious way to spend idle time. Perhaps his relative success in reading class is due to the special attention that is afforded him there. Billy Charles scores fairly well on most standardized tests, but he was placed in a "special education" reading class because he had been "disruptive" in other classes and was considered more "manageable" in smaller groups. He is reportedly less abusive and obnoxious to the reading teacher.

For the most part, though, school and the world of Billy Charles do not over-lap. On weekdays, he is locked in his school's embrace, but he is often dreaming of another time, another place, imagining that he is free, his own man in a future when every day is Saturday. His is a vision awash in nostalgia, adamantly culling out for celebration only the pleasant features of the past—the thrill of the catch, the pan-fired trout, and the time spent under his father's benign tute-lage—while screening out the unbearable: his father's scowl, his friend's limp body, or anything (like, say, a car or a classroom) invented since the Industrial Revolution. But the selectivity of Billy Charles's memory is understandable, and it represents, I believe, a hopeful sign. For it is only when his defenses break down and the grim ghosts of episodes past invade his psyche that Billy Charles seems most seriously at risk of abandoning more than just a formal education.

Does his vision of the future include earning a living? Billy Charles is utterly convinced that his own talents at tapping the bounty of nature will be sufficient to provide the necessities of life. As if to seal his argument, he points to his father, who works at odd jobs (currently selling bait out of a small store) to supplement his "natural" income. Others in the area are skeptical about the possibility of living only off the land these days, pointing to stringent enforce-ment of the legal limitations regarding season and size of catches.

And is Billy Charles foreseeing the possibility of a future family whose hungry mouths demand more than he can provide? Odds are that Billy Charles will once again find his hours divided into time lived and time served, as the time clock replaces the clock on the classroom wall. Still, his expectations are so robustly romantic, so close to those that even members of my branch of our frontier culture were so recently forced to abandon, that I have found myself hoping along with him: maybe there is a way. What if, for example, he changed his mind about the ethics of teaching for a living? Billy Charles recently forked over $100 for a week-end of instruction in a "trapping school." He found it rather useless (as would any advanced student in a remedial class). "But," I asked, "have you ever thought of opening a school of your own or becoming a guide to earn your own money?"

Grinning, Billy Charles answered, "Oh no, I don't believe that it's right to sell just words, to sell what you know, to make a living."

When I pointed out to him that words are precisely what his teachers sell, his reply was another grin. But Billy Charles is young, so we may hope for future compromises of his rigorous ethical standards. Getting paid for opening up his treasure chest of backwoods wisdom to weekend sportsmen still seems to me both pragmatic and honorable.

Of course, Billy Charles wouldn't need any more formal schooling for such an occupation. On the contrary, if this were his goal, school might then be precisely what he already believes it to be: an unwarranted roadblock on the path to the "good life." This is an unsettling notion to those of us who work devotedly toward fulfilling those goals of universal mandatory schooling. But what are those goals? By the time such academically disinclined students such as Billy Charles reach the middle grades, we think we see their future just ahead. To paraphrase the vice principal at his school, Billy Charles will, at best, become a common laborer like his stepfather, perhaps working nights operating within a forklift. And seldom, if ever, will he read a newspaper or a novel or a book of poetry.

So we abandon any lingering hopes for Billy Charles's conversion to a world of erudition and instead focus on *our* version of the basics. Teenagers unlikely ever to attend college must, we assume, be equipped with the mental skills appropriate to a working-class life: minimal competence in the basics; maybe an additional dash of content from the dominant culture (what *every* American needs to know); the basic skills of a trade, which we hope will be acquired in a high school vocational track; and, certainly, the employee's attitude, a demeanor tacitly encouraged by the organizational structure of the school and composed of a nexus of behavioral norms (such as perseverance, promptness, diligence, and intellectual docility) needed for the industrial workplace. If the non-college-bound acquire these learnings, we the taxpayers are placed at lower risk of having to fork over welfare money, and prospective employers are placed at lower risk of having to provide remedial education for candidates for employment.

But, I ask myself again, what of students such as Billy Charles who have equipped themselves to eke out a living (maybe even legally) within the cracks of the modern global economy? Billy Charles is not illiterate (and perhaps no more aliterate than the average citizen), and he possesses much more than the minimal knowledge needed for his own way of life. Could it be that Billy Charles's economic well-being is jeopardized only by our persistent attempts to inculcate values and behaviors that are, in fact, counterproductive to the successful conduct of his line of work? What use, after all, are passivity and punctuality to denizens of the forest?

Stated flatly, is Billy Charles at risk only if he stays in school? On those moments when I forget about the purposes of schooling that transcend the narrow focus on careers, my answer is yes. Then I am visited by Maria Montessori's vivid metaphor of students in rigid rows of desks as butterflies pinned to a display case. I confess to entertaining, at those moments, the impossible fantasy of pulling the pin and setting Billy Charles free.

How many other Billy Charleses are there—potential dropouts with the wits and wherewithal to survive financially in a world that worships the high school diploma? The conventional wisdom—the wisdom of my subculture, the legitimated wisdom—says "not many." There are other exceptions to the rule, of course, including the future stars of stage, screen, or playing field, the youthful heirs of family fortunes, or even the honest entrepreneurs-to-be. But I am incapable of imagining many stories like that of Billy Charles.

Nevertheless, I am reluctant to abandon the promises of schooling, even for such an exceptional case as Billy Charles. Indeed, his very exceptionality invites us to look beyond the narrowly pragmatic, utilitarian objectives of schooling to recollect a more substantial notion of the purposes of education. His case revives our fading dreams of a broader sort of empowerment that schools once hoped to provide for *all* American children, regardless of their economic or social backgrounds. This included the power to use the disciplines for penetrating more deeply into one's own past and present world, the power to imagine a wide range of alternative worlds in other times and places, and the power to express these understandings by employing many forms of literacy—verbal, visual, musical, kinesthetic, and so on.

This is where the exceptionality of Billy Charles ends and his commonality begins. For these are powers of thought and expression so often denied not only to the Billy Charleses among us, but also to the many respectable students for whom schooling is merely endured for the payoff of financial security and social standing. Them I have known much longer, those classroom drones who remain (like Billy Charles) seriously at risk of never becoming truly educated. They may pass their courses, but they are just as inevitably failed by their schools.

The institution of the school has also failed to facilitate mutual acquaintance among the people who inhabit it. I will not document the obstacles that have kept teachers and administrators from seeing Billy Charles as I have been privileged to see him. I leave it to other essays to explore the kind of restructuring that is needed before schoolpeople can pay closer attention to the life histories of other students like Billy Charles. His relatively benign experiences in a less crowded reading class and in a livelier social studies class only hint at the directions of that restructuring.

But even educators like Billy Charles's reading and social studies teachers will usually need help in acquiring the kind of knowledge that I lacked when I first met that scruffy stranger under McDonald's golden arches. Cocooned in the world of the middle-class educator, we are insulated from unfamiliar norms and ways of life. We have lost—indeed, we have been systematically encouraged to lose—the ability to reach out to honor the places (whether the barrio, the ghetto, the reservation, the Appalachian holler, or simply the peaks and pits of adolescence) where our students live.

Of course, a restructuring that gives teachers the time, the resources, and the motivation to learn about the individual worlds of their students will be only a beginning. Empathy alone is not enough. It is merely a necessary condition for a second element crucial to good teaching: the development of educational activities that can broaden students' horizons. Teachers in a school with a Billy Charles Barnett will not only need to understand the importance of making turtle soup, they will also need to entice students to study cuisines from other cultures. Math teachers will need the curricular finesse to lead students outward from field-and-stream economics to numeracy in other contexts. However, as John Dewey wisely noted long ago, one cannot effectively lead students outward without starting from the place where they currently reside.

Empowering teachers (and students) in this way may require more resources than our society is willing to provide. We will need to reeducate teachers, to reduce their workload, and to purchase material resources to link the local community with the larger one. Thus far, we have lacked the vision and the will to commit the resources necessary to this effort. Instead, we have sometimes resorted to gimmicks to lure our children back to school. In some Florida schools, pizza is offered as an incentive to attend classes. In one Kentucky district, a snazzy car is raffled off as a door prize for students with good attendance records. But should such bribery succeed in filling classrooms with warm bodies, will this no longer be a nation at risk of losing the hearts and wasting the minds of its young people? I think not.

I venture to suggest the heresy that we would not necessarily be better off were the dropout rate to decrease dramatically tomorrow. We conveniently forget the role of the traditional American school in perpetuating a seriously impoverished notion of what constitutes an education. Before we could say that a lower dropout rate is good news, we would need to know whether the reasons for not leaving school are valid ones. Are students remaining because we have become serious about introducing meaning into the life of the classroom? Are they staying because we have equipped our teachers with the means for knowing and respecting their students' pasts even as they attempt to open up their futures? And why would we need to know whether these things are occurring? Because Billy Charles Barnett has reminded us that doing anything less is still a very risky business.

Chapter 8

What Are Some Criteria for Assessing Arts Based Research?

We turn now to the assessment or appraisal of arts based research. In order to appraise the degree to which a piece of arts based research is a success, and therefore worth sharing with members of an audience, we must return momentarily to the discussion regarding the meaning of success in relation to arts based research. What constitutes success in arts based research? We have argued that a good piece of arts based research succeeds in enticing a reader or viewer into taking another look at dimensions of the social world that had come to be taken for granted. This may result in a surprise for the viewer and even in the promotion of an interrogative disposition, one in which the viewer questions the usefulness of the "usual kind of picture" and the set of values that had served to support that perhaps stale perspective. This, in turn, may lead a community of viewers or readers into a conversation about the utility of alternative ways of interpreting and understanding social events and issues.

SUCCEEDING AS ART AND AS RESEARCH: CRITERIA VERSUS STANDARDS

We suggest that, to be useful, a piece of arts based research must succeed both as a work of art and as a work of research. It must be, that is, of sufficiently high quality to lead members of an audience into a powerful experience, into a *researching* of social phenomena. But in order to accomplish this, certain aesthetic qualities must be present within the work. Lacking these qualities, the work may fail to attract the viewer into vicariously experiencing the phenomena portrayed within the text of the work and thus fail to stimulate a reconsideration of those phenomena.

The assessment of a work of arts based research requires the use of *criteria*. Criteria are essentially reminders to an assessor of what can be paid attention to in the evaluation of a work. Criteria facilitate the perusal and the judgment made by someone regarding the significance or value of what has been created. Consider, for example, the criteria used to assess the quality of a fictional short story such as that by Gordimer (1985; also see Chapter 6). These criteria may serve as indicators of the degree to which the various literary elements of "A City of the Dead, A City of the Living" are likely to entice readers into rethinking important social issues, such as those related to privacy, oppression, and the fear and defeatism of the subjugated in a police state.

For a work of literature such as Gordimer's (1985), critics may disagree on the sufficiency of the presence of pertinent criteria for achieving that outcome. When there are differences among critics concerning the significance of what has been judged, deliberation among judges may follow. A strong consensus among critics—one way or another—may aid potential readers in deciding whether to spend time and energy in reading (or viewing) the work for themselves.

The same is true for a work of arts based research submitted to a journal. A set of criteria may be offered to reviewers by editors for their assessment of the work. An editor then may, on the basis of the judgments of the reviewers, make a determination as to whether the work succeeds in that for which arts based research is designed and whether it is, therefore, worthy of publication. Is the work, that is, worth the time and effort of readers in reading or viewing it? A process of this sort was likely employed, for example, as the editors of the *Harvard Education Review* reviewed and deliberated regarding the suitability of Sullivan's (2000) article for publication in their journal. Very often, a journal will supply a list of criteria for judging the quality of a submission that is compiled by the authors and sent to outside reviewers deemed qualified by the editors.

The use of criteria in judging the qualities within a work of arts based research is not the same as the use of *standards*. The distinction between criteria and standards is not broadly understood in many research and evaluation communities. Our propensity to want to quantify information has led to neglect in identifying other means through which the assessment of the quality of some performance or object could be made. But John Dewey, writing in *Art as Experience* (1934/1958) made the distinction between criteria and standards clear, at least in relation to works of art. He wrote,

Standards define things with respect to quantity . . . The standard, being an external and public thing, is applied physically. The yard-stick is physically laid down upon the things measured to determine their length . . . When, therefore, the word "standard is used with respect to judgment of works of art, nothing but confusion results . . . The critic is really judging, not measuring physical fact. He is concerned with something individual, not comparative—as is all measurement. His subject matter is qualitative, not quantitative.

If there are no standards for works of art and hence none for criticism . . . there are nevertheless criteria in judgment, so that criticism does not fall in the field of mere impressionism . . . But such criteria are not rules or prescriptions. They are the result of an endeavor to find out what a work of art is as an experience: the kind of experience which constitutes it. (pp. 307, 309)

Standards, therefore, imply the employment of a quantitative metric that enables one to enumerate or to summarize quantity. One can count the number of literary flourishes—say, the number of times a particular metaphor is employed—in a short story, but the significance of those literary design elements are not revealed simply by their number. What matters is the capacity for enabling members of an audience to reexperience the world from a previously unavailable vantage point, and the use of criteria is a way for an assessor to be reminded of what to pay attention to in judging that capacity.

Standards are indeed measures of quantity. And as such, they can, more or less, be easily applied and used universally. Criteria are much more slippery. Criteria demand judgment regarding significance or value. Art critics do not seek a universal standard for making judgments about the quality of a work. What they do seek are achievements related to whatever the criteria are that are appropriate for the work being assessed. The particular criteria that are applicable to a work depend, at least in some measure, on the particular character of the work. Appraising the quality of a skater doing figure eights require criteria that are quite different than those applied to the same skater doing improvisational dance on ice. Similarly, criteria used to make judgments about Saldana's (2005) ethnodrama may be somewhat different from those used to assess the usefulness of a work of grounded theory. A part of the mark of expertise is having available a variety of criteria that suit a variety of performances or works. Sometimes precision and assessment is both desirable and appropriate. At other times, it may be inappropriate. We are reminded of Aristotle's comment that "the educated man seeks only as much precision as the subject matter will admit. It is as foolish to seek precision from a poet as it is metaphor for a mathematician."

GENERAL CRITERIA FOR JUDGING ARTS BASED RESEARCH

In his discussion of the use of criteria, Dewey (1934/1959), of course, was talking about criticism in relation to works of art. Although arts based research may seldom secure a level of achievement represented by the phrase *work of art*, the function of criticism in relation to the criteria which guides it is, we believe, as relevant for arts based research as it is for paintings, novels, or dance performances. But while appropriate criteria may be different for judging various genres of arts or arts based research, assessment is not necessarily idiosyncratic. There are some general criteria that serve well in judging the quality of most arts based research. These include but are not limited to the following:

- Incisivenss
- Concision
- Coherence
- Generativity
- Social significance
- Evocation and illumination

Incisiveness

What do we mean by incisiveness? By incisiveness, we mean that the research gets to the heart of a social issue. It goes to its core. It does not get swamped with details that have no inherent significance and do little to increase the cogency of the research itself. Incisiveness means that the work of research is penetrating; it is sharp in the manner in which it cuts to the core of an issue.

An incisive observation was made to Elliot Eisner during a visit to a junior high school in Poughkeepsie, New York, by the principal of that school. Eisner had been doing some work for the National Endowment for the Humanities. This worked pertained to the role, if any, that the humanities played in the curriculum of this junior high school. Early on in his visit to the school, Eisner was told by one of the secretaries sitting behind a long metal counter that when he was through at the end of the day the school principal would like to see him. The end of the day came, and he dutifully went back to the office in which he had entered when he arrived and was told that the principal would see him.

Eisner and the principal had a conversation about his visit in which he tried to be informative without violating any methodological considerations that needed to be honored. The principal looked at him at one point and said, "You know, there is a particular feature of schools that has always intrigued me." Eisner asked what that was, and the principal turned around and looked at him and said, "Schools are places with very few soft surfaces."

Now it is the case that Eisner had spent 40 years in schools of one kind of another but believed that he had never encountered a comment so incisive and so revealing. He did not need to go out to the field to visit schools to count the numbers of soft surfaces versus hard surfaces in them. He already knew what the surfaces of schools looked like, and the principal's comment simply gelled for him the reality that had been tacit rather than explicit in his experience. This is an example of an incisive comment made by a perceptive practitioner to a professor whose major focus was on the conceptual development of language and thought about education.

When it comes to a work of art—or arts based research—incisiveness may be found through the observations that are embedded in the research text. This sort of cultural text may lack the directness of the individual incisive statement like the one uttered by that school principal. But could Saldana, Finley, and Finley's ethnodrama "Street Rat" be any more incisive as it gets at the heart of issues related to homeless teenagers? Could its descriptions of the manner in which these young people adapt to the dire circumstances in which they find themselves be any more telling? Could the depiction of the strategies they invent and deploy for maintaining a semblance of normalcy in a scattered and scary existence be any more keen and piercing? The incisiveness that permeates the script and production does indeed offer the potential for waking the reader up to a strange world that appears new and yet always existed in the shadowy corners of the city that they had never explored on their own. The incisiveness of the work enabled someone who was once a relatively privileged youth—Tom Barone—to vicariously experience the conditions of lives as lived in parts of the city in which he was raised but lives of which he was previously (for whatever reason) ignorant. The production of *Street Rat* that he witnessed in Arizona—and not Louisiana—helped him to begin to understand how certain social and economic forces operate at a very local level to victimize young people.

Concision

Another quality of a work of art—or arts based research—pertains to the degree to which it occupies the minimal amount of space or includes the least amount of verbiage necessary for it to serve its primary, heuristic purpose of enabling members of an audience to see social phenomena from a fresh perspective. Any additional material simply diminishes the capacity of the piece to achieve that purpose, waters down the power of the work, and hence its effectiveness. In his *Poetics*, Aristotle (1961) reminded us that one of the worst epithets that can be hurled at a story is to call it *episodic*; indeed, any work of narrative art or research that rambles or meanders aimlessly fails in terms of the criterion of concision. Rather than offering tight-fisted power, it may be instead an invitation for readers' minds to wander or become confused. A really good arts based research text may therefore be characterized as lean, insofar as every single word contributes to the whole of the text. Such works avoid any unnecessary padding that adds little to the gestalt.

What allows for concision is the presence of a controlling insight—some would call it a theme—that serves as a guide for the artist or researcher in making judgments about which material to include and which to exclude. For a reader or viewer of a work, the theme may only emerge after some degree of immersion within the work; it may not be immediately obvious. Similarly for the artist or researcher the theme may arise only after some time spent in the field. But an inability to concisely address a theme may result in what some qualitative researchers call a "data dump," a text in which all facts uncovered or observations offered in the research process are seen as equal in significance. Concision requires a kind of intelligent discrimination based on a sense of what sorts of questions the researcher would raise in the minds of the audience about the social phenomena being researched.

Concision may be found in many of the examples of art and arts based research mentioned in this book. Had not Doisneau's (1973) photograph of the two patrons in a Parisian café been focused in tightly and skillfully enough, all sorts of extraneous images would surely have diminished its effectiveness. Similarly, in the literary essay by Barone (2000), the focus was on only certain dimensions of the life story of a potential school dropout and not all that Barone had learned about him in the conduct of the research. The theme of "at riskness" (as adumbrated in the title of the piece) served the author–researcher as a qualitative mediator that allowed for him to select the most telling details and omit reams of other field notes and to thereby tell the story in only a few pages. It aims to encourage readers to think about what it means for a student to be at risk in a manner that cuts against the usual way of thinking about a phrase that has acquired the status of a cliché. Barone attempted to omit any verbiage that did not contribute to that aim.

Coherence

A third criterion that can be used to perceive and assess arts based research deals with matters of coherence. By coherence, we mean the creation of a work of arts based research whose features hang together as a strong form. Gestalt psychologists often refer to the law of *pragnanz*, a law that pertains to the way components in a complex form hang together. Does the piece of music display coherence? That is, do its forms work together to provide a musical image that is satisfying. Does a short story hang together so that the reader has a sense of completion in reading the story? Does a painting "work"? Does it represent a "good gestalt"? One of the lessons that the arts teach—especially with good teachers—is to enable students to look at the whole of the work and to see the kinds of interactions that exist between and among the qualities that the individual has created. The color might be a little too bright, the line a bit too strong, the form a bit too light to provide a good gestalt.

Consider the power of a film such as *Pan's Labyrinth*. The theme of that profoundly insightful movie may be seen as the role of the imagination in political resistance. Each of the artistic dimensions of the film—the plot, the pacing, the musical score, the cinematography, the sets, the acting, and especially the fantastic imagery—were all parts of an intricate puzzle that stimulate the viewer to think about mythology in relation to issues of political repression. For Tom Barone, the manner in which its parts cohered promoted one of the greatest cinematic experiences of his lifetime. Moreover, part of the wonderment of such a film is that it may be returned to repeatedly to reexperience the manner in which the parts do indeed cohere—and thereby to think again about the significance of the theme in contemporary terms.

Part of the business of learning to make forms that hang together is learning how to see and respond to the ones that the individual artist and other artists have made. The same is true in dealing with arts based research. Arts based research is, as we have suggested, the result of a creation of expressive form that reveals qualities of life that might otherwise not have been experienced. So, as with the other criteria mentioned so far, the reader is invited to apply this criterion of coherence to the various examples of art and arts based research included in this book. Consider the literary style autoethnographic essay by Ruth Behar (1996). One may find this essay to be not only incisive and concise but one may also notice the manner in which it continuously circles back on itself as the author returns to a theme that is manifested both in the storytelling and in the more "scholarly" commentary that adds an additional dimension to the relevant themes and subthemes implicit and explicit within the piece.

Generativity

The fourth criterion pertains to the generativity of the arts based research itself. By generativity, we mean the ways in which the work enables one to see or act upon phenomena even though it represents a kind of case study with an n of only 1. Generativity is not to be confused with the traditional research notion of generalizability, although the two notions are similar.

In many traditional forms of scientific research, the "rules" of statistical inference require a random selection process in order to draw appropriate conclusions from the sample that pertained to the population from which they were drawn. Such a mandate certainly has its utilities and is employed in virtually all statistically driven studies. But arts based research is not primarily relevant for what can be measured and made statistical. Indeed, we believe that "generalizations" take place all of the time without randomly selecting the "units" intended to represent some population. In other words, we "generalize" not only from an $n = x$ but from a sample that is represented by $n = 1$.

The arts typically project an image that reshapes our conception of some aspect of the world or that sheds light on aspects of the world we had not seen before. Good arts based research generalizes in such a fashion. It has "legs," allowing you to go someplace. It does not simply reside in its own backyard forever but rather possesses the capacity to invite you into an experience that reminds you of people and places that bear familial resemblances to the settings, events, and characters within the work.

Aristotle once commented that poetry is "truer" than history because poetry deals with the world in its most general sense while history focuses on particulars. In the play, *Death of a Salesman* (Miller, 1967), the central character, Willie Loman, is portrayed as a failing salesman. Now if the play is simply about a fictional character whose name is Willie Loman, then the significance of the play as a work of art is diminished. But if *Death of a Salesman* is about middle age and about the ways in which failing salesmen cope with getting older and losing one's job and having disappointments with one's children, then the meaning of the play becomes significant. Although not nearly as important a work as *Salesman*, a similar sort of generativity may be found in the reading of Barone's (2000) literary essay on Billy Charles Barnett. Some teachers who have read the story/essay have reported that it has generated reflections about the "Billy Charleses" in their midst—their own students who may not possess much of the symbolic capital honored within the dominant culture yet who are bright and capable in ways not appreciated within their school settings. If generating questions about the taken-for-granted definitions of at riskness may be said to be the aim of the piece, then at least for some readers it apparently succeeds.

Social Significance

Social significance is the fifth criterion we identify in our efforts to describe what can be attended to in the appraisal of arts based research. Significance pertains to the character, meaning, and import of the central ideas of the work. It seems to us foolish to pursue at great cost what is intellectually or aesthetically trivial in doing arts based research. What makes a work significant is its thematic importance, its focus on the issues that make a sizable difference in the lives of people within a society. What one is looking for is something that matters, ideas that count, important questions to be raised.

Determining what is significant requires a frame of reference that gives significance or secures significance from the phenomena that is being examined. Significance doesn't speak for itself. It requires an interpretive or thematic frame, and part of the preparation of arts based researchers is to acquire the frames of reference that they can employ in doing research in general and arts based research in particular. Thus, we want to know not only what happened but why it is important. If it isn't important in the eyes of its readers, it will be dismissed as something trivial. We believe that arts based researchers want to avoid such a verdict.

Think about the important issues that are highlighted in the examples of arts based research mentioned in this book. They include issues of homelessness, of racial divides, of political oppression and the nature of freedom, of adolescent alienation and the curriculum of the school, of the relationship between "attention" and the sensory details of the empirical world, of the possibilities of informal education by a parent, of female empowerment, of the nature of forgiveness, of the insecurities of immigrants in a new world, of the culture clash between a new teacher and the school, and townspeople from another social class, region of the county, race, and so on.

Of course, we are not insisting that any arts based work is to be completely dismissed if the topic it addresses is less than earth shattering. But we are suggesting that it may be unfair to readers and viewers to take up their time by trying to focus their attention on the insignificant and trivial. We believe that the best arts based research aims to make a difference in the world.

Evocation and Illumination

The sixth criterion that we identify for the assessment of arts based research pertains to its evocative and illuminative qualities. Evocation is important because it is through evocation and illumination that one begins to *feel* the meanings that the work is to help its readers grasp.

In using the term *readers*, we are not restricting our comments to people who read books or articles or newspapers; we mean people who secure meaning in whatever form it needs to be read. Paintings are read, music is read, and dance is read. Evocation is therefore an epistemological means for the acquisition of meaning. If a person is numbed to the visual world, it will remain an unreachable source for that individual. If the visual text does not possess the capacity for reaching that individual, then again there is no communication.

Evocation pertains to feeling. It may signify an aesthetic experience. Its contrast is the anesthetic, a process that dulls pain or that suppresses feeling. The arts traffic in feeling, and they are often anesthetic to those who have not yet learned to "read" them.

What sorts of feelings are evoked as one views and reads the examples of arts based research included in this book? The evocation of that feeling may result not merely in a cognitive understanding of the material being viewed or read. Arts based works do, of course, like all art, possess a cognitive dimension. Indeed the criterion of "illumination" as applied to arts based research pertains to the ways in which the work illuminates a terrain, a process, an individual. It sheds light often by defamiliarizing an object or a process so that it can be seen in a way that is entirely different than a way in which customary modes of perception operate. It calls attention to itself and when generative, to the processes or events that the creator of the work is attempting to reveal. It is not for nothing that we often talk about a work and its "shedding light" on something. Given the limiting influence of customary forms of perception, the ability to discover new angles from which to see is no trivial accomplishment. In fact, it is often through such observation that we learn to problematize the customary and to see something as general rather than as an individual event or object. Sight can be promoted, and evocation moves that process forward. But when illumination is combined with the quality of evocation within a vivid experience, the work will serve both to illuminate cognitively and to prompt the percipient to respond emotionally, as well. And the whole of the experience may serve to motivate the viewer or reader to reflect more deeply about the issues that are embodied so vividly within the particulars of the work and even to act differently in the nearby world outside of the work.

"Broken and Buried in Arkansas" is an example of a short story that evokes a sense of what it is like to be a Teach For America volunteer in a cultural setting that is foreign to her. Its details from a "nonfictional" setting are effectively selected and arranged to enable readers to experience—that is understand and feel—what it is like to live and to struggle to make a difference through teaching in such a situation. Its power to evoke and illuminate can lure a reader into reconsidering a vague but somewhat settled set of judgments about a national program such as Teach For America.

AVOIDING A STATIC CRITERIOLOGY

Each one of these criteria we have offered functions as a cue for perception. It may remind the assessor of what to look for across the board of all arts based research genres, serving as a kind of common basis for the assessment of all arts based research. But it is not altogether clear at this stage of the development of this form of research whether such a "common basis" would be an asset or a liability. We can well imagine that assessment practices in arts based research could become standardized. This is, after all, what most social programs seek. There is utility in commonality, to be sure, but there is also liability. One can get locked into criteria that constrain innovation and that dampen imagination. Technological orientations to success and to the assessment of programmatic success are attractive aspirations for those who seek standardization. For those whose values and aspirations are closer to the arts, local innovation—indeed, individual innovation—is far more attractive.

There is, of course, a lack of efficiency in an individualized approach to assessment. A lack of efficiency often is the result of a difficulty in making comparisons across performances of individuals whose performance significantly differs in form, intent, and quality. Comparability is compromised when standardization is diminished.

So we offer these criteria merely as a starting point for thinking about the appraisal of works of arts based research. We do not believe that we can have an effective arts based research program without some degree of common reflection over what might be attended to in looking at such work. Thus, in a certain sense, we compromise between, on the one hand, common criteria and, on the other, criteria that are idiosyncratic to the work itself. This may appear as a dilemma, but it is also a reality. Recipe books will give you the means and the sequence needed to produce a chocolate cake to a particular standard. The more detailed and prescriptive the recipe, the more likely that the cakes made from that recipe will be indistinguishable from one another. We prefer innovation. We prefer surprise. We prefer imagination, even though such aspirations may cost us what in the measurement literature is referred to as reliability.

So, finally, we invite you, the readers, to use your own judgment in applying these criteria to the examples of the works of arts based research included in this book and to those many that are not included. But we also urge you to use your imagination in ascertaining other criteria that may emerge from your encounters with arts based work in the future. As an informed and imaginative reviewer and critic of examples of arts based research, you may serve to ensure that those works positioned to achieve the purpose of raising questions about important social issues in a powerful manner will more likely to be made available to others.

Chapter 9

Is There a Place for Theory in Arts Based Research?

One does not normally associate arts based research with deep theoretical conceptions. Is this "neglect" justified? Is arts based research an a-theoretical enterprise? To answer that question, we first need to be clear about the meaning of theory in any enterprise. We think it is useful to draw a distinction between theory as an effort to *account for* some set of empirical relationships and theory as an effort to give an *account of* the world as it is. Most of what we have talked about in this book thus far has pertained to descriptive efforts to make vivid what one had not noticed. Can nondiscursive forms give us an account of something? The answer seems clear. Art forms describe all of the time. Consider plays such as *A Raisin in the Sun* or photographs by Dorothea Lang. These works do a great deal to call attention to aspects of reality that in some cases we would rather not see. In a deep sense, they give us an account of a state of affairs that command our attention. But can they explain? Can they account for what they have given an account of? Again, it depends on what one means by understanding. If understanding depends upon the forms that promote it and if these forms are diverse in character—that is, if they come in varieties—then it is reasonable to assume that there are different forms of understanding that are promoted by different forms of representation. These forms of representation need not be discursive, although in our culture they probably would have a discursive character to them. Discursiveness, however, is not a required feature of the form. The presence of nondiscursive experience provides for an awareness that when artistically crafted enables us to grasp some aspects of the meaning of things. Nondiscursive theory is not an oxymoron as long as our conception of theory is expanded beyond the narrower confines of traditional scientific discourse.

THE DIDACTIVES OF THE IMAGE

In looking at theory this way, we can recognize the fact that there is a kind of didacticism in much nondiscursive material. How a teapot is designed, what it says about its owners, the period in which it was made, can all be revealed in experiencing the pot. We mention this simply to illustrate the idea that we do not wish to incarcerate theory in a scientific model exclusively. We want to say about theory that it is an effort to explain. Such explanations can come through the generation and communication of images. Indeed, the presence of images are often more powerful in explaining a situation than a discursive rendering of the same situation. As we know, a picture is worth a thousand words.

There is another sense in which theory functions in arts based research. That other sense pertains to the fact that forms of representation are expressive and make their contribution by rendering vividly some aspect of the world at hand. How, for example, a family converses around the dinner table is something that requires more than attention to language, it requires attention to body language, to those subtle cues that people use to learn about the deeper meanings of the conversation. Arts based research can make such body language vivid in ways that discursive language is unlikely to reveal. Arts based research can provide the stuff that researchers can use to promote theoretical understanding of the traditional sort. Thus, out of connoisseurship come opportunities to generate conventional theory.

The process is something that can be likened to the perspective secured from the peak of Mount Everest. To have such an opportunity is to see the world from another angle, and by seeing the world from another angle, other explanations of the world can be built. Theory is both a tool for representing and a means for securing perspectives that make understanding possible.

Is this effort of ours to secure a place for theory in arts based research a strained effort to do what shouldn't have been done in the first place? Some readers might find that so. We, however, are interested in expanding our understanding of the varieties of ways in which explanations are given. We wish to give to the world of research another perspective of the means through which research can be undertaken. It seems to us that we have much greater tolerance for diversity in our commonsensical efforts to understand the world than we have in our discipline-oriented approaches to the study of human understanding.

When we look at the world through the eyes of diverse forms of representation, we find understanding promoted by film, poetry, the novel, narratives of all kinds, and dance. Now none of these, one might claim, are concerned with matters of truth; they are merely expressive options that can be chosen to provide one's impression of things. Such an objection is, we think, invalid. We do not seek certainty through arts based research but plausibility, and it is a plausibility that is promoted through the deliberations that occur and that are prompted by art forms. Arts based research is closer to the idea of "let us reason together" than it is about the swift pursuit of a certain outcome. Arts based research is intended to open up possibilities rather than to converge upon a single correct and true answer to a question or solution to a problem.

In some ways, arts based research reflects a mix of the ancient Greeks' conception of the productive domain, that domain concerned with making something, and the practical domain, that domain concerned with the execution of action. In both of these orientations to knowledge, the process of deliberation is central. The Greeks were not interested in measuring the speed of a bullet in flight; they were much more interested in understanding the flight of a butterfly.

Here again, the concern was with context-based knowledge and with forms that do not result in a single conception of uniformity to an absolutely true ideal. Deliberation, inquiry, and imagination are the values that give direction to arts based research. It is not helpful, we believe, to conceive of inquiry as a process that can be understood outside of the context in which it is to function. Arts based research provides a view of that context.

The major point we have emphasized thus far in this chapter pertains to the ways in which nondiscursive forms—forms such as music, narrative, film, and the like—enable us to grasp meanings that are in no way limited to discursive forms of language. As Michael Polanyi once commented, "We know more than we can tell." The limits of our language do not define the limits of our understanding. In fact, it can be argued—and we would so argue—that for literal language, for example, to be meaningful, it must be referenced in the reader or speaker to phenomena that are essentially qualitative in character. To speak about a tree as being green requires that the statement be understood by referencing greenness with the tree to the color green. To say that the color of a tree is "grue," one would leave readers without the ability to determine what grue is like, and how, for example, it compares with green. Our point is that language secures its meaning in part because of the way it denotes or connotes qualities. These qualities collectively in the use of language serve as the basic constituents of theoretical understanding. Language becomes meaningful when one is able to see the connection between the language as such and its referents. Language for the most part, but not exclusively, is dependent upon one's ability to imagine that to which the language refers. This is certainly as true for theoretical material as it is for what we think of as being nontheoretical. Another way of putting it is that language depends upon imagination to be meaningful. If a reader cannot imagine that to which language refers, the likelihood the language will be meaningful is low.

There is another sense in which the language employed in arts based research informs, and that other sense pertains to the expressive character of the language. The language used in art forms is expressive. One reads about the Crucifixion, but one can also see the Crucifixion in a 13th century painting. In both cases, the language is expressive, but it is expressive in different ways. Part of the artist's task, whether as a researcher or as a painter, is to shape language so that it conveys what words in their literal form cannot address. Artistically rendered forms contribute to the enlargement of human understanding because they do what poetry has been said to do, to say in words what words can never say.

TOWARD A WIDER CONCEPTION OF LANGUAGE

In writing about the theoretical contributions of the qualitative, we have said relatively little about the fact that the theoretical in its conventional form as a language-bearing enterprise and qualitatively constructed images can both be used in the same work. One does not have to pick one over the other; both can be employed to provide the forms of understanding that researchers seek. In fact, this is what criticism in the arts is intended to do. The critic looks at a situation, say a play or a painting, and brings to these two events a perspective that is informed by the events but that is also made possible by the ways in which what is brought to those events affect one's understanding of it. Critics write about the works they address. Teachers talk about the work and bring a bevy of language to bear upon those works. The interaction between the work and language can provide not a distraction from the work (although it could) but an enrichment of one's experience with the work.

In the field of education, images of classroom life can be made articulate by what the arts based researcher sees in the situation and what he or she makes of it. The task is a constructive one; we *make* sense of the world. In making sense, we give a certain power to what we have described. We gradually become smarter about those aspects of the world we have learned to address. The language we have acquired or invented to address those worlds has a payoff in more refined experience.

We hope it is clear that the most qualitative of practices have theoretical significance. To the extent to which those qualitative practices awaken us to meanings that otherwise would be buried under the rubble of language, to that extent, the arts as the quintessential qualitative achievement is also a vehicle for theoretical insight. Theory estranged from the qualitative is empty, just as the qualitative divorced from theory is meaningless. Concepts without percepts are blind, and percepts without concepts are empty.

There is another sense in which theory has its place in arts based research. That sense pertains to the fact that through arts based research we notice relationships that might not otherwise be seen. In doing so, our attention is called to other possibilities beyond those that exist for talking about or writing about the work or problem or issue at hand. To the extent to which arts based research heightens our consciousness to aspects of the world, it provides the material out of which theory, in its more conventional sense, can be generated. In other words, we can theorize about phenomena that we had not experienced earlier. To the extent to which arts based research is a way to widen and deepen our vision, to become wide awake, to notice what is subtle but significant, it provides the material for theoretical explanation in its more conventional form. This is no trivial accomplishment. Consider the concept of social structure. The concept of social structure is not a concept that grows on trees or that is found in a field of flowers. It is a human-made way to characterize the way in which people and places organize themselves. By becoming aware of such connections, it becomes possible to say something about what accounts for their existence as well as what is given an account of. This is an example of how theory, in its more abstract sense, follows awareness.

Of course, awareness also follows theory. This oscillation between the awareness of the world that arts based research makes possible and the uses of arts based research to help individuals become aware is something like an oscillating pendulum. The pendulum swings from one end to the other retracing its steps in the process. Once someone conceptualizes something called social structure, we can notice it in places we never did before. At the same time, the awareness of social structure is something that a novel, a painting, or a poem might promote.

The central theme of this book is that the enlargement of human understanding is the child of many forms of representation, not all of which are literal. Aesthetic and artistic material also perform a critical function in human understanding.

It is useful to note that the term *theory* comes from the Greek and refers to a process of considering, speculating, looking at. The roots of the term suggest a kind of visualization related to speculation and contemplation—that is, to look at. Now looking at some aspect of the world is a nondiscursive process. It is made discursive as individuals attempt to detect the rules and principles that guide the creation of the process. In its initial stages, we should not forget that theory is a mental image, something one makes in order to understand. We argue in this book that such making is not limited to discursive language but refers to any form used for purposes of representation and explanation.

The argument we mount here is that theory is not limited to statements or to propositions; it is not necessarily fettered to the linguistic. We argue that theory is a structure for the promotion of understanding, or, as Nelson

Goodman used to say, for the enlargement of mind. This argument depends on the ability to recognize that communication takes place through a variety of forms and that each of these forms—visual, auditory, olfactory, mathematical—sheds its own distinctive light on what is being attended to. Thus, putting together a complex form that promotes understanding can be said to be a theoretical enterprise.

You will recall that we indicated that theory at its root is a process that involves contemplation. It also involves action. Designing a play, or organizing a story, or choreographing a dance are all efforts that are subject to appraisal regarding the extent to which what has been created and experienced engenders some insight. This insight might refer to a form that is qualitative in character. With the aid of an artistically shaped form of representation, insight and understanding can be promoted. The argument of this book is that such forms of understanding are specific and unique.

There are a multitude of examples one can point to. For example, consider the ways in which advertising design firms shape a product, say an advertisement, for television, in order to promote sales. The music, the tempo of the visuals, and the character of what is being portrayed are all designed to influence; and they do. Such works do not meet at least one crucial aspect of arts based research: They are basically designed to persuade the "reader" to accept a conclusion that is already known by the person or group that designed the ad. But putting that aside for the moment, what we have in the well-designed ad is an image that is shaped qualitatively and that is intended to convey certain meanings, certain images, and certain statuses in order to sell a product. Who can deny that our view of the world is profoundly shaped by what advertisers create?

Consider film as a source of understanding. In film, we have a plot, we have characters who learn their roles in particular ways, we have lighting, and we often have music. In short, we create films by integrating a variety of resources—all of which are designed to capture interest and to generate experience that the readers of such material will find interesting, indeed satisfying. In school, we have a strong tendency to break down such contributions into their component parts. We tend to look at a subject one way and then move to another subject and look at it another way. This is ironic because the power of the film, or the play, or the dance is found in the relationships that are created by their authors. Again, paradoxically, we start with the whole and then gradually take it apart.

One of the important considerations in assessing the quality of research in the social sciences pertains to the determination of its validity. The meaning of the term *validity* is not self-explanatory. We do get some insight, however, by comparing the term *validity* to its antonym. That antonym is "invalid."

Now an invalid is someone who is handicapped or in some other way weak and without power. The term *invalid* is also used to signify that a document or ticket will no longer be honored in order to get access to, say, a symphony or a movie. In research in the social sciences, there is substantial interest in determining how a study could increase its validity. This is done by making a distinction between two types of validity: internal validity and external validity. The internal validity of a study pertains to the way in which a study was designed and whether, in principle, conclusions can be drawn from the premises or values of the conditions for which it was undertaken.

External validity, on the other hand, is intended to assess the relevance of the study to conditions the study was intended to address. The question asked here is, Is this study relevant to the population and the conditions it was intended to address? In this research paradigm, what one seeks overall are studies that have both internal and external validity—that is, they are studies that are designed to enable one to draw conclusions that will withstand logical scrutiny and they are designed to be relevant to a population in which one is interested. A study can have internal validity and no external validity. A study can also have external validity but no internal validity. How shall we think about validity for arts based research? Is arts based research simply an "anything goes" process for which there are no criteria?

To avoid arts based educational research being an anything goes process that evokes little credibility among its readers, we can think about increasing the validity of such research. There are two concepts relevant to promoting credibility in arts based research. We address them now. The first of these pertains to what is called structural corroboration. Structural corroboration relates to the preponderance of evidence located within the study that enables one to support its conclusion. Circumstantial evidence is an example of the study having structural corroboration. Even though direct evidence of a crime has not been identified, there are enough pieces in the evidence gathered to persuade a jury to convict or to pardon someone accused of a crime.

In arts based research structural corroboration is located in the preponderance of evidence located in the study itself. What one is seeking in the pursuit of structural corroboration is a set of questions that will have the effect of deepening one's analysis of the situation. Instead of merely looking at a photograph of a person who might be referred to as a "derelict," evidence could be found in the work that this is not the case. Structural corroboration is a gathering of many pieces of evidence that enable one to create a compelling whole. At its best, as we indicated, it deepens the conversation. It makes the analysis more sensitive; it yields an array of questions that will make more complex the analysis that was initially undertaken.

We sometimes say of a story that it will hold no water, by which we mean that is a sufficient number of problems with the analysis so that it undermines any cogency or credibility that one might otherwise secure.

A study has referential adequacy when one is able to find in the situation studied the qualities and meaning that an arts based research study should possess. The story rings true. The analysis is cogent and credible. The tale is coherent. The meanings are generalizable. In sum, the study persuades because of its validity. These criteria cannot be applied with a set of rules or as parts of operational definitions. They must be deliberated or discussed; one needs to exercise judgment in the absence of rule. To expect operational definitions of criteria is to expect what cannot be provided. When the criteria addressed material whose meanings are influenced by the way in which words have been shaded and observation offered, one uses forms that suit the conditions.

Poetry and literature are two ringing examples of the ways in which poets and writers shape language in order to convey meanings that would otherwise not be expressible. This absence of operationalism in poetry and in literature has never been a condemnation of their uses in sharing meanings and in providing powerful insights in the world. The form has to shape the meaning as much as the meaning of a statement must be formed so that it fits the circumstance. When Elizabeth Barrett Browning wrote, "How do I love thee? Let me count the ways." she was speaking metaphorically and not literally. It would be foolish to expect someone to take a tape measure to determine how much she loves someone. Life doesn't work that way. Indeed, most of the most profound experiences we have in life are fundamentally unmeasurable. This is not a liability; it is a recognition of the particular characteristics of the form of representation one is going to use that one believes is appropriate for the content one wishes to express.

Chapter 10

What Are Some Fundamental Ideas From Arts Based Research?

Throughout this book, we have identified important concepts and ideas that underlie arts based research. We are aware of the fact that some of the writing has an abstract quality to it that some readers might find difficult to access. We are, therefore, in this chapter, identifying 10 basic concepts from arts based research and providing a relatively brief— but, we hope, illuminating—discussion of their meaning and significance. We do not want to reduce everything we have written to paragraph length statements, but we are interested in making a distillation of the basic ideas upon which arts based research is built. It is our hope that this distillation will enable readers who are unfamiliar with arts based research to have a firmer grasp on the issues involved in its use. We turn to these "fundamental ideas" now.

1. Humans have invented a variety of forms of representation to describe and understand the world in as many ways as it can be represented.

This proposition emphasizes the idea that we *make* sense of the world and we do so by working with a form of representation. Music is a form of representation—so is visual art, so is mathematics, so are the various sciences. The world, we argue, is largely a construction, and the forms of representation we have access to plays a fundamental role in shaping that construction.

The implication of this view is that the technologies we know how to use, from pencil to computer, play a basic role in shaping what we can represent and what we can know. For example, the absence of the ability to read diminishes many aspects of the world for the person who cannot read. The inability to experience the expressive forms of a painting or a piece of music curtails the individual's ability to experience the expressive character of both the music as such and what it expresses. The constructive character of cognition is made particularly vivid if you reflect upon the impact of those technologies of mind that humans have invented. Each new technology has its own strengths and limitations, and each makes possible a distinctive way in which the world can be represented. Thus, photography stills a moving image; cinematography captures movement and makes it a focus of its work. These technologies of mind open up the possibilities of representation. The existence of neon tubes for lighting has made possible neon sculpture that Michelangelo himself could not have imagined.

What we have on a more micro-level is the use of the "same technology" by different individuals who, in the course of their work, impress their own intellectual thumbprint on the images or language they choose to use. Thus, diversification is not only something that occurs at a macro-level of, say, comparing music to the visual arts or poetry to the novel; they also exist within the same genre of work but are exercised differently by different individuals. Diversification awakens a sleepy eye to a wide awakeness, as Maxine Greene (1994) might say, to features of the reality in which we live to a form that suits both the expressive temperament of the individual and the capacities of the form of representation to express itself.

Of course, one must have the requisite skills to be able to use a medium as a representational vehicle. Put another way, technique must be available. If there is no skill, there is no technique. If there is no technique, there is no expressivity. If there is no expressivity, there is no art.

Let us return again to reading. The ability to read alleviates the necessity of memorization. One can inscribe meanings and return to them over and over again. Without the availability of a language to be read and the ability to read it, our cognitive skills would change. When reading is not an option, ideas must be remembered. The limitations of remembering are substantial.

The American philosopher Nelson Goodman (1968) reminds us that each construction of the world with a specific form of representation yields a different world. This view is not one that is widely shared in the community. It is widely held there is one world and many ways to see it. Goodman argues there are many worlds and many ways to see them. In fact, he argues there are as many worlds as there are ways to describe them. Goodman's position places great emphasis on the inventive or creative aspect of inquiry. What we come to know is what we make of something. What we make of something depends upon the tools we use and the conceptions we work with. Individuals who have new tools are often stimulated to do work that previously could not have been done. The casting of bronze made it possible to create vessels that could not have been imagined before the invention of bronze itself.

2. Each form of representation imposes its own constraints and provides its own affordances.

Constraints pertain to activities that are made difficult or impossible given the features or character of any particular medium, while affordances refer to the moves that can be made with the invention of new material. For example, technology made possible by the computer also makes possible images that would not otherwise be seen. Slow motion and images that are speeded up in the time frame could not be employed until these processes came to light. We are now able, through cinematography, to show the way in which a bullet pierces a plate glass window, something we could not see without the technology. Similarly, we are able to see the growth of a flower by speeding up the frames we can use to make it visible. In a more prosaic way, we have Day-Glo paints that make it possible to create a vividness and color that otherwise would be impossible. The marriage of technology and art here is very clear.

Each form of representation, as we said, imposes its own constraints and provides its own affordances; artists are people who exploit the expressive potentialities of the medium to "say" what otherwise could not be "said." For educational research, this idea suggests that the invention of and use of new media might give us images of social life that would otherwise be impossible to see. Just what are the patterns of behavior one finds in a public marketplace? Would an audio–video image reveal its features? What kind of skills and talents must an individual have to use such a medium effectively?

3. The purpose of arts based research is to raise significant questions and engender conversations rather than to proffer final meanings.

A third idea from arts based research concerns the fundamental purpose for engaging in it. The purpose of engaging in arts based research is not to add to a "knowledge base" or to proffer truth claims regarding social phenomena. It is rather the purpose that we have repeatedly noted throughout the book, and it has been described in a variety of ways. Arts based research is designed to enable readers and viewers to see aspects of the social world that they might have overlooked otherwise. Engaging in an arts based research text may thereby raise questions about conventional, commonsensical, orthodox ways of perceiving and interpreting the meaning of social phenomena.

Arts based research is based on the notion that any perspective on the world is always partial and therefore incomplete. We sometimes talk in the research community about securing a comprehensive view. If comprehensive means "total," it is an illusion. All perspectives have a slant on things, and what that slant omits may be as important as what it includes. One thing we can be sure of it that it is never total. The absence of totality is, on the other hand, a potential asset. It makes it possible for individuals to discuss their different perspectives and through such discussion and deliberation can arrive at conceptions that a single unified view would not provide. The virtue of partiality is to enter a universe of deliberation so that ideas can be challenged, elaborated, extended, and crafted into an argument that itself can be examined for the amount of weight an argument holds.

If arts based research serves to generate conversations about that which it represents, it may even, sometimes, serve as a catalyst for action. But that will ultimately be up to the reader or viewer of the work, since good arts based research—even when dealing with overtly political issues—never offers propaganda or agitprop.

Nevertheless, arts based research may possess the power to persuade an audience to "rethink" aspects of the social world by *reexperiencing* them. This reexperiencing is not merely a cognitive act. It also contains a powerful emotional element that can motivate viewers and readers to replace parts of an unexamined value system with new appreciations, attitudes, and even behaviors toward other people(s) who have previously been regarded as alien Others. The power to lure an audience into an alternative experiencing of the world suggests the capacity of the arts for doing that which other discursive formations cannot.

4. Arts based research can capture meanings that measurement cannot.

To measure is to ask how much. The strong virtue of measurement is that it provides a degree of precision that is difficult to achieve in most other forms. It has a standard against which qualities are quantified, and therefore, it provides utilities that can be secured no other way. There are, of course, varieties of measurement—correlation, length, weight. These varieties pertain not only to what can be measured but to what units can be employed to describe what has been measured.

It is believed by many that measurement takes the subjectivity out of description. Common units should reveal common qualities when qualities are common. But as we all know, how what is quantified is to be interpreted is another matter. The *meaning* of a number does not speak for itself. Furthermore, virtually all numerical systems applied to empirical phenomenon engage in a reduction of those phenomena. Consider the difference between temperature and heat. Temperature is the result of a measurement in terms of, lets us say, Fahrenheit. Heat is the feel of warmth that an object or event may possess. To feel the heat is not the same as measuring the temperature.

The point here is significant for research. To expect all or most outcomes in school, for example, to be rendered in terms of measurement is to reduce the information that one would secure if other forms of representation were employed. Arts based research is inquiry designed to exploit the epistemological capacities of a form of representation. Those potentialities are represented in nonquantitative forms. Thus, a poem can convey meaning in ways what measurement cannot capture. One must immediately add "and vice versa."

It is widely believed that research and especially evaluation practices must employ quantification in order to have validity. Quantification through measurement provides a description of a state of affairs pertaining to magnitude. But you will recall the distinction we drew between temperature and heat. Qualitative experience is experience by sensory information. To experience something as hot is not to experience it as the measurement of heat but as an experience as such. Much of the experience that we cherish the most is not mainly something that pertains to magnitude but something that pertained to qualities. The arrangement of qualities is something all of the arts have in common. Artists, you will recall that we commented, are people who qualify qualities. They are people who use component qualities in combination to generate a total quality that possesses certain satisfying forms of experience. Arts based research is inherently qualitative in character.

This does not mean that one cannot combine measurement with qualitative forms that are, in some ways, constructive. Again, there is no prohibition, just the ability to make judgments and to ground one's judgments in good reasons.

5. As the methodology for the conduct of research in the social sciences expands, a greater array of aptitudes will encounter forms that are most suited to them.

When the only game in town is basketball, those who are 5'5" are likely to have something of a handicap. One of the long-term potential benefits of arts based research is the fact that it employs forms of representation that cover the entire spectrum of representational possibility. In so doing, it affords individuals an opportunity to use aptitudes that might otherwise not be usable in conventional forms of research. Conventional forms of research are largely quantitative and statistical; those whose aptitudes reside in the use of number have a distinct advantage compared to their peers whose aptitudes reside, say, in the use of visual form as a source of representation. As the character of forms for arts based research expand, so, too, will it afford individuals with new opportunities to use forms that previously were not thought of as being relevant as a research tool. This should "democratize" research efforts so that not everyone needs to walk down the same yellow brick road.

6. For arts based research to advance, those who prepare researchers will need to diversify the development of skill among those who are being taught.

For example, the ability to use film may very well be one of the important resources for describing and understanding the world or some aspect of it. One of the ramifications of the growth of diversification among forms of representation will be the need in universities and other institutes to prepare individual researchers who possess the skills and talents necessary to do work that is useful. If storytelling, for example, is an important tool under the general umbrella of arts based research, learning how to write good stories is a necessity. If videotape becomes a powerful means of addressing the particular circumstances of a particular episode or event, those who use video will need to be able to use it effectively. What this means is that the demands on the preparation of researchers is going to become wider and more diversified, more complex, and more revealing. It may seem strange at the moment, but we can foresee departments of education collaborating with departments of English, communications, and the arts to jointly develop projects in which the diversity of skills that are represented in these departments have an opportunity to come to the fore. This should only enrich our understanding of what life is like in the situations we study.

7. Arts based research is not only for arts educators or professional artists.

Of course, arts based research can indeed be pursued by members of both of those groups. It is not, however, exclusively their province. With the kind of training, education, practice, and dedication previously alluded to—whether acquired and engaged in formally or informally—anyone might become a skilled arts based researcher. This does not mean that when it comes to the quality of arts based research that anything goes. The quality of a piece of arts based research depends on its capacity to enable percipients of the work to see aspects of the social world anew, thereby prompting them to reexamine the value and usefulness of their own prevailing perspective regarding those features. In making judgments about the success of a particular piece of arts based work, an evaluator is concerned less about the personal characteristics and background of the researcher than the quality of the work itself. That means, again, making judgments about whether the work is likely to serve as a catalyst for the kind of questionings, reexaminations, and conversations, and maybe even activism that is to be expected of a useful piece of this sort of social research.

8. In arts based research, generalizing from an *n* of 1 is an acceptable practice.

One of the foundational ideas in conventional statistically driven research is the importance of random selection of a sample from a population in order to draw conclusions that apply to the population from which the sample was drawn. The basic assumption is that generalization can only occur with validity when random selection is the method for securing the data one acts upon.

This view is not contrary to the view that we will put forward but is inadequate as a conception of the process of generalization. Generalizing takes place in various ways and an *n* of 1 can be used to secure knowledge of a process or an outcome that can serve as a guide for work in the future. Novels, for example, are not random samples of someone's life but generalize by providing an image, a picture, a narrative that stands for situations like it. The character in the novel itself is a surrogate or proxy for characters like him or her and thus provide guidance to the reader that enables the reader to find the novel's hero in situations outside of the novel. In fact, Aristotle pointed out that fiction is truer than history, since history deals with events that pass while fiction addresses situations that apply to what is enduring. Put another way, we secure our view of the heroic by reading *Ulysses*. We obtain our image of uncertainty by reading *Hamlet*. We secure our image of blind persistence by reading *The Old Man and the Sea*. Great art gives us enduring images that influence our conception of some aspect of the world. Few readers we know of secure their view of life by randomly selecting the images that populate their culture.

9. The aim of arts based research is not to replace traditional research methods; it is to diversify the pantry of methods that researchers can use to address the problems they care about.

The primary aim of arts based research is to expand the variety of resources that researchers can use to understand the social world. Its aim is *not* to replace old methods with new ones; its aim is to supplement, to enlarge, to expand, and to diversify the tools researchers can use and through such diversification to both see what might not otherwise have been seen and to be able to say what otherwise might not have been able to be said. We seek to contribute to a plurality of paradigms for doing research. This will require, of course, acceptance on the part of scholars that such methods are useful and this expectation is entirely justifiable. At the same time, it is not to be expected that new methods will be highly refined when they begin their journey in the professional marketplace. Nevertheless, one must often start small in order to grow large. This largeness refers to the availability of diversity in research methodology so that it suits both the researchers' aptitudes and the situation that is being addressed.

In many cases, new methods will yield problems that had not been conceptualized before. This is all to the good. Genuinely effective research methods in arts based research are known by the questions they engender. Put another way, the major aim of arts based research is not to have the correct answer to the question or the correct solution to the problem; it is to generate questions that stimulate problem formulation. The skilled arts based researcher is known by the insight and the quality of questions he or she promotes among those who read or see or hear his or her work.

10. Utilizing the expressive properties of a medium is one of the primary ways in which arts based research contributes to human understanding.

We save this observation for last because we believe that it is this essential feature in form that differentiates the aesthetic from the anesthetic. The expressive properties of a medium are a function of the way in which relationships in the work influence each other. It is through this relationship that we come to feel what the work is about and to know it, therefore, in ways that cannot be known with strictly discursive features. The nondiscursive has its affective utilities and it is in the marriage of these affective utilities and the more literal and less affective structures that the work functions as a work of art. In the process, the researcher, regardless of the field, becomes an artist, someone who works artfully with a material or process.

Much of what we have written in this book is iconoclastic. It takes a contrarian to try to make the case that the arts can be a deep source of understanding. The press of the culture pushes in another direction. It is only science, some would argue, to which we must appeal, in order to understand the world in which we live. The arts might be an assist, but they are clearly not on the first team. We have taken the view throughout this book that the arts should not try to replace science as the only mode of inquiry that produces human understanding. What we do argue is that there are different ways of understanding the human condition. The arts are among them, and with their virtual absence, the research community pays a dear price. Indeed, their absence diminishes our capacity for understanding.

All understanding has a frame of reference, a bias if you will, that frames the way we think and express what we have learned. The issue is not one of seeking an unbiased view. There is no view that does not have a slant on things. The issue is making it possible for the diversity of ways in which humans have constructed the world to find their appropriate place in the research community. What we have done in this book is to try to identify some examples of how such understanding has been generated and what it has revealed.

We fully expect the ideas we have put forth to be modified and altered over the coming years. Indeed, we would consider it a failure if change in ideas by those who employ them did not occur. The changes we seek are most likely to be in the form of fresh questions rather than certain conclusions. By arts based research, we are more interested in puzzlements than certitudes. We hope there is enough interest in these ideas to generate a community of scholars who collectively would explore the parameters and possibilities of arts based research.

References

Agger, B. (1990). *The decline of discourse: Reading, writing, and resistance in post modern capitalism.* New York: Falmer.

Aristotle. (1961). *Poetics.* (S. H. Butcher, Trans.). New York: Hill & Wang.

Bakhtin, M. (1981). *The dialogic imagination: Four essays.* Austin: University of Texas Press.

Bakhtin, M. (1984). *Problems of Dostoevsky's poetics.* (C. Emerson, Ed. and Trans.). Minneapolis: University of Minnesota Press. (Original work published 1965).

Baldwin, J. (1962). *The creative process.* New York: Ridge Press.

Banks, A. & Banks, S. (1998). *Fiction and social research.* Walnut Creek, CA: AltaMira Press.

Barone, T. (2000). Ways of being at risk: The case of Billy Charles Barnett. In T. Barone, *Aesthetics, politics, and educational inquiry: Essay and examples.* New York: Peter Lang.

Barone, T. (2001). *Touching eternity: The enduring outcomes of teaching.* New York: Teachers College Press.

Barone, T. (2002). From genre blurring to audience blending: Reflections on the field emanating from an ethnodrama. *Anthropology and Education Quarterly, 33*(2), 255–267.

Barone, T. (2008). Going public with arts-inspired social research: Issues of audience. In A. Cole & G. Knowles (Eds.), *Handbook of the arts in social science research* (pp. 485–492). Thousand Oaks, CA: Sage.

Barrett, T. (1985). Photographs and contexts, *Journal of Aesthetic Education, 19*(3), 51–64.

Becker, C. (1994). Introduction: Presenting the problem. In Becker, C. (ed.), *The subversive imagination: Artists, society, and social responsibility.* New York: Routledge.

Behar, R. (1996). The girl in the cast. In Behar, R. *The vulnerable observer: Anthropology that breaks your heart,* (pp. 104–132). Boston: Beacon Press.

Belsey, C. (1980). *Critical practice.* London: Methuen.

Caputo, J. D. (1987). *Radical hermeneutics: Repetition, deconstruction, and the hermeneutic project.* Bloomington: University of Indiana Press.

Case, S. (2010). *Broken and buried in Arkansas: A nonfiction short story.* Unpublished document.

Chappell, S. (2009). *Evidence of utopianizing toward social justice in young people's community based art works.* Unpublished doctoral dissertation, Arizona State University.

Coulter, D. (1999). The epic and the novel: Dialogism and teacher research. *Educational Researcher, 28*(30), 4–13.

Denzin, N. (1997). *Interpretive ethnography: Ethnographic practices for the 21st century.* Thousand Oaks, CA: Sage.

Denzin, N., & Lincoln, Y. (1998). Introduction. In N. Denzin & Y. Lincoln (Eds.), *The landscape of qualitative research: Theories and issues* (pp. 1–34). Thousand Oaks, CA: Sage.

Denzin, N. & Lincoln, Y. (2000). *Handbook of qualitative research.* Thousand Oaks, CA: Sage.

Dewey, J. (1929). The later works of John Dewey, Volume 4, 1925–1953. In J. A. Boydston (Ed.), The quest for certainty: A study of the relation of knowledge and action. Carbondale, IL: Southern Illinois University Press.

Dewey, J. (1934/1958). Art as experience. New York: Capricorn Books.

Dickens, C. (1854/1964). Hard times. New York: Bantam Books.

Diefenbeck, J. A. (1984). A celebration of subjective thought. Carbondale, IL: Southern Illinois University Press.

Doisneau, R. (1973). At the café, Chez Fraysee, Rue de Seine, Paris, 1958. In J. Szarkowski, Looking at photographs: 100 Pictures from the collection of the Museum of Modern Art (p. 172). New York: The Museum of Modern Art. Photograph also found at: http://community.livejournal.com/adski_ kafeteri/1505452.html or http://www.flickr. com/photos/manuelitro/2472981672/

Dunlop, R. (1999). Boundary Bay: A novel. Unpublished doctoral dissertation, University of British Columbia, Vancouver, Canada.

Ecker, D. (1966). The artistic process as qualitative problem solving. In E. Eisner & D. Ecker (Eds.), Readings in art education (pp. 57–68). Waltham, MA: Blaisdell.

Eisner, E. W. (1979). The educational imagination. New York: Macmillan.

Felshin, N. (1995). But is it art? The spirit of art as activism. Seattle: Bay Press.

Finley, M. (2000). Street rat. Detroit, MI: Greenroom Press, University of Detroit Mercy.

Finley, S., & Finley, M. (1999). Sp'ange: A research story. Qualitative Inquiry, 5(3), 313–337.

Frye, N. (1967). Anatomy of criticism. Princeton, NJ: Princeton University Press.

Geertz, C. (1974). The interpretation of cultures. New York: Basic Books.

Geertz, C. (1983). Local knowledge: Further essays in interpretive ethnography. New York: Basic Books.

Gombrich, E. (2000). Art and illusion. Princeton, NJ: Princeton University Press.

Goodman, N. (1968). Languages of art. Indianapolis, IN: Bobbs-Merrill.

Goodson, I. (1995). The story so far: Personal knowledge and the political. In J. Hatch & R. Wisniewski (Eds.), Life history and narrative (pp. 89–98). London: Falmer Press.

Gordimer, N. (1985). A city of the dead, a city of the living. In N. Gordimer (Ed.), Something out there. London: Penguin Books.

Gordimer, N. (1989). The gap between the writer and the reader. New York Review of Books, 36(14), 59–61.

Gosse, D. (2005). Jackytar. St. John's Newfoundland, Canada: Jesperson.

Greene, M. (1977). Toward wide-awakeness: An argument for the arts and humanities in education. Teachers College Record, 19(1), 119–125.

Haley, A. (1977). Roots: The saga of an American family. New York: Doubleday.

Iser, W. (1974). The implied reader. Baltimore: Johns Hopkins University Press.

Iser, W. (1980). The reading process; A phenomenological approach. In J. P. Tompkins (Ed.), Reader-response criticism: From journalism to post-structuralism. Baltimore: Johns Hopkins University Press.

Iser, W. (1993). The fictive and the imaginary: Charting literary anthropology. Baltimore, MD: Johns Hopkins University Press

Jacoby, R. (1987). The last intellectuals: American culture in the age of academe. New York: Basic.

Kaufman, M. (2001). The Laramie project. New York: Vintage Books.

Kozol, J. (1991). Savage inequalities. New York: Harper Perennial.

Krathwohl, D. (1993). Methods of educational and social science research: An integrated approach. New York: Longman.

Kristeva, J. (1982). Powers of horror: An essay of abjection (L. Roudiez, Trans.). New York: Columbia University Press. (Original work published 1980).

Kristeva, J. (1996). A conversation with Julia Kristeva. In R. Guberman (Ed.), Julia Kristeva interviews (I. Lipkowitz & A. Loselle, Trans., pp. 18–34). New York: Columbia University Press. (Work originally published 1985).

Kristeva, K. (2000). Sense and non-sense of revolt (J. Herman, Trans.). New York: Columbia University Press. (Work originally published 1996).

Kuhn, T. (1970). The structure of scientific revolutions (2nd ed., enlarged). International

Encyclopedia of Unified Science, 2(2). Chicago: University of Chicago Press.

Kuhn, T. (1977). *The essential tension.* Chicago: University of Chicago Press.

Langer, S. K. (1957). *Problems of art.* New York: Scribner's.

Lather, P., & Smithies, C. (1997). *Troubling the angels: Women living with AIDS.* Boulder, CO: Westview Press.

Lyotard, J.-F. (1979). *The postmodern condition: A report on knowledge.* (G. Bennington, Trans.). Minneapolis: University of Minnesota Press.

McNergney, R. F. (1990). Improving communication among educational researchers, policymakers, and the press. *Educational Researcher, 20*(10), 3–9.

Miller, Arthur. (1967). *Death of a salesman.* New York: Viking Press.

Nash, R. (2004). *Liberating scholarly writing: The power of personal narrative.* New York: Teachers College Press.

Nietzsche, F. (1887/1968). *The will to power.* New York: Vintage.

Nisbet, Robert A. (1976). *Sociology as an art form.* New York: Oxford University Press.

Pepper, S. (1945). *The basis of criticism in the arts.* Cambridge, MA: Harvard University Press.

Phillips, D. C. (1994). Telling it straight: Issues in assessing narrative research. *Educational Psychologist, 29*(1).

Poetter, T. (2006). *The education of Sam Sanders.* Lanham, MD: Hamilton Books.

Pope, D. C. (2001). *Doing school: How we are creating a generation of stressed out, materialistic, and miseducated students.* New Haven, CT: Yale University Press.

Puzo, M. (1969). *The godfather.* New York: G.P. Putnam's Sons.

Richardson, L. (2000). Writing: A method of inquiry. In N. Denzin & Y. Lincoln (Eds.), *Handbook of qualitative research* (2nd ed.). Thousand Oaks, CA: Sage.

Roiphe, A. (1988, February 14). This butcher, imagination: Beware of your life when a writer's at work. *New York Times Book Review,* 3, 30.

Rorty, R. (1979). *Philosophy and the mirror of nature.* Princeton, NJ: Princeton University Press.

Rorty, R. (1989). *Contingency, irony, and solidarity.* Cambridge, UK: Cambridge University Press.

Saldana, J. (Ed.). (2005). *Ethnodrama: An anthology of reality theatre.* Walnut Creek, CA: AltaMira Press.

Saldana, J., Finley, S., & Finley, M. (2002). *Street rat.* Unpublished manuscript.

Sarkowski, J. (1973). Robert Doisneau. In *Looking at photographs: 100 pictures from the collection of The Museum of Modern Art.* New York: The Museum of Modern Art.

Sartre, J.-P. (1988). *What is literature? And other essays.* Cambridge, MA: Harvard University Press. (Original work published 1948).

Saye, N. (2002). *More than "once upon a time:" Fiction as a bridge to knowing.* Unpublished doctoral dissertation, Georgia Southern University, Statesboro.

Simon, L. (Director). (1997). *Fear and learning at Hoover Elementary.* POV series. [Television broadcast]. New York: Public Broadcasting Service.

Smith, A. D. (1993). *Fires in the mirror: Crown Heights, Brooklyn, and other identities.* Garden City, NY: Anchor.

Smith, A. D. (1994). *Twilight, Los Angeles, 1992.* Garden City, NY: Anchor.

Smith, N. (2006). The edge of each other's battles newsletter. Personal electronic communication: nsmith@igc.org

Snow, C. P. (1993). *Two Cultures and the Scientific Revolution.* London, New York: Cambridge University Press.

Springgay, S. (2003). Cloth as intercorporeality: Touch, fantasy, and performance and the construction of body knowledge. *International Journal of Education and the Arts, 4*(5). Retrieved from http://ijea.asu.edu/v4n5/

Stone, L. (2005). Perspective 9: Poststructuralism on the Sullivan study. In J. L. Paul, *Introduction to the philosophies of research and criticism in education and the social sciences* (pp. 311–314). Upper Saddle River, NJ: Pearson.

Stone, R. (1988). The reason for stories: Toward a moral fiction. *Harper's, 276*(1657), pp. 71–78.

Sullivan, A. M. (2000). Notes from a marine biologist's daughter: On the art and science of attention. *Harvard Educational Review, 70*(2), 211–227.

Taylor, P. (2003). *Applied theatre: Creating transformative encounters in the community.* Portsmouth, NH: Heinemann.

Toulmin, S. (1953). *Philosophy of science.* London: Hutchinson University Library.

Wicomb, Z. (1991). An author's agenda. In P. Mariani (Ed.), *Critical fictions: The politics of imaginative writing* (pp. 13–16). Seattle, WA: Bay Press.

Williams, B. (1972). Rene Descartes. In P. Edwards (Ed.), *The encyclopedia of philosophy* (pp. 344–354). New York: Macmillan and The Free Press.

Additional Readings

Angrossino, M. V. (2002). Babaji and me: Reflections on a fictional ethnography. In Arthur P. Bochner, & Carolyn Ellis (Eds.), *Ethnographically speaking: Autoethnography, literature and aesthetics* (pp. 327–335). Walnut Creek, CA: AltaMira Press.

Bach, H. (1998). *A visual narrative concerning curriculum, girls, photography, etc*. Edmonton, Alberta: Qualitative Institute Press.

Barone, T. (1992) Beyond theory and method: A case of critical storytelling. *Theory into Practice, 31*(2), 142–146.

Baskwill, J. (2001). Performing our research and our work: Women principals on stage. In L. Neilsen, A. L. Cole, & J. G. Knowles (Eds.), *The art of inquiry*. Halifax, Nova Scotia, Canada: Backalong Books.

Belliveau, G. (2006). Engaging in drama: Using arts-based research to explore a social justice project in teacher education. *International Journal of Education & the Arts, 7*(5). Retrieved from http://www.ijea.org/v7n5/index.html

Blumenfeld-Jones, D. S. (1995). Dance as a mode of research representation. *Qualitative Inquiry, 1*(4), 391–401.

Brady, I. (2000). Three Jaguar/Mayan intertexts: Poetry and prose fiction. *Qualitative Inquiry, 5*(4) 58–64.

Buttingnol, M., Jongeward, C., Smith, D., & Thomas, S. (1999). The creative self: Researching teaching through artistic expression. In A. L. Cole, & J. G. Knowles (Eds.), *Researching teaching: Exploring teacher development through reflexive inquiry* (pp. 98–137). Boston: Allyn & Bacon.

Cahnmann, M., & Siegesmund, R. (Eds.). (2007). *Arts-based research in education: Foundations for practice*. New York: Routledge.

Chappell, S. (2009). A rough handshake or an illness: Teaching and learning on the border as felt through art-making. *Journal of Curriculum and Pedagogy*, 10–21.

Clifford, J., & Marcus, G. E. (Eds.) (1986). *Writing culture: The poetics and politics of ethnography*. Berkley: University of California Press.

Cole, A. L., & Knowles J. G. (2001). *Lives in context: The art of life history research*. Walnut Creek, CA: AltaMira Press.

Conway, J. K. (Ed.) (1992). *Written by herself, autobiographies of American women: An anthology*. New York: Random House.

Coulter, C. (2003). *Snow white, revolutions. The American dream and other fairy tales: Growing up immigrant in an American high school*. Unpublished doctoral dissertation, Arizona State University.

Davies, B. (2000). *(In)scribing body/landscape relations*. Walnut Creek, CA: AltaMira Press.

Denzin, N. K. (1989). *Interpretive biography*. Newbury Park, CA: Sage.

Diamond, C. T. P., & Mullen, C. A. (Eds.). (1999). *The postmodern educator: Arts-based inquiries and teacher development*. New York: Peter Lang.

Donmoyer, R., & Yennie-Donmoyer, J. (1995). Data as drama: Reflections on the use of readers theatre as a mode of qualitative data display. *Qualitative Inquiry, 1*(4), 402–428.

Dunlop, R. (1998). Written on the body. In S. Abbey, & A. O'Reilly (Eds.). *Redefining motherhood: Changing identities and patterns.* Toronto: Second Story Press.

Dunlop, R. (1999). *Boundary bay: A novel as educational research.* Doctoral dissertation. University of British Columbia.

Dunlop, R. (2008). *White album.* Toronto: Inanna Publications and Education, Inc.

Ellis, C. (2000). Creating criteria: An ethnographic short story. *Qualitative Inquiry, 6*(2), 271–277.

Ellis, C., & Bochner, A. P. (Eds.). (1996). *Composing ethnography: Alternative forms of qualitative writing.* Walnut Creek, CA: AltaMira Press.

Finley, S. (2000). Dream child. *Qualitative Inquiry, 6*(30), 432–434.

Finley, S. (2001a). Painting life histories. *Journal of Curriculum Theorizing, 17*(2), 13–26.

Finley, S. (2001b). Arts-based inquiry in QI: Seven years from crisis to guerrilla warfare. *Qualitative Inquiry, 9*(2), 281–296.

Geertz, C. (1988) *Words and lives: The anthropologist as author.* Stanford, CA: Stanford University Press.

Glesne, C. (1997). That rare feeling: Re-presenting research through poetic transcription. *Qualitative Inquiry, 3*(2), 202–221.

Goodall, H. L., Jr. (2000). *Writing the new ethnography.* Walnut Creek, CA: AltaMira Press.

Gray, R. E. (2003). Performing on and off the stage; The place(s) of performance in arts-based approaches to qualitative inquiry. *Qualitative Inquiry, 9*(2), 254–267.

Irwin, R. L., Bickel, B., Triggs, V., Springgay, S., Beer, R., Grauer, K., et al. (2009). The city of Richgate: A/r/tographic cartography as public pedagogy. *International Journal of Art and Design Education, 28*(1), 61–70

Knowles, J. G., & Cole, A. L. (2007). *Handbook of the arts in qualitative research: Perspectives, methodologies, examples and issues.* Thousand Oaks, CA: Sage.

Lawrence-Lightfoot, S., & Hoffmann Davis, J. (1997). *The art and science of portraiture.* San Francisco: Jossey-Bass.

Leggo, C. (2001). Writing lines is more than writing lives: Postmodern perspectives on life writing. *Language and Literacy, 2*(2). Retrieved from http//educ.queensu.ca/~landl/

Marín, C. (2007). A methodology rooted in praxis: Theatre of the oppressed (TO) techniques employed as arts-based educational research methods. *Youth Theatre Journal, 21,* 81–93.

Prendergast, M., Leggo, C., & Sameshima, P. (Eds.). (2009). *Poetic inquiry: Vibrant voices in the social sciences.* Rotterdam, Netherlands: Sense.

Prendergast, M., Lymburner, J., Grauer, K., Irwin, R. L., Leggo, C., & Gouzouasis, P. (2008). Pedagogy of trace: Poetic representations of teaching resilience/resistance in arts education. *Vitae Scholasticae: The Journal of Educational Biography, 25,* 58–76.

Saldana, J. (2003). Dramatizing data: A primer. *Qualitative Inquiry, 15*(4), 431–446.

Sameshima, P. (2007). *Seeing red—a pedagogy of parallax: An epistolary bildungsroman on artful scholarly inquiry.* Amherst, NY: Cambria Press.

Sameshima, P., Vandermause, R., Chalmers, S., & Gabriel, R. (2009). *Climbing the ladder with Gabriel: Poetic inquiry of a methamphetamine addict in recovery.* Rotterdam, Netherlands: Sense.

Sanders, J. H., III. (2006.) Performing arts-based education research: An epic drama of practice, precursors, problems, and possibilities. *Studies in Art Education, 48*(1), 89–107.

Sinner, A., Leggo, C., Irwin, R. L., Gouzouasis, P., & Grauer, K. (2006). Arts-based educational research dissertations: Reviewing the practices of new scholars. *Canadian Journal of Education, 29,* 1223–1270.

Springgay, S., Irwin, R., Leggo, C., & Gouzouasis, P. (Eds.). (2008). *Being with a/r/tography.* Rotterdam, Netherlands: Sense.

Spry, T. (2001). Performing autoethnography: An embodied methodological praxis. *Qualitative Inquiry, 7*(6), 706–732.

Sullivan, A. (2000). The necessity of art: three found poems from John Dewey's Art as experience. *International Journal of Qualitative Studies in Education, 13*(3) 325–327.

Taylor, P. (2003) *Applied theatre: Creating transformative encounters in the community.* Portsmouth, NH: Heinemann.

Index

About the Authors

Over 30 years ago, **Tom Barone's** doctoral dissertation at Stanford University investigated the possibilities of literary nonfiction for researching and writing about educational matters. Since then, he has explored, conceptually and through examples, a variety of narrative and arts based approaches to contextualizing and theorizing about significant educational issues. He has published widely and is the author of two books: *Aesthetics, Politics, and Educational Inquiry: Essays and Examples* is a collection of his early writings; *Touching Eternity: The Enduring Outcomes of Teaching* (Outstanding Book Awards from Division B of American Educational Research Association [AERA] and the AERA Narrative Research Special Interest Group) is an ironically titled narrative study that questions the possibility of heroic transfers of learning. As professor of education in the Arizona State University Mary Lou Fulton Teachers College, Barone teaches courses in curriculum studies and qualitative research methods. Barone was the recipient of the 2010 Lifetime Achievement Award of Division B of the AERA.

Elliot W. Eisner is the Lee Jacks Professor Emeritus of Education and Art at Stanford University. His major educational interests are in the role of the arts in the development of cognition. He is also interested in the ways in which art forms illuminate and promote understanding of the qualitative world. These interests are reflected in seventeen books, including *Educating Artistic Vision*, *The Educational Imagination*, and *The Arts and the Creation of Mind*. Professor Eisner's interest in the connection between the arts and cognition developed early in his career. It is reflected in the effort to expand our conception of cognition so that works that are nonlinguistic have an important place in the armamentarium scholars use to study the qualitative world. For his efforts in this arena, he has been the recipient of numerous significant awards. Some of these include the Jose Vasconcelos Award given by the World Cultural Council, the McGraw Prize, the Brock Medal, and most recently the prestigious Grawmeyer Award.

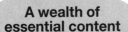